Migration, Minorities and Citizenship

General Editors: **Zig Layton-Henry**, Professor of Politics, University of Warwick; and **Danièle Joly**, Professor, Director, Centre for Research in Ethnic Relations, University of Warwick

Titles include:

Muhammad Anwar, Patrick Roach and Ranjit Sondhi (*editors*)
FROM LEGISLATION TO INTEGRATION?
Race Relations in Britain

James A. Beckford, Danièle Joly and Farhad Khosrokhavar
MUSLIMS IN PRISON
Challenge and Change in Britain and France

Thomas Faist and Andreas Ette (*editors*)
THE EUROPEANIZATION OF NATIONAL POLICIES AND POLITICS OF IMMIGRATION
Between Autonomy and the European Union

Thomas Faist and Peter Kivisto (*editors*)
DUAL CITIZENSHIP IN GLOBAL PERSPECTIVE
From Unitary to Multiple Citizenship

Adrian Favell
PHILOSOPHIES OF INTEGRATION
Immigration and the Idea of Citizenship in France and Britain

Agata Górny and Paulo Ruspini (*editors*)
MIGRATION IN THE NEW EUROPE
East-West Revisited

James Hampshire
CITIZENSHIP AND BELONGING
Immigration and the Politics of Democratic Governance in Postwar Britain

John R. Hinnells (*editor*)
RELIGIOUS RECONSTRUCTION IN THE SOUTH ASIAN DIASPORAS
From One Generation to Another

Danièle Joly
GLOBAL CHANGES IN ASYLUM REGIMES (*editor*)
Closing Doors

Zig Layton-Henry and Czarina Wilpert (*editors*)
CHALLENGING RACISM IN BRITAIN AND GERMANY

Jørgen S. Nielsen
TOWARDS A EUROPEAN ISLAM

Pontus Odmalm
MIGRATION POLICIES AND POLITICAL PARTICIPATION
Inclusion or Intrusion in Western Europe?

Aspasia Papadopoulou-Kourkoula
TRANSIT MIGRATION
The Missing Link Between Emigration and Settlement

Jan Rath (*editor*)
IMMIGRANT BUSINESSES
The Economic, Political and Social Environment

Carl-Ulrik Schierup (*editor*)
SCRAMBLE FOR THE BALKANS
Nationalism, Globalism and the Political Economy of Reconstruction

Vicki Squire
THE EXCLUSIONARY POLITICS OF ASYLUM

Maarten Vink
LIMITS OF EUROPEAN CITIZENSHIP
European Integration and Domestic Immigration Policies

Östen Wahlbeck
KURDISH DIASPORAS
A Comparative Study of Kurdish Refugee Communities

Migration, Minorities and Citizenship
Series Standing Order ISBN 978-0-333-71047-0 (hardback) and 978-0-333-80338-7 (paperback)
(*outside North America only*)

You can receive future titles in this series as they are published by placing a standing order. Please contact your bookseller or, in case of difficulty, write to us at the address below with your name and address, the title of the series and the ISBN quoted above.

Customer Services Department, Macmillan Distribution Ltd, Houndmills, Basingstoke, Hampshire RG21 6XS, England

The Exclusionary Politics of Asylum

Vicki Squire
The Open University, UK

First published 2009 by
PALGRAVE MACMILLAN

Palgrave Macmillan in the UK is an imprint of Macmillan Publishers Limited, registered in England, company number 785998, of Houndmills, Basingstoke, Hampshire RG21 6XS.

Palgrave Macmillan in the US is a division of St Martin's Press LLC, 175 Fifth Avenue, New York, NY 10010.

Palgrave Macmillan is the global academic imprint of the above companies and has companies and representatives throughout the world.

Palgrave® and Macmillan® are registered trademarks in the United States, the United Kingdom, Europe and other countries.

ISBN-13: 978-0-230-21659-4   hardback
ISBN-10: 0-230-21659-5   hardback

This book is printed on paper suitable for recycling and made from fully managed and sustained forest sources. Logging, pulping and manufacturing processes are expected to conform to the environmental regulations of the country of origin.

A catalogue record for this book is available from the British Library.

Library of Congress Cataloging-in-Publication Data

Squire, Vicki, 1974–
    The exclusionary politics of asylum / Vicki Squire.
        p. cm. — (Migration, minorities and citizenship)
    Includes bibliographical references and index.
    ISBN 978-0-230-21659-4
    1. Asylum, Right of—Great Britain.   2. Asylum, Right of—European
    Union countries.   3. Refugees—Government policy—Great Britain.
    4. Refugees—Government policy—European Union countries.
    5. Refugees—Legal status, laws, etc.—Great Britain.   6. Refugees—
    Legal status, laws, etc.—European Union countries.   I. Title.
    JV7682.S68 2009
    323.6′31—dc22   2008053014

10   9   8   7   6   5   4   3   2   1
18   17   16   15   14   13   12   11   10   09

Transferred to Digital Printing 2011

Contents

Acknowledgements

There are many people that I need to thank, for I have been lucky to have had a lot of support along the way.

First, I would like to thank those people whose invaluable comments have been central to the development of this book. In particular, I would like to thank Engin Isin, Aletta Norval and David Owen for their encouragement and insightful comments. Claudia Aradau, Barry Hindess, David Howarth, Jef Huysmans, Jason Glynos and John Bartle have all commented on various chapters, for which I am grateful. Thanks to Danièle Joly for her support and encouragement, as well as to Thomas Diez, Steve Peers and Yasemine Soysal who have all commented on chapter drafts. The constructive comments of my reviewers are also much appreciated.

Particular thanks are extended to my former colleagues at the University of Birmingham, in particular to Anca Pusca, Laura Shepard and Nicki Smith, whose encouragement has been invaluable. Thanks also to the inspiration of my fellow PhD students at the University of Essex, especially Mette Marie Roslyng, Mercedes Barros, Mike Strange, Emilia Palonen, Jansev Jemal, Tim Appleton and David Payne.

I would like to give special thanks to Dave Stamp, whose abiding support and encouragement is not always as openly appreciated as it is inwardly appreciated. Special thanks also to my ever-inspiring children, Jamila Squire and Jake Squire, who have moved over very generously while I have nursed this book. I am most grateful for the continuing support of my Mum, Penny Squire, as well as of my sisters, Louise Squire and Charlotte Squire. Thanks also to all of my friends who have helped me through both the challenging and rewarding times – most notably Rachel Clements, Lynette Canervaro and Kara Powell.

This book is clearly not mine alone. I'd like to extend thanks to all those people that I interviewed, especially those who helped me to begin to think and act beyond an exclusionary politics.

This research was generously funded by the Economic and Social Research Council, for which I am most grateful (PTA-030-2002-00452, PTA-026-27-1294).

This book is dedicated to two people who were sadly lost along the way: David Squire and Pat Stamp.

Part I Introducing the Exclusionary Politics of Asylum: The Management of Dislocation

1
A Dislocated Territorial Order? Introducing the Asylum 'Problem'

This book tells two stories. The first story has as its primary character a sovereign state. This state strives to protect its citizens against the negative imposition of uninvited non-citizens, while the latter risk life and limb in order to steal the benefits of which the former are the rightful recipients. As we will see, there is seemingly no end to this story, because the sovereign state effectively generates the 'problem' or 'threat' to which it is opposed. The second story has as its primary figure the 'asylum seeker', who is defined according to his or her 'unauthorised' entrance into a foreign territory. This mobile character, in risking life and limb, serves as an exemplary figure that renders visible the exclusionary practices employed by the state in its attempt to maintain a territorial order. The ending of this story remains unclear. Will the asylum seeker be consigned to the role of a scapegoat, or will s/he constitute herself/himself as a political agent within a broader movement towards a 'post-national' or 'post-territorial' citizenship?

In juxtaposing these two stories, this book critically explores how the territorial political community is defined against those mobile subjects who fit neither its norms nor its exceptions. The 'abusive' asylum seeker is a key figure in this respect, particularly in the European and UK contexts. Often assumed to be an economic migrant who enters without authorisation in order to reap the benefits of living in a wealthy state, this figure is largely perceived as a 'bogus' one that 'poses' as a refugee in need of protection. On this reading, the asylum-seeker-cum-illegal-immigrant does not fit the norm of a citizen who is protected by his or her own state, but neither does s/he fit the exceptional status of the refugee who requires protection within a 'civilised' state from one that is 'rogue' (Owen, 2005). It is in exploring the political, popular and technical constructions of this ambiguous figure as a 'problem' or

3

'threat' that this book shows how the exclusionary politics of asylum get entangled in a self-fulfilling cycle of restriction and control. In particular, it shows how the exclusionary politics of asylum precariously reconstructs the territorial political community in the face of its dislocation by constituting asylum seekers as scapegoats for 'problems' that are the political community's 'own'. Although the asylum seeker may be seen as a semi-autonomous agent who challenges the territorial norms of the sovereign state, s/he can thus also be conceived of as a subject who is prohibited and subsequently punished for his or her transgressions. It is when mobile subjects come up against their restricted doubles that this book observes the potential for a move beyond the reactionary confines of exclusionary politics.

Asylum, citizenship and sovereignty

In exploring the exclusionary politics of asylum, this book entails a broader engagement with questions surrounding citizenship, governance and belonging. As theorists such as Bonnie Honig (2001) have shown, the 'foreigner' plays a founding role through which a broader imaginary of citizenship is constructed, and in this respect citizenship *qua* belonging is defined in relation to 'foreign' figures such as the asylum seeker. Rather than approaching the political community and its citizen-body as pre-given entities that need to be defended against 'threatening' foreigners, this book approaches citizenship as variously constituted through relations with 'alien others' and 'immanent outsiders' (Isin, 2002). Its opening assumption is thus that the production of 'foreign' figures plays a constitutive role in defining the limits of citizenship and political community. Indeed, it suggests that the drawing of lines between foreigners and citizens does not only delineate those who belong to the political community from those who do not, but it also entails processes of governance or government through which the movement of citizens and non-citizens is regulated by the state and its subsidiary agents. In this respect, citizenship can be understood as a regime of inclusion/exclusion that creates units of belonging through which populations are governed (see Hindess, 1998).

It is in exploring how these limits are drawn through an opposition to asylum that this book seeks to contribute to existing debates surrounding citizenship and immigration (e.g. Brubaker, 1989; Castles and Davidson, 2000; Hampshire, 2005; Hansen, 2000; Joppke, 1999; Koopmans, Statham, Giugni and Passy, 2005; Layton-Henry, 1992; Spencer, 1994). Asylum shot up the political agenda in the UK and across Europe from the 1990s, rendering the asylum seeker a key 'foreign' figure by which the limits of citizenship are drawn. In this context, attention has been drawn to the paradoxical role that asylum plays in constituting liberal democratic citizenship. On the one hand, a commitment to the provision of protection for those fleeing persecution is key in articulating a liberal democratic way of life as morally superior to that of refugee-producing states or to that of states that are not signed up to the 1951 United Nations Convention for Refugees (Schuster, 2003a). On the other hand, the articulation of asylum as a security issue necessitating intensified border controls undermines the very freedoms that are central to a liberal democratic way of life (Huysmans, 2006). According to Matthew Gibney's (2004) reading, liberal democratic citizenship is thus constituted in 'schizophrenic' terms, because it combines a moral attachment to the principle of asylum with a practical attachment to measures that are designed to ensure that asylum seekers don't reach the territory where they can receive protection.

This book approaches this paradoxical liberal democratic formulation of citizenship as indicative of a tension at the very heart of the territorial order. This tension, it suggests, is central to the workings of the sovereign state and its subsidiaries. The primary focus in this book is thus on the restrictive impulse which Gibney highlights, which is conceived of as characteristic of the sovereign state as much as of the liberal democratic state. Immigration control is one of the defining features of the modern sovereign state and, as such, serves as an important means by which a territorial order is constituted in terms of state governance and national belonging (Bartleson, 1995). This territorial articulation of governance and belonging can be interpreted in terms of the inscription of an opposition between sovereignty and anarchy, in which the domestic sphere is conceived as one of peace and order and the international sphere is conceived as a dangerous and threatening anarchy (Ashley, 1988). As we will see, however, there have been significant disruptions, transgressions and dislocations of this distinction between the inside and the outside over recent years (Kostakopoulou and Thomas, 2004). This renders the drawing of limits around citizenship highly complex. Indeed, it often leaves the distinction between those who belong and those who do not, as well as the distinction between those who require restriction and those who do not, in a relation of tension with the territorial frame of the nation state (Joppke, 1998).

It is in relation to these varied disruptions, transgressions and dislocations of a territorial order that this book explores the contemporary articulation of asylum as a 'problem' or 'threat'. It is now firmly established that a framing of free movement as a security issue has led to its construction as a 'threat' in the post-Cold War context (Huysmans, 2006). Indeed, it has been suggested that the securitisation of migration signals a 'disembedding' of liberalism, particularly in a post-9/11 context (Hampshire and Saggar, 2006; Hampshire, 2008). This is particularly evident in relation to asylum, not only in the UK but also more widely across Europe and beyond. As Guy Goodwin-Gill (2001) suggests, the articulation of asylum as a security issue has diluted the language of refugee protection, while facilitating a move away from an individual rights-based approach. These developments have led some to claim that a 'new asylum paradigm' may be emerging as an alternative to the post-war international refugee regime (Crisp, 2003; Koser, 2001; Schuster, 2005a). Whether or not contemporary developments in the area of asylum signify a qualitatively 'new paradigm' remains open to debate, but the analysis in this book clearly supports the suggestion that a 'hostile new agenda' has emerged over recent years (Joly, Kelly and Nettleton, 1997). Running parallel to managed migration, this agenda can be conceived of as part of a wider attempt to manage complex and mixed migratory flows 'at a distance' (Geddes, 2000). With asylum seeking perceived as 'threatening' the very success of managed migration (Flynn, 2005), an exclusionary approach has emerged in which asylum seekers are subject both to restrictive measures of surveillance and control (see Pratt, 2005; Pickering and Weber, 2006), as well as to hostile narratives of exclusion (Ahmed, 2004; Nickels, 2007). It is where these dimensions become intertwined in what Heaven Crawley (2005:15) describes as a 'vicious cycle' that the exclusionary politics of asylum can be identified.

The emergence of the asylum 'problem'

Asylum has a long and varied history in both the UK and the European contexts, but it only became a focus of primary legislation in the UK in 1993 (Schuster, 2003a). It was at this point that the Asylum and Immigration Appeals Act incorporated the 1951 United Nations Geneva Convention Relating to the Status of Refugees into British law, and the UK was formally obliged to acknowledge Article 14 of the Universal Declaration on Human Rights, which refers to the right of asylum. The 1993 act thus constituted a commitment on UK's behalf to provide an individual with the right to claim asylum on its territory and, if successful in his/her claim, with the right to enjoy asylum. Prior to this legislation the granting of asylum remained a more *ad hoc* process, which was developed according to the needs of particular groups. Such was the case in relation to Chilean and Vietnamese refugees during the 1970s (e.g. Joly, 1996).

Notably, the 1993 commitment to the UN Convention came at a time when there had already been a shift towards the 1951 Convention's more 'restrictive interpretation' (Castles and Miller, 1998:89). This is reflected in what Roger Zetter (2007:189) describes as the 'fractioning' of the refugee label, whereby a complex legal plethora of temporary protections statuses have emerged that conceal the political agenda of *restricting access* to refugee status'. Supporting this claim, this book shows how a complex legal picture tends to be precluded by a more simplistic distinction between 'desirables' and 'undesirables', both at the level of political and popular debate as well as at the level of technical practice (see Parts II and III). While a restrictive approach to refugee protection is widely conceived as emerging in response to an increase in 'territorial asylum seeking' during the 1980s and 1990s, this analysis seeks critical distance from the assumption that restriction has been a 'natural' response to increased numbers of individuals physically entering the country in order to claim asylum. Rather than interpreting restriction as *necessarily* emerging in the face of growing numbers of asylum claims, it contends that it is important to develop a more complex understanding of the shift towards restriction. This can be developed through the consideration of various events and processes that serve as the conditions under which restrictive asylum discourse emerged.

The end of the Cold War is generally seen to be the most important event that conditioned the emergence of restrictive asylum policy. As Liza Schuster (2003a; 2003b:244) suggests, asylum became of declining political utility in a post-Cold War context, because it no longer benefited the interests of powerful states. Indeed, the literature on asylum widely recognises the declining political efficacy of asylum after 1989. In a context where asylum no longer refers to those fleeing communist regimes, a commitment to political migration would seem to be of secondary concern (Castles and Miller, 1998). Nevertheless, asylum entails new political efficacy in its movement from an issue of 'low' politics to an issue of 'high' politics. Specifically, its articulation as a 'problem' or 'threat' facilitates a specifically *exclusionary* territorial reconstruction of political community in a context marked by increased cross-border mobilities. This process has a longer history than is sometimes assumed, but could be said to have taken on a new intensity after 9/11 and, in the UK, after the 7/7 London bombings in 2005.[1] While the direct articulatory linkage of asylum seeking and terrorism would seem to be unfounded, the analysis in this book suggests that associational links between various types of 'cross-border threat' remain efficacious. This is evident, in particular, where we consider the consequences of the framing of asylum as a security issue for those seeking to claim asylum in EU states such as the UK (Guild, 2003).[2]

The end of the Cold War and the Global War on Terror (GWOT) are not the only factors that have conditioned a move towards an increasingly restrictive asylum agenda. Various events and processes need to be addressed if we are to understand more fully how a restrictive approach to asylum has come to have such a hold within the European and UK context today. First, there are economic conditions. A longer history is required here: beginning in the 1970s, a period of economic instability led to the shrinkage of guest worker programmes across Europe, and paved the way for a restrictive approach that retains its resonance even today. Indeed, the shrinkage of guest worker programmes led to the greater visibility of asylum, which increased proportionately in relation to overall immigration figures. Economic factors are thus important in developing an understanding of the emergence of a restrictive agenda that targets asylum seekers specifically.

Also important in understanding this restrictive agenda are changing political conditions within Europe. The break-up of the former Yugoslavia during the 1990s was a key factor conditioning concerns about increasing the numbers of asylum seekers, while the opening of internal borders and a corollary expansion and tightening of the Union's external borders reframed restriction in terms that largely work against the inclusion of asylum seekers (Kostakopoulou, 1998).[3] Although integration has led to a significant liberalisation of migration within the EU, it has thus been coupled with a strong emphasis on the restriction of migration from outside of the Union (c.a.s.e. collective, 2006). Despite the EU's explicit ongoing commitment to asylum and to human rights, and despite its attempt to prevent a 'race to the bottom' in terms of asylum reception standards, European integration could thus be conceived as moving asylum policy in a broadly restrictive direction.

This analysis thus suggests that a range of events and processes have emerged as conditions for the emergence of a restrictive approach to asylum within the European context. Indeed, this restrictive approach is particularly strong in the UK, whereby an influential right-wing popular press has often engaged in a campaign against asylum seekers (Kaye, 1998). Such a campaign arguably thrives on an authoritarian nationalism which emerged in the UK under the leadership of Margaret Thatcher in the 1980s (Hall, 1983), and which found in the asylum seeker a convenient scapegoat during the 1990s. This antagonistic approach to asylum needs to be understood in relation to wider political and popular hostility surrounding a human rights framework, which is often articulated as granting rights to 'foreigners' over citizens. Such hostility is, for example, evident in political debates surrounding whether or not the UK should renege on its commitment to the European Convention on Human Rights (Joint Committee on Human Rights, 2006). A concerning concoction of anti-asylum, anti-European and anti-judiciary sentiment would seem to have conditioned the emergence of a restrictive asylum agenda in the UK (see Chapter 4).

It is, thus, in relation to various economic, social and political conditions that asylum has been constructed as a 'problem' or a 'threat' that necessitates intensified controls. Such a discourse rests on several key assumptions. First, it assumes that there is, or has generally been, an increase in the numbers of asylum seekers, and that this constitutes a problem for receiving states. Second, it assumes that the asylum system has been subject to widespread 'abuse' by economic migrants who want to enter, reside and work in the UK. Third, it assumes that intensified restriction or control will help in successfully resolving 'problems' that are associated with increased numbers of asylum seekers.

One of the main aims of this book is to challenge these assumptions, each of which are conceived to be highly problematic. With regard to the first assumption, it is clear that there have generally been higher numbers of asylum claimants since the 1990s, although this rise in numbers has been punctuated and has dropped recently. However, rising numbers do not necessarily constitute a 'problem' for receiving states such as the UK, particularly given its ageing population and its requirement for migrant workers in certain sectors. With regard to the second assumption, it is critical to note that the question of whether an asylum seeker is 'deserving' or not is impossible to establish in fact, and is imbued with judgements regarding his or her 'desirability' or 'undesirability'. A focus on 'would-be' migrants who 'abuse' the asylum system plays on this ambiguity in terms that foreclose questions regarding the rationale on which decisions about asylum claims are made. This is highly problematic because it closes down opportunities for a more open debate surrounding the issue of asylum. With regard to the final assumption, it is important to note that the specific effects of restriction are difficult, if not impossible, to judge because of the wide range of factors that condition contemporary migrations (Castles and Miller, 1998:19–29). Going further, it seems that many of the 'problems' associated with asylum are not, strictly speaking, problems of asylum seeking but that they are, in fact, often produced or aggravated by restrictive controls (see Part III). Such are the exclusionary politics of asylum, which constitute scapegoats for the wider dislocation of a territorial order.

Exclusionary politics and the dislocation of a territorial order

Rather than working with the assumption that restrictive controls serve as a 'natural' response to increased numbers of asylum seekers, this book suggests that it may be more adequate to interpret restriction as symptomatic of a wider dislocation of a territorial order of governance and belonging. It has often been suggested that we are witnessing the displacement of a territorial order in which the sovereign state reigns supreme. Some researchers emphasise economic and social factors that are related to the demand for flexible labour, the development of a global market, the internationalisation of finance and to the autonomy of corporations (Thompson, 2000). Others focus on social and technological factors, such as the development of transport and communication systems that foster interactions between peoples at a global scale (Appadurai, 1996). Others still draw attention to political and legal shifts such as the development of human rights norms and modes of multilevel governance (Habermas, 1992, 1998). These various strands of research suggest that there is what might be described as a 'meta-discourse' of globalisation that is characteristic of our times.

It is in relation to these wider processes of globalisation, neoliberalism and transnationalism that questions have emerged regarding new forms of governance and belonging that undermine the authority of the sovereign state and the national articulation of citizenship (Bhabha, 1999; Soysal, 1994; Linklater, 1998, 2007). Migration or human mobility is of particular interest in relation to such debates, because it entails complex and often contradictory rearticulations of governance and belonging (Tastsoglou and Dobrowolsky, 2006). Human mobility might thus be conceived of as a 'turbulent' force that disrupts territorial borders, to which the sovereign state has often responded defensively (Papastergiadis, 2000; Mezzadra and Nielson, 2003). It has frequently been noted that a neoliberal commitment to the free movement of goods has not been met by a similar commitment to the free movement of people (Harris, 2003). In this context, the sovereign state's response to the 'turbulence of migration' can be seen as mixed, if not blatantly contradictory. Thus, 'desirable' migrants are warmly welcomed while 'undesirables' clearly are not (Newman, 2003).

Indeed, Anne McNevin (2007) suggests that these ambivalences are central to the development of restrictive asylum policy. She argues that the sovereign state's closure of asylum routes can be interpreted as part of a process of assuaging domestic anxieties provoked by neoliberal restructuring. In this respect, McNevin draws attention to the ways in which asylum has been central to the neoliberal adaptation of the sovereign state. While her analysis draws on the Australian case, this book develops a similar reading of the UK. As we have already seen, the 1980s were marked by the resurgence of a nationalistic, authoritarian-populist discourse of citizenship, which ran alongside a pervasive neoliberalism. Despite their significant rearticulation, there has been a continuation of both of these dimensions under recent Labour governments. Such conditioning factors – authoritarian nationalism and neoliberalism – run both in parallel and also in contradiction with one another. Thus, the neoliberal demand for flexible labour serves to open up migration routes, while domestic anxieties (often articulated in nationalistic terms and related in part to the pressure for flexible labour and related job insecurity) demand their partial closure. It is in this ambiguous context that the conditions have been ripe for a constitution of the asylum seeker as a scapegoat for wider shifts in governance and belonging.

If exclusionary asylum discourse functions to assuage anxieties in a context marked by neoliberal restructuring, it could also be said to assuage anxieties in a context marked by a range of dislocations of a territorial order of governance and belonging. European integration is of particular interest in this regard, because it potentially entails a post-territorial mode of governing (Weiner, 1998) and a post-national mode of belonging (Soysal, 1994). In other words, European integration itself potentially dislocates a territorial order. This raises questions as to whether asylum is constituted as a scapegoat at the European level, and as to whether an emergent 'post-national' or 'post-territorial' polity such as the EU facilitates a movement beyond the framing of governance and belonging in the territorial terms of exclusionary asylum discourse. This book engages with such questions through analysing asylum discourse in both the UK and the EU contexts. The UK can be conceived as an exemplary case by which such questions can be considered, both because of its tradition of Euro-scepticism (which suggests that European integration is particularly dislocatory in this context), and also because of its specific focus on asylum. While concerns regarding 'illegal immigration' have generally tended to dominate in the southern and eastern European contexts, a concern with asylum has been particularly heightened in the UK. As such, an analysis of

UK asylum discourse is not only of interest in its own right, but also is of interest in its relation to the articulation of asylum at a wider European level. Indeed, it is an important case by which we can develop an understanding of exclusionary politics more generally. On this reading, UK asylum discourse can be approached as a story of what happens when the sovereign state and its national community come together in responding to territorial dislocations in distinctly exclusionary terms.

Analysing the exclusionary politics of asylum

The UK's exclusionary focus on the 'threat' or 'problem' of asylum in part reflects its geographical positioning.[4] As an island 'buffered' by various EU member states, the UK does not face 'illegal immigration' in such an immediate way as countries such as Italy and Spain in the south, or the more recently acceded EU states in the east. Much of the concern in the UK has thus been about those who have passed through other EU states, including those who have been trafficked or smuggled, and also as asylum seekers. The prominence of asylum seeking, over illegal immigration, reflects this concern, although the revised Dublin Convention has lessened this emphasis in the UK since it requires that asylum seekers be dealt with by the first safe country that they entered. Notwithstanding these important specificities, however, the differences between UK and other EU (and non-EU) states should not be overstated. Asylum discourse is characterised by a 'frequent conflation' of asylum with issues of immigration (Lewis and Neal, 2005:436). Indeed, an exclusionary politics that takes asylum as its primary target of control may be less distinct than it initially appears from an exclusionary politics that takes 'illegal immigration' as its primary target of control. It is with this in mind that restrictive asylum discourse can be conceived of as part of a wider exclusionary politics in which the focus of control shifts between various 'threatening' mobile subjects.

This book draws critical attention to the conflation of asylum and 'illegal immigration' through referring to the *asylum-seeker-cum-illegal-immigrant*, as well as to asylum-cum-illegal-immigration or illegal-immigration-cum-asylum. Where such terms are used, they specifically refer to the conflated categories of asylum and 'illegal immigration', which often form a focus of concern in political and popular debates. Nevertheless, it is important to remember that the two are in fact separate subcategories of migration, which have distinct legal meanings. *Migration* broadly refers to the movement of humans across borders, whether forced or unforced, whether political or economic and whether authorised or not. While the *migrant* is a traveller or a worker who moves from one region to another, the *immigrant* seeks settlement within the 'host' region or country. *Asylum seeking* in its territorial variant applies only to those migrants who have physically reached the state's territory or its port, and who have lodged a claim for refugee protection. On successfully being granted protection the asylum seeker is redefined as a *refugee*, who according to the 1951 Convention, is 'a person outside of his or her country of nationality who is unable or unwilling to return because of persecution or a well-founded fear of persecution on account of race, religion, nationality, membership of a particular social group, or political opinion' (United Nations High Commissioner for Refugees, 1996:16). If s/he does not meet the criteria of the Convention, s/he may instead be granted with subsidiary protection, often of a temporary nature.

In contrast to asylum, *'illegal immigration'* refers to the unauthorised residence of migrants within a 'receiving' state. The 'illegal immigrant' may enter without authorisation or s/he may enter legally and breach his or her visa conditions by staying after his/her visa has expired. Although 'illegal immigration' is primarily represented in relation to asylum as a problem of entrance without authorisation, it can thus also refer to those who have reached the end of the asylum process without having their claims accepted by the state. This serves as just one of the ways in which illegality is produced by the state (De Genova, 2002, 2004). An acknowledgement of the various processes of 'illegalisation' that come into play through the extension and reinforcement of restrictive policy initiatives is expressed in the use of quotation marks around the term 'illegal immigration' throughout this book.

It is important to note that the asylum seeker is protected in international law from being defined as an 'illegal immigrant'. However, there have been moves to criminalise those asylum seekers entering without correct documentation over recent years, despite the 1951 Convention's emphasis on the right of an asylum seeker to enter a territory without legal documents (Guiraudon, 2003). Reflecting such developments, the term 'asylum-cum-illegal-immigration' is employed here through a critical engagement with the restrictive discourse of control, which is dominant in the UK and elsewhere. In contrast, the term 'irregular migration' is employed in order to signify a critical *disengagement* with such a discourse. Where the book refers to the *irregular migration*, it thus employs its own term to refer to disruptive 'acts' in which state borders are crossed and territories are inhabited without authorisation (Isin and Nielsen, 2008). This term is thus not used in a legalistic sense, nor does it refer to a specific category of migrants. Rather, the irregular migrant is perceived as a figure who potentially interrupts an exclusionary discourse through which a territorial order of governance and belonging is precariously reconstructed. The term 'irregular migration' is thus indicative of the critical distance that this book strives to develop between the analysis and the object of the analysis.

A growing number of works have emerged over recent years that develop a critical understanding of the way in which EU states such as the UK respond to asylum within the international or global sphere. Whether from a legal (Goodwin-Gill, 1996), political (Boswell, 2003a; Geddes, 2003) or sociological perspective (Morris, 2002), and whether taking as a primary focus domestic (e.g. Hansen, 2000) or EU developments (e.g. Lavenex, 1999; Guild and Niessen, 1996), asylum policy and practice have been subject to detailed investigation. An analysis of the securitisation of free movement can contribute to this critical body of literature by examining the way in which the framing of asylum as a security issue legitimises the extension of restriction developments within, and beyond, 'host' states such as the UK (Bigo, 2000a, b, 2002b; Huysmans, 2006; van Munster, 2009). This analysis contributes to the literature on securitisation by focusing on its exclusionary processes and consequences in relation to asylum-seeking more specifically. In this regard, it can be linked to a wider literature on criminalisation (Cuneen, 2000; Garland, 2001). Rather than producing a detailed and comprehensive analysis of asylum policy *per se*, it engages with policy developments specifically in terms of the way that they shed light on the framing of asylum as a security or criminal 'threat'. Conceptualising securitisation as related to criminalisation (or 'illegalisation') in terms of its exclusionary narrative and technical operations, the book conceives both as similarly entailing a logic of selective opposition. This, it suggests, can be understood in terms of the articulation of asylum as a 'threatening supplement' against which the territorial political community is defined (Derrida, 1997; Smith, 1994). Such an articulation is conceived both in terms of the exclusionary reconstruction of a nationalistic conception of belonging, as well as in relation to the exclusionary reconstruction of a state-centric conception of governance. Indeed, this analysis suggests that restrictive migration controls precariously reconstruct the state where it is disrupted by the increased role of subsidiary regulatory agencies, while at the same time the nation is reaffirmed against disruptive or turbulent transnational and regional identifications.

In analysing these exclusionary politics from a critical perspective, this book strives to move beyond a restrictive discourse of control in which some migrants are included, only for others to become scapegoats. In so doing, it has four key objectives. First, it aims to consider how an exclusionary approach to asylum has become dominant in the UK and the EU today. While the centrality of restrictive (and often draconian) policy developments is relatively widely charted in the literature on asylum, the process by which a restrictive approach has become dominant is less clearly understood. This book addresses this limitation through developing a historical analysis of the conditions of emergence for restrictive asylum policy, and through undertaking a discursive analysis of the interrelation between the political and popular legitimisation and the technical and institutional embedding of such developments. In so doing, it develops a discursive approach to securitisation in which narratives of control and technologies of control are approached as distinct practices that come together as part of a wider exclusionary asylum discourse. Such an approach enables us to consider how words and actions come together to constitute asylum as a 'problem' or a 'threat' necessitating restrictive controls.

Related to this, the second objective of the book is to examine how exclusionary asylum discourse is manifest across the political, popular, public and technical spheres. Various commentators have pointed to linkages between press and policy debates regarding asylum (Kaye, 1999) and to the co-option of various non-governmental and private organisations within an exclusionary agenda (Zetter, Griffiths and Sigona, 2005). A discursive approach facilitates a detailed analysis of these processes, because it allows both for a consideration of the ways in which exclusionary narratives of control are manifest across EU, governmental, party political and press discourse (Part II), as well as for a consideration of the technical operations through which various agencies enact restriction (Part III). In exploring these processes, the book draws on a wide range of texts and interviews in order to show how processes of securitisation and criminalisation serve to legitimise and extend restrictive controls while delegitimising alternative discourses of asylum. This not only allows it to shed light on the way in which an exclusionary asylum discourse maintains dominance even where restrictive measures are subject to significant contestation, it also shows how the increasing dominance of exclusionary asylum discourse at the domestic level tends to preclude a more radical rethinking of asylum at the European level.

The third objective of the book is more concerned with the effects or consequences of exclusionary asylum discourse than it is with the operations and processes by which exclusionary asylum discourse has become dominant. Specifically, the book explores the effects of restrictive controls in relation to asylum seeking, both in conventional and critical terms. First, the book assesses policy initiatives in their 'own terms'. It does this by drawing out a range of exclusionary narratives of control in Part II, through which key initiatives examined in Part III are then assessed. Drawing on interviews with asylum seekers, community representatives, asylum support workers and immigration officers, the analysis shows how policy initiatives often produce and reproduce the 'problems' that serve as justification for such practices. From this, the book develops a second line of critique in which it is suggested that asylum seekers are constituted as scapegoats onto whom various 'problems' are projected. This process is, it suggests, an inherent dimension of exclusionary politics in which processes of securitisation and criminalisation get entangled in a self-fulfilling cycle.

It is in the attempt to break out of this self-fulfilling cycle that the final objective of the book comes into play. While the primary aim of the analysis is to consider how, and with what effects, exclusionary politics have become dominant in and beyond the UK today, attention is also paid to how the space for a more 'inclusionary' approach to asylum can be opened up. Throughout the book, the analysis draws attention to various contestations that emerge in relation to the restrictive measures and threatened/threatening subjectivities that such a discourse inscribes. In considering how such contestations might be engaged with critical effect, Part IV of the book shows how a reinvigorated conception of the political subjectivity of asylum seekers serves as an important starting point for any movement beyond exclusionary politics. It suggests that such a move not only requires a rereading of asylum, but also a rethinking of citizenship more broadly. Drawing attention to the European Union as a key site by where this re-enactment of citizenship and asylum might proceed, the book suggests that any movement beyond exclusionary politics of the reactive and territorial form outlined here requires a rearticulation of citizenship in terms that takes mobility seriously.

An outline of the exclusionary politics of asylum

This book is divided into four parts, the first and last of which are primarily theoretical in nature and the middle two of which combine empirical analysis with theoretical discussion. Part I goes forward from this introductory chapter into Chapter 2, which develops the conceptual and theoretical tools by which the empirical analysis proceeds. The first part of the chapter shows how a focus on asylum is important in drawing attention to the exclusionary tendencies of 'managed migration', and suggests that both liberal and critical analysts risk reaffirming a discourse of the asylum 'problem' where they do not critically distance themselves from the exclusionary operations of a managerial approach. Introducing securitisation theory as one starting point for such a critique, Chapter 2 suggests that a discursive theory of securitisation enables us to critically examine the exclusionary processes through which the territorial political community is constructed against the 'threatening supplement' of asylum-cum-illegal-immigration. Going further, it suggests that a discursive approach is able to bridge a methodological and empirical gap that has opened up between speech act and governmental theories of securitisation, because it is able to examine the exclusionary interactions between narratives of control and restrictive techniques of control. This is critical in showing how restriction becomes decontested or depoliticised through the discursive sedimentation *and* the institutional embedding of an exclusionary politics.

Part II of the book explores how exclusionary asylum discourse has become dominant in the UK and the EU, and outlines the key securitising and criminalising narratives that emerge across political, public and popular debates. Chapter 3 further charts the historical emergence of restrictive asylum developments in the UK, and considers how emergent European policies have been legitimised at both the domestic and EU levels through an opposition to asylum and associated 'threats'. The first part of the chapter situates restrictive asylum developments in relation to a longer historical trajectory of restriction in post-war Britain. In so doing, it suggests that contemporary asylum politics might be conceived of as an exclusionary reiteration of post-war immigration politics. Situating the exclusionary politics of asylum in relation to European integration, the second part of the chapter goes on to show how the tensions and dislocations that emerge between European and domestic articulations of political community are mediated or covered over by exclusionary asylum discourse at both the domestic and at the European levels. Specifically, it examines European Council, European Commission and UK government discourse in order to show how the construction of asylum-seekers-cum-illegal-immigrants as 'threatening' or 'culpable' subjects both naturalises and normalises the extension of restrictive controls in terms that bring together the UK and the EU in an exclusionary relation of equivalence. This, Chapter 3 concludes, serves to precariously reconstruct a territorial order while covering over dislocations that are in part produced by the process of integration.

Chapter 4 moves from this focus on the EU in order to examine the dominance of restrictive asylum policy at the domestic level. More specifically, it charts public contestations of restrictive policy measures and explores how exclusionary narratives of asylum that cross governmental, party political and popular press texts legitimise restrictive developments at the level of practice. The first part of the chapter shows how recent governments have limited the scope and effectiveness of contestation by developing a populist and exceptionalist style of government. The second part of the chapter shows how this style of government needs to be understood in relation to a broader shift towards restriction across the party political spectrum, which in turn needs to be understood in term of the dominance of exclusionary narratives of control in which asylum is constructed as 'threatening'. Charting these narratives in further detail, the analysis shows how political community is defined as socially stable and morally benevolent, precisely through an opposition to asylum. This contradictory reconstruction of political community is indicative of a productive tension at the heart of exclusionary asylum discourse in which the dislocations of a territorial order are selectively covered over in reactionary terms.

While Part II of the book begins with restrictive practices and moves through to the analysis of exclusionary discourse, Part III of the book starts with exclusionary discourse and moves through to an analysis of restrictive practices. Specifically, Part III develops a more detailed assessment of the effects of exclusionary politics by assessing two control initiatives in both conventional and critical terms. Chapter 5 focuses attention on 'external' techniques of control that prohibit the entrance of asylum seekers *en route* to EU states such as the UK. The first part of the chapter introduces interception as part of a managerial approach that entails a range of institutional and technical processes of securitisation and criminalisation, and shows how the managerial development of migration control signals a process of depoliticisation in which restrictive controls are moved away from the sphere of public scrutiny. The second part of the chapter considers the effects of such developments in relation to asylum. Showing how asylum is constituted as a 'problem' of unauthorised entrance through the development of interdictive controls, it challenges the assumption that external regulatory practices respond to a pre-existing 'threat' of unauthorised entrance. Specifically, it argues that interceptive techniques are better understood as interdictive control technologies that pre-emptively *refoule* 'undesirables' such as asylum seekers.

Chapter 6 focuses attention on 'internal' techniques control that discipline asylum seekers who have already entered EU states such as the UK. The first part of the chapter introduces asylum reception practices such as dispersal, detention and deportation (or removal) as punitive technologies that form part of a wider deterrent rationality. Going on to critically analyse the punitive techniques that characterise the dispersal initiative, it shows how a range of organisations have become co-opted within the diffuse practice of policing asylum seekers. The second part of the chapter develops a critique of dispersal by showing how the initiative aggravates many of the 'problems' that it is designed to resolve. Specifically, it shows how dispersal tends to reproduce the 'threat' of service strain and social tension, while constituting asylum seekers *en mass* as 'culpable' subjects who have no right to complain. Claiming that this process reduces the scope for solidaristic political engagement by creating a hostile environment in which asylum seekers are vulnerable to both political and economic exploitation, Chapter 6 concludes that dispersal feeds into a self-fulfilling cycle of securitisation and criminalisation, the only route which would seem to move in the direction of abjection.

Part IV shifts the focus back to a more theoretical level, while considering the potential for a movement beyond the exclusionary politics of asylum. Chapter 7 opens by considering how far Giorgio Agamben's theorisation of sovereign power facilitates a specifically critical diagnosis of exclusionary politics. While it accepts that Agamben's work is important in facilitating a conceptualisation of the exclusionary processes of securitisation and criminalisation in relation to the production of abject spaces, it warns against an approach that precludes a consideration of the 'turbulent' resistance of irregular migrants. Instead, the analysis suggests that sovereign-bio-power produces multiple abject spaces, which are crossed through with a range of contestations. The second part of the chapter develops this claim by considering how the critical inhabitation of abject spaces by the *No Borders* and *No One Is Illegal* movements enact citizenship, governance and belonging in terms that exceed a territorial frame. Such actions are important, the chapter suggests, because they critically intercede an exclusionary politics by producing solidaristic relations between citizens and irregular migrants through the 'misplaced' claiming of rights and obligations.

Chapter 8 closes the book by considering how a more 'inclusionary' approach to asylum might be developed. Summarising the critical diagnosis of the exclusionary politics of asylum as a specifically reactionary, depoliticising and divisive politics of differential inclusion, the first part of the chapter suggests that a simple move beyond a territorial political frame is inadequate to the task of rethinking asylum. Suggesting that a critique of both the oppositional relations and also of the discursive and institutional depoliticisations of an exclusionary politics is critical in any 'post-territorial' rethinking of citizenship and asylum, the second part of the chapter goes on to draw attention to the limits of human rights and open borders approaches in critically interceding exclusionary politics. As an alternative, the chapter argues for a distinctly *political* engagement of asylum *qua* irregular migration and for a mobile re-enactment of 'post-territorial' citizenship in terms of acts of solidarity. Pointing to the European Union as a fertile ground for such developments, the chapter concludes that such political engagements potentially open the space for a dialogue that does not become caught in an exclusionary cycle.

2
Challenging Managerial Operations: Developing a Discursive Theory of Securitisation

An analysis of the contemporary politics of asylum brings to the fore both exclusionary practices of governance and exclusionary articulations of belonging. For example, a raft of measures that are designed to restrict and deter access to asylum systems have become standard across Europe in recent years, while the criteria for recognising asylum claims have widely been tightened (Boswell, 2003b). Indeed, such measures are largely conceived of as legitimate in the face of unauthorised entrance (Boswell, 2007). It is this assumption of the legitimacy of restrictive controls that this analysis seeks to challenge. It shows how the construction of asylum as a 'problem' or 'threat' needs to be understood in relation to the wider articulation of political community as a territorially defined entity that requires protection from 'alien' incursion. In this book political community is thus shown to be precariously reconstructed in territorial terms through the development of exclusionary relations of governance and belonging. While the book works from the assumption that both the inevitability and desirability of a territorial rendering of political community is open to debate, the book also conceive its contemporary rearticulation in relation to asylum to be highly problematic because of the exclusionary tendencies such a relation entails. This analysis thus seeks to challenge the articulation of the asylum seeker as a scapegoat figure onto which various dislocations of the territorial order are projected (see Chapter 1).

Current theories of securitisation are particularly useful in developing such an analysis, because they address a number of important theoretical and empirical issues that arise in relation to exclusionary politics. At a conceptual level, theorists of securitisation have raised important questions about how the 'exceptionalism' of a security-orientated approach can be critically challenged (Aradau, 2004a, 2008). This concern with

21

developing a 'politics out of security' is important in the struggle to move beyond the confines of a sovereign power that has turned biopolitical, which this book conceives as inherently related to exclusionary politics (see Chapters 7–8). At an empirical level, analysts of securitisation have raised important questions about how migration or human mobility has been articulated or embedded as part of a security frame (Bigo, 2000a, b, 2002, 2005; Bigo and Tsoukala, 2006; Huysmans, 2006; van Munster, 2009). Such questions are important in understanding the operations and effects of an exclusionary politics, which have been of particular concern since 9/11 but which have a much longer and more complex trajectory (see Chapters 3–6). It is through an engagement with this second set of questions that the book introduces a discursive approach to securitisation.

The discursive approach to securitisation outlined in this chapter can be understood both as a challenge to the 'managerial' account of asylum as a 'problem' sketched in Chapter 1, and also as an attempt to bridge the gap that seems to have emerged between the so-called Copenhagen and Paris 'schools' of securitisation theory. The first part of the chapter shows how a focus on asylum is important in drawing attention to the exclusionary tendencies of 'managed migration', and suggests that both liberal and critical analysts risk reaffirming a discourse of the asylum 'problem' where they do not critically interrogate and distance themselves from the exclusionary operations of a managerial approach. The second part of the chapter introduces securitisation theory as one starting point for such a critique, and shows how a discursive theorisation of exclusionary politics suggests the territorial political community is constructed against the 'threatening supplement' of asylum-cum-illegal-immigration. The third part then goes on to claim that such analysis can bridge a methodological gap that has opened within the field of securitisation theory, because it requires an analysis of both the speech acts of political elites and the governmental techniques of security professionals. Indeed, it argues that such a move is critical in understanding exclusionary politics, because it facilitates a consideration of the oppositional interactions between technical or technological processes of securitisation and linguistic or narrative processes of securitisation (Balzacq, 2008).

Challenging exclusionary politics? Liberal and critical readings of 'managed migration'

As suggested in Chapter 1, 'managed migration' has become the dominant paradigm by which European states such as the UK have responded to complex and mixed migratory flows over recent years.

Indeed, migration management is not confined to the European context, but rather it can be conceived of as an emergent global system that is designed to manage the cross-border movement of people (Duvell, 2003). This part of the chapter opens the discussion of migration management by drawing attention to its exclusionary dimensions. In particular, it suggests that a managerial approach to migration is problematic because, in defining 'unproductive' migrants as 'undesirable' migrants, it entails both selectively restrictive dimensions and highly exclusionary tendencies. The analysis then goes on to show how the exclusionary renderings of a managerial approach are often reaffirmed by analysts of migration control, both liberal and critical. As such, it concludes that any critique of the managerial response to migration needs to carefully interrogate managed migration while critically challenging its exclusionary tendencies.

Migration management and exclusionary politics

There are two slightly different ways in which 'managed migration' can be conceptualised, both of which are interrelated and both of which are important for an analysis of the exclusionary politics of asylum. First, managerialism can be conceptualised as an approach through which the state extends its administration of human mobility (see Clarke and Neuman, 1997). On this reading, managed migration signals a shift in state practices of control, both in terms that grant technocratic and non-state actors a more central role and also in terms that extend and disperse disciplinary techniques of surveillance and control (Bigo, 2002, 2005). As the analysis in Part III of this book suggests, such developments are problematic because they significantly reduce the scope for the political contestation of restrictive controls. Related to this first reading, but slightly different from it, managed migration can also be conceptualised in terms of differentiated migratory routes (Mezzadra and Nielson, 2008). It is this second formulation that we focus on here, in which managerialism is conceptualised both in terms of the discrimination between various types of migrants as well as by their differential regulation. It is against the backdrop of these complex processes of differentiation that the exclusionary politics of asylum need to be understood.

Managed migration has often been conceived as a relatively 'liberal' or 'open' approach to migration, primarily because it introduces new migration routes that were previously foreclosed by a zero-immigration approach (Veenkamp, Buonfino and Bentley, 2003). However, there are important limitations to the liberal credentials of a managerial approach, and these do not only relate to its restricted provision of refugee protection routes. Managed migration has primarily been developed in terms of the utilitarian and neoliberal rubric of maximising the economic and social benefits of migration, and as such can only be defined as open, liberal or inclusive in a highly selective sense (Duvell, 2003). The converse of this selectively inclusive approach is, of course, a selectively exclusive approach in which 'unproductive' migrants become subject to restrictive controls. This can be understood in terms of an exclusionary rubric of deterrence or prevention. It is important to note that distinctions made between 'productive' and 'unproductive' migrants are complex, ambiguous, often contradictory and sometimes paradoxical. Nevertheless, a dualistic distinction remains important as a broad frame of reference according to which migrants are differentially categorised. While it is fair to say that managed migration is a relatively liberal approach in terms of its articulation according to a logic of selective inclusion, it is also fair to say that managed migration is a highly restrictive approach that is articulated according to a logic of selective exclusion. Managed migration, in other words, is not as liberal as some would have us assume.

Although this book is critical of the utilitarian and neoliberal renderings of migration management, this is not its main line of critique. Rather, its primary concern is with the way in which the political processes of differentiation that are inherent to managed migration become depoliticised through reactionary means. This process signals the moment where an exclusive politics moves into the realm of an exclusionary politics, and occurs where 'unproductive' migrants are identified as 'undesirable' migrants. There are three points that are central to this exclusionary reformulation of exclusive processes. First, it is in the rearticulation of 'unproductive' migrants as 'undesirable' migrants that exclusionary processes of securitisation and criminalisation come to the fore. These processes can be conceived of as tendencies that are inherent to the operations of a managerial approach, but not as its inevitable outcome. Second, a key effect of such exclusionary processes is that political decisions in which 'productive' migrants are distinguished from 'unproductive' migrants are subject to processes of depoliticisation. This is particularly the case where the identification of migrants as 'undesirable' works through exclusionary processes of securitisation, because the scope for political debate surrounding differential categorisations is likely to be further reduced where fear predominates. Third, the process of rearticulating 'unproductive' migrants as 'undesirables' serves to cover over the transgressions of territorial belonging and governance that managed migration entails. This is particularly the case where territorial transgression (or unauthorised entrance) is articulated as the defining feature of 'undesirables', and where managed migration is articulated as a system of control that is designed to resolve this 'problem' or 'threat'. On this reading, a managerial approach to migration is not only problematic because it entails a selectively restrictive dimension, but is problematic also because of the exclusionary tendencies that are inherent to, if not necessary outcomes of, its operations.

Slipping into exclusionary politics

Analysts of migration control often tend to reaffirm the exclusionary assumptions of a managed migration approach, despite the critical concerns of many researchers within the field. This partial slippage into the realm of exclusionary politics is evident, for example, in Sarah Spencer's (2003) introduction to a special edition of *The Political Quarterly*. It is important to note that Spencer is primarily concerned with the effective management of economic migration in this piece. She calls for 'optimal management' as opposed to a response that denies opportunities for immigration, and in this respect contributes towards the theorisation of a more liberal approach towards migration at large (Spencer, 1994). However, while her approach might be conceived as moving away from exclusionary politics in relation to the issue of immigration, if we focus on asylum more specifically it would seem that Spencer's approach is less liberal. Suggesting that asylum systems in the EU are under strain to the detriment of all concerned (2003:1), Spencer indirectly articulates asylum as 'problem' of 'abuse'. Thus, she claims that 'As one of the few channels of legitimate entry into Europe, the asylum route designed for those seeking protection has been taken also by those wanting a chance to better their lives' (2003:1–2). Even while she makes the case for a more liberal approach to immigration, Spencer treads a more restrictive line on the issue of asylum.

That Spencer slips so easily into reaffirming exclusionary renderings of asylum perhaps says as much about the contemporary operations of managerialism as it does about Spencer's politics. Managed migration is produced through a play of inclusion and exclusion, because its founding rationale is to provide 'productive' migrants with a legal route (while closing down all avenues for the 'unproductive'). Indeed, a liberal or inclusive approach to migration always has limits, however these are defined. These limits are clearly evident in Spencer's approach. While she calls for the opening up of legal migration routes for economic migrants and refugees, Spencer also supports forceful intervention in countries of origin 'where necessary' (2003: 3–4). In addition, she calls for the development of an effective asylum determination system in order to remove 'the huge incentive the current system provides to make unfounded applications' (2003:22). It is in this implicit rearticulation of asylum seekers as 'undesirable' migrants that Spencer tends to slip from her support of the (inherently exclusive) liberal politics of managed migration into an exclusionary politics of asylum. Indeed, this slippage would seem to be characteristic of managed migration more generally.

While Sarah Spencer develops a liberal approach to migration in terms that remain firmly within the realms of a managerial framework, Liza Schuster develops a more critical reading of exclusionary renderings of managed migration. In this respect, her work is closely related to the approach developed here, particularly in her analysis of the criminalisation of asylum seeking (Schuster and Welch, 2005; Welch and Schuster, 2005). Indeed, Schuster's work is influenced by a similar tradition of work as the analysis in this book, namely that which challenges the subjection of various 'immigrants' to processes of racialisation and criminalisation (Hall, Critcher, Jefferson, Clarke and Robert, 1979; Collyer, 2005). Nevertheless, there are important differences between Schuster's analysis of exclusionary politics and that developed here, primarily because this book undertakes a critique based on a discursive analysis while Schuster bases her critique on a constructionist analysis. The effectiveness of Schuster's critique of the exclusionary politics is limited by her use of this analytical framework. Specifically, her rather 'thin' development of a constructionist approach risks drawing her back towards managerialism, while also limiting her ability to radically rethink asylum (2003a:261–79).

Although she claims that 'reality is constructed' (2003a:57), Schuster would seem to assume that state interests are pre-given variables that explain the development of a control agenda. For example, she claims that asylum is of declining political utility to the state in a post-Cold War context, and that it is for this reason (rather than because of an increase in the number of claimants) that asylum has come to be defined as a 'problem' (2003b:244). While this book develops a similar reading of the importance of the end of the Cold War in accounting for the emergence of the exclusionary politics of asylum, it approaches this dislocatory event in relation to a wide range of conditioning events and processes (see Chapter 1). In so doing, it does not conceive state interests as pre-given factors that dictate the pattern of processes of differential inclusion and exclusion. Rather, it perceives state interests as constituted *through* such processes. The approach developed here could thus be said to differ from that of Schuster, because it develops a more thoroughly contextualised, discursive analysis of exclusionary politics.

While the differences between the approach developed in this book and that developed by Schuster are subtle, they are important to the development of an effective critique of the exclusionary politics of asylum. Specifically, Schuster's 'thin' constructionist approach is problematic because it tends to draw her back into the realm of exclusionary politics. This occurs precisely in her critical analysis of its operations, such as in relation to the interpretation of asylum statistics. To her credit, Schuster develops a strong critique of the political debate surrounding asylum statistics that became dominant in the 1990s and early 2000s. In arguing that asylum statistics have fluctuated since the early 1990s, she questions the dominant narrative in which asylum figures are conceived as 'on the rise' (2003b:236). Going further, she argues that increasing numbers of asylum seekers reflect shifting political and economic circumstances, rather than the failure of immigration controls (2003a:145–6). Thus, she criticises the announcement by the former Prime Minister, Tony Blair in 2002, in which he suggested that the number of asylum applications would be halved within a year. Schuster argues that the former Prime Minister's claim demonstrates a failure to acknowledge external factors, such as difficult political and economic living conditions, which impact on asylum application figures (2003b:237). In making this claim, Schuster undertakes a critical move by identifying asylum seekers as forced migrants, whether as a result of political or economic circumstances.

Despite the important contributions that Schuster makes in terms of her critical interpretation of asylum statistics, however, her critique runs the risk of reaffirming the managerial assumption that 'numbers matter' in relation to asylum. For example, in claiming that asylum statistics have not risen straightforwardly over recent years, Schuster opens up the terrain for managerialists to contend that a longer-term statistical analysis shows an overall rise in the numbers of asylum applicants. Similarly, in claiming that increased numbers reflect political and economic 'push' factors rather than domestic 'pull' factors, Schuster implicitly suggests that numbers matter. Whether or not Schuster's claims are accurate is not the critical issue here. Rather, what is critical is whether or not Schuster reaffirms exclusionary managerial assumptions by contributing to a debate surrounding the *extent* of the asylum 'problem'.

It seems that Schuster runs the risk of so doing, despite her critical attempt to reframe the nature of the asylum 'problem'. In this respect, her development of a 'thin' constructionist approach limits Schuster's ability to create critical distance between the exclusionary operations of managerialism, and her analysis of such operations.

This book suggests that any challenge to the exclusionary politics of asylum needs to couple a careful interrogation of the exclusionary operations of a managerial approach with a critical distance of its workings. A 'thicker' constructionist or discursive approach is particularly well placed to do just this. Indeed, such an approach is arguably able to develop a more critical reading of contemporary contestations of exclusionary politics than Schuster's 'thin' constructionist approach. Rather than idealistically appealing to 'dreams' of an existence beyond the confines of the nation state (Schuster, 2003a:276), a discursive analysis shows how contemporary contestations of exclusionary asylum discourse can be conceived as creative moments of political intervention that potentially move governance and belonging in an inclusionary direction (see Part IV). This book thus strives to move through a critical analysis of asylum discourse in order to consider how asylum and citizenship can be rethought beyond the territorial confines and exclusionary operations of managerialism. The effectiveness of such a critique is, of course, a matter of debate.

A discursive theory of securitisation: From the 'existential threat' to the 'threatening supplement'

Liza Schuster brushes rather quickly over the securitisation literature in her analysis, claiming that internal criticisms have rendered the framework inappropriate to the study of migration (2003a:31–2). This is partially true, since some security analysts have been criticised in terms of their potential validation of the articulation of migration as a 'threat' (Huysmans, 1995a). Indeed, it remains important that a security-based approach does not preclude alternative readings of migration (Boswell, 2007, 2008). Nevertheless, the focus in this part of the chapter reflects the insight that securitisation theory can be developed in order to critique the exclusionary operations of managed migration. The first part of the analysis introduces the Copenhagen School's theory of securitisation as a speech act, and suggests that this serves as critical starting point for the analysis of the exclusionary rendering of asylum as a 'problem' or a 'threat'. Developing a distinctly discursive approach to securitisation, the second and third sections go on to show how securitisation is characterised by a logic of selective opposition in which the territorial political community is precariously reconstructed against the 'threatening supplement' of asylum. In so doing, it shows how securitisation can be theorised alongside criminalisation in terms of an exclusionary politics whereby state governance and national belonging are reactively reconstructed in the face of their territorial dislocation.

Securitisation as a speech act

The Copenhagen School's speech act theory securitisation has been highly influential in extending the analysis of security studies in a post-Cold War context (Wæver, Buzan, Kelstrup and Lemaitre, 1993; Wæver, 1997). In particular, the framework developed by Barry Buzan, Ole Wæver and Jaap de Wilde (1998) has facilitated a widening of the security studies field beyond a traditional focus on the military. Working from a constructivist perspective, Buzan et al. approach securitisation as a type of intersubjective process that occurs between an actor and his/her audience through the performative 'speech act' (see Austin, 1975). There are two dimensions central to the definition of securitisation in this formulation. First, securitisation is characterised by the construction of an oppositional relationship between an 'existential threat' (here: asylum or asylum-cum-illegal-immigration), and a 'referent object' (here: 'the state' or 'the nation'). Second, it is characterised by the existence of an 'emergency condition' whereby 'the established rules of the game' do not apply (Buzan, Wæver and Wilde, 1998:22–3). In this formulation, the grammar of securitisation reflects the Schmittian political grammar: both are characterised by the construction of a dichotomous relation between friend and enemy, and by the sovereign exception as residing above 'normal' politics.

A speech act theory of securitisation serves as an important starting point for a critique of exclusionary asylum discourse, because it allows us to create critical distance between our analysis and the managerial rendering of asylum as a 'problem' or 'threat'. In particular, the constructivist lens of securitisation theory enables us to approach the exclusionary articulation of asylum as a socio-historical construction that is open to contestation, and thus to change (Howarth, 2000). Buzan et al. state that: '"Security" is thus a self-referential practice, because it is in this practice that the issue becomes a security issue – not necessarily because a real existential threat exists but because the issue is presented as such a threat' (1998:24). In this formulation, securitisation theory does not only serve as an analytical framework by which we can examine the oppositional logic and exclusionary processes through which asylum is constructed as a 'problem' or 'threat'. So also does it allow us to critically examine the way in which such articulations legitimise 'exceptional' measures in terms that lessen the scope for political debate (Wæver, 1995). For this reason, a speech act theory of securitisation remains an important starting point for this analysis.

While securitisation theory facilitates a critical analysis of the oppositional logic and justificatory mechanisms that are central to the exclusionary politics of asylum, it would seem that Buzan et al. tell only part of the story regarding the articulation of asylum as a 'problem' or 'threat'. As Jenny Edkins (2002) suggests, they risk leaving the status of the referent object unquestioned, at least in their early formulation of securitisation theory. According to Jef Huysmans (1995b:54–7), securitisation is not only characterised by the twin mechanisms of the existential threat and its referent object or objects, but so also is it characterised by the *maintenance of the referent object's identity*. A consideration of this third dimension is critical, for it draws attention to the way that the referent object is constructed through the very process in which the existential threat is opposed. A conceptualisation of securitisation where the referent object is analytically excluded from the processes of construction is thus epistemologically problematic. Indeed, it is also politically dangerous, because it risks overlooking the exclusionary or reactive processes that are inherent to the articulation of asylum as a 'problem' or 'threat'. This analysis thus differs from a constructivist reading of securitisation, which fails to adequately challenge the objectivism that is central to a managerial approach.

If we approach both the referent object(s) *and* the existential threat as constructed through processes of securitisation, we can turn Buzan et al.'s model of securitisation on its head. That is, we can show how the referent object is constructed through its opposition to a specified threat, just as the threat is constructed as such through its opposition to the referent object. It is in relation to this deconstruction of the referent object that a discourse theoretical approach can contribute to the critical development of securitisation theory (Campbell, 1998; Hansen, 2006). Discourse theory has both affinities and tensions with the securitisation framework that is developed by the Copenhagen School. In epistemological terms the two approaches do not necessarily conflict with one another, for both might be interpreted as anti-objectivist or constructionist of sorts. However, a discourse theoretical approach potentially poses a greater challenge to the articulation of asylum as 'problem' or 'threat', because it breaks with objectivism in both epistemological *and* ontological terms. This potentially facilitates a more far-reaching critique of the exclusionary operations of a territorial order.

A discursive theory of exclusionary politics

The discursive theory of securitisation that is developed in this book is informed by the work of Ernesto Laclau and Chantal Mouffe and, as such, does not develop a straightforwardly constructivist epistemology. Rather, it is based on the presupposition that there exists a world and objects that are independent of discourse, but that these are only accessible through a discursive frame. When it comes to the process of analysis, such an approach is thus decidedly anti-objectivist, because it is based on the assumption that 'natural facts are also discursive facts ... [and that] they are so for the simple reason that the idea of nature is not something that is already there, to be read from the appearances of things, but is itself the result of a slow and complex historical construction' (Laclau and Mouffe, 1987:84). In critically analysing the exclusionary politics of asylum from an anti-objectivist perspective, this book does not direcly challenge the claim that there has been a general (if inconsistent) rise in the numbers of asylum seekers since the 1990s. It does, however, challenge the claim that such a trend is threatening or problematic. Rather than focusing direct attention on the exclusionary interpretation of asylum statistics, the analysis thus strives to develop a more thoroughgoing critique of the exclusionary processes and effects of articulating asylum as a 'problem' or a 'threat'.

Discourse theory works on the ontological assumption that any attempt to create a social or discursive order of objective meanings and identities remains incomplete or precarious (Laclau and Mouffe, 1987:87). It thus couples its epistemological anti-objectivism with ontological anti-objectivism (Torfing, 1999). Specifically, it challenges a totalising conception of social order by drawing attention to the centrality of relational processes of articulation in the construction of meaning and identity (Laclau and Mouffe, 2001). There are thus two ontological assumptions on which an anti-objectivist theory of securitisation is based. First, it rests on the assumption that any *purely* objective meaning or identity is impossible. Rather, it examines the relational processes that are inherent both to the construction of meaning and to the construction of identity. Second, it rests on the assumption that a discursive order can never be complete, or that it can never reach the point of absolute closure. To borrow a phrase from Laclau and Mouffe: 'the incomplete character of every totality necessarily leads us to abandon, as a terrain of analysis, the premise of 'society' as a sutured and self-defined totality' (2001:111). By coupling epistemological anti-objectivism with ontological anti-objectivism, this book approaches the territorial articulation of political community as an inherently unstable social order of governance and belonging that undergoes constant change.

It is in relation to this inherent instability that the exclusionary politics of asylum can be seen as one specific strategy in the struggle to stabilise the meaning and identity of a territorial political community. In this book, there are two dimensions that define this strategy. First, exclusionary politics can be conceived as a totalising ideological strategy that attempts to mask the inevitable failure of a territorial order to fully constitute itself (Glynos, 2001; Glynos and Howarth, 2007). While this process is inevitable in the sense that any social order fails to fully constitute itself, what is not necessarily inevitable is that such a failure needs to be ideologically masked. Nevertheless, the process of ideological masking is conceived by discourse theorists as an inherent tendency, which is perhaps more likely to occur in certain circumstances, such as where a social order is subject to a dislocation by processes that precede or exceed its discursive frame (Laclau, 1990). These processes of dislocation are, arguably, characteristic of the contemporary situation within which the exclusionary politics of asylum arise (see Chapter 1). This leads us to the second dimension of exclusionary politics to which this book draws attention. This rests on the suggestion that the strategy associated with the exclusionary politics of asylum is not simply an ideological one through which the dislocation of a discursive territorial frame is masked. It is also a *reactive* one, in which the dislocations of a territorial order are blamed on a scapegoat 'other'. It is thus important to note that, even in a context that is marked by a heightened dislocation of the territorial order, the exclusionary politics of asylum are not inevitable. Rather, exclusionary politics should be understood as one, specifically reactionary, ideological strategy that needs to be critically challenged.

Securitisation and the threatening supplement

This book conceptualises securitisation, alongside criminalisation, as central to the workings of an exclusionary politics that responds reactively to 'internal' and 'external' dislocations of the territorial order. It has already been suggested that this exclusionary process is evident where asylum seekers are identified as 'undesirable' migrants. This insight is developed throughout the course of this book, which shows how 'undesirable' migrants such as asylum seekers are constructed as 'threatening' or 'culpable' subjects. Such exclusionary processes occur through the intertwinement of processes of securitisation and criminalisation, which come together in relation to the logic of selective opposition. The analysis in this book explores this logic through theorising securitisation in relation to the 'threatening supplement'. In order to clarify the meaning of this theoretical category, a more detailed exposition of the discourse theoretical categories of nodal points, the empty signifier, antagonism, dislocation and the logics of equivalence and difference is required. Let us take each one of these in turn, before considering how the exclusionary or oppositional logic of securitisation can be identified as constituting asylum as a 'threatening supplement' of (rather than as an 'existential threat' to) the territorial political community.

A discourse theoretical reading of securitisation conceptualises referent objects as signifiers that have become partially fixed as *nodal points* within a territorial order. Nodal points are defined by Laclau and Mouffe as 'privileged discursive points' through which a discourse or social order is constituted (2001:111). To translate this statement in relation to our object of analysis, one could say that referent objects such as 'the state' and 'the nation' are partially fixed nodal points through which the territorial political community is precariously constructed. Political community, on the other hand, is better understood in relation to the discourse theoretical category of *the empty signifier*, which might be conceived of in terms of a 'master signifier' that unifies a range of nodal points or referent objects within a wider social order (Laclau, 1996). In this book, this discursive process of unification can thus be understood in terms of the constitution of a social formation, which entails both processes of identity construction and also processes of governance or regulation.

We can further develop an understanding of this articulation of a territorial order in relation to the discourse theoretical category of *antagonism*. 'Antagonism', Laclau and Mouffe suggest, 'far from being an objective relation, is a relation wherein the limits of every objectivity are shown' (2001:125). It is in developing a theory of securitisation with reference to the category of antagonism that this analysis shows the 'referent object' and its 'existential threat' to be mutually constituted through processes of exclusion and inclusion (or of equivalence and difference). Indeed, discourse theory rests on the assumption that there can be no strict division between a social order and it's 'outside' (Norval, 1997). While antagonism is often conceived of as a normatively imbued analytical concept that implies that all identity formations are exclusionary, it is perhaps more adequately conceived as an analytical concept that refers to the complex relations of inclusion/exclusion (of difference/equivalence) through which frontiers are drawn around an 'always precarious, always threatened' social order (Laclau cited in Norval, 1997:53; Norval, 2000). On this reading, Laclau and Mouffe's theorisation of antagonism implies that identity construction, like the process of constructing social order, always has an exclusive dimension. However, it does not imply that such processes *necessarily* entail an exclusionary dimension.

It is on moving from the theoretical category of antagonism to the theoretical category of *dislocation* that this book conceives exclusive social formations as potentially moving in an exclusionary direction. Laclau (1990) conceptualises dislocation as a material dimension that the discursive or conceptual can never fully grasp. Thus, dislocation refers to the process by which the inherent instability of a discursive formation becomes evident because the social order is unable to incorporate emerging material elements (Howarth, 2000:132). One could perhaps say that, while antagonism focuses attention on the complex play of inclusion/exclusion through which one territorial political community is distinguished from another, dislocation focuses attention on the failure of this play of inclusion/exclusion to successfully constitute the territorial order. In relation to our object of analysis, contemporary dislocations of the territorial articulation of state governance and national belonging can be conceived of both in terms of 'external' forces that 'precede' such articulations (e.g. cross-border mobilities), as well as in terms of 'internal' forces that transform such articulations (e.g. extraterritorial regulations of free movement). Asylum, on this reading, is not dislocatory of the territorial order because it serves as an 'existential threat' to state governance or national belonging. Rather, asylum is dislocatory of a territorial order because it brings into visibility the instabilities that are inherent to the social formation through which state governance and national belonging are constituted. It is where this failure of the territorial order to fully constitute itself is *projected* onto a supplementary 'other' that an exclusionary politics emerge (Zizek, 1990). In this book, securitisation is thus conceived of as a specifically reactive strategy that is characterised by an exclusionary logic of selective opposition.

This exclusionary logic can be further theorised in terms of the logics of equivalence and difference, where the logic of equivalence is understood as a broadly exclusive logic and where the logic of difference is understood as a broadly inclusive logic. Laclau and Mouffe conceive the logics of equivalence and difference as central to the construction of the frontier between that which is part of any order of governance and belonging, and that which is not (2001:127–30). They define the *logic of equivalence* as emerging where an unstable identity is redefined alongside a series of other elements in relation to a negative and external 'something', and suggest that the effect of this process is that various identities are rendered the equivalent through their opposition to an 'other'.[1] Numerous examples of this exclusive or oppositional logic emerge through this analysis, which suggests that it is predominant in contemporary asylum discourse. For example, in Chapter 5 we will see how the EU, the UK and Bosnia Herzegovina are rendered equivalent through their articulation in opposition to the 'threat' of asylum-cum-illegal-immigration (and equivalent 'others'). In contrast, examples of the inclusive or pluralising logic of difference are much harder to identify. Laclau and Mouffe define the *logic of difference* as emerging where there is a proliferation of antagonisms and a multiplication of political space.[2] An example in this regard might be drawn out of the analysis in Chapter 7, whereby irregular immigrants and citizens engage as 'workers', 'activists' and 'people' in terms that disrupt the categories of the exclusionary renderings of a territorial order.

The dominance of the logic of equivalence in contemporary asylum discourse is suggestive of an exclusionary politics that is characterised by a selective logic of opposition. While discourse theory works on the assumption that equivalence and difference (or exclusion and inclusion) always remain present in a relation of tension with one another, this analysis suggests that different discourses and social formations entail more or less exclusive/inclusive articulatory relations. As such, asylum discourse, like governance and belonging more widely, can be articulated in broadly exclusionary or in broadly inclusionary terms (see Part IV). This book defines processes of securitisation and criminalisation in relation to the dominance of the oppositional logic of equivalence, the selective application of which betrays a complex play of inclusion/exclusion that is conceived as inherent to any exclusionary politics. In exploring how processes of securitisation and criminalisation emerge as part of an exclusionary strategy through which the territorial order is precariously reconstructed in the face of its dislocation, we develops a reading of the exclusionary politics of asylum based on the threatening supplement.

There are two parts to the process by which an 'other' is constructed as a *threatening supplement*, which need to be analytically distinguished from one another. First, the referent object is named as an object (here: the nation or the state); this process can work in relation to an 'other' that the object is defined against. In this respect, the 'other' (here: asylum) is *supplementary* to the meaning or identity of the referent object in question. Second, there is a struggle to separate the referent object from its supplementary other. Because the frontier between the object and the supplement is indefinite, the other forms a subversive *threat* to the meaning or identity of the object (Laclau and Mouffe, 2001:127). In other words, that which is articulated as a threat to the referent object *at the same time* serves to make the meaning or identity of that object possible by supplementing its essential lack (Derrida, 1997). By approaching asylum as a threatening supplement, this analysis is able to shed critical light on the exclusionary constitution of political community. The latter can also be conceived of in two stages. First, migrants are selectively included or excluded as supplementary to a territorial order of governance and belonging. The book conceives this to be a process marked by inclusion and exclusion, which does not necessarily move into the realm of exclusionary politics. Second, 'unproductive' others are marked as 'undesirable' and are transformed into 'threatening' or culpable' subjects. The book suggests that it is in this second move that an exclusionary politics takes hold, because it is here that processes of securitisiation and criminalisation come together as dimensions of the logic of selective opposition.

A discursive analysis of securitisation: Bridging a methodological divide

A discursive approach to securitisation not only facilitates a critical retheorisation of securitisation in relation to exclusionary politics, but also contributes to the development of a distinctive methodology in which both linguistic and non-linguistic processes of securitisation can be analysed. This is important, because it potentially bridges a divide that seems to have opened up between the 'speech act' theory of securitisation associated with the Copenhagen School and the 'governmental' theory of securitisation that has been developed by Didier Bigo. While there remain important and irreconcilable theoretical differences between these two approaches, this part of the chapter suggests that a discursive theory of securitisation facilitates a consideration of the interaction between technical or technological processes of securitisation, and linguistic or narrative processes of securitisation. This, it claims, is critical, because it enables us to consider how linguistic and non-linguistic processes of securitisation come together in exclusionary terms by legitimising the extension of restrictive controls, while limiting the scope for their political contestation.

From the speech act to governmental technologies

Drawing on, and developing, Rens van Munster's distinction between speech act and risk-based theories of securitisation (2005, 2009), this book approaches Bigo's reading of securitisation as differentiated from that of the Copenhagen School in terms of his theorisation of the following dimensions: (a) the representation of 'threat'; (b) the strategy for dealing with the 'threat'; (c) the objective in dealing with such a 'threat'; (d) the agents of securitisation; and (e) the practices of securitisation (see Table 2.1). Let us briefly examine each of these dimensions

Table 2.1 Five differences between speech act and governmental theorisation of securitisation

	Securitisation as a speech act	Securitisation as governmental practice
Representation of threat	Friend/Enemy opposition and personification of the enemy.	Friend/Enemy continuum and impersonal correlation of factors liable to produce risk.
Measures or strategy	Exceptional measures that bypass normal political procedures; measures counteract existential threat.	Routine or normalised measures such as surveillance and risk profiling; measures contribute to the social control of large populations.
Objective	Elimination of threat; the elimination of a threat secures the collective survival of a socio-political order.	Management of risks against the background of uncertainty and contingency; risk management seeks to prevent risks from developing into existential threats.
Agents	Political elites and their audiences.	Security professionals including military agencies, secret services, customs, police forces and immigration agencies.
Practices	Linguistic speech acts: performative social practices that are announced by the securitising agent and accepted by the securitising audience.	Techniques of government: power/knowledge devices, discipline and expertise gestures, manoeuvres and rituals of demonstration.

Source: Developed from Rens van Munster's (2005) 'Three differences between securitisation and risk management. Logics of security: The Copenhagen School, risk management, and the war on terror', Political Science Publication, 10/2005, University of South Denmark.

in turn, before discussing in further detail how a discursive approach can bridge the methodological gap between the two theories of securitisation in order to develop a more thoroughgoing critique of the exclusionary politics that this book conceives as central to a managerial approach.

In terms of his conceptualisation of the *objective* of securitisation, Bigo suggests that the aim of a risk-orientated rendering of security is to prevent the development of a represented threat, rather than to eliminate its existence (Bigo, 2004). He thus tends to conceive securitisation in more proactive terms than those analysts drawing on the Copenhagen School theory of securitisation. Moreover, while a speech act theory of securitisation suggests that the *representation* of the threat works through opposition to an 'enemy', Bigo conceives securitisation as working through a continuum in which a slippage can easily occur between those who are represented as a 'friend' and those who are represented as an 'enemy'. This has implications for Bigo's conceptualisation of the *strategy* applied in dealing with threats. While Copenhagen School analysts tend to focus on the exceptional nature of policies that are framed according to a security logic, Bigo conceives securitisation more in terms of the wider government of populations, which is developed through the drawing up of 'a "common" list of threats' (2000a:171–3). For Bigo, security *practices* are thus better conceived of as routinised 'techniques of government' than as exceptional 'speech acts', while the *agents* of security are more adequately conceptualised as 'security professionals' than as elite politicians.

Despite the irreconcilable differences in the theoretical frameworks through which the speech act and the governmental theories of securitisation are developed, it is not clear that all of the differences outlined above are unbridgeable. Whether preventative and eliminative strategies of securitisation are best conceived of in terms of contradictory logics or in terms of intertwined technologies remains a matter for further investigation (see Chapter 5). Indeed, the differences and similarities between a risk-orientated approach to governmentality and an exceptionalist reading of the politics of security is a rich area requiring further consideration (see Aradau and van Munster, 2007, 2008). Where a discursive approach might contribute to this theoretical debate is in its consideration of the way in which a security frame entails an exclusionary politics. In this book, the exclusionary politics of asylum are not straightforwardly exclusive, but emerge within a broader managerial frame of differential inclusion that is composed of complex processes of inclusion/exclusion. Bigo's continuum of threats might thus be conceived in relation to a wider exclusionary politics of differential inclusion that is characterised by a logic of selective opposition.

What we are left with, then, is an empirical and methodological gap that is left when the analysis of securitisation is pulled towards that of Bigo or the Copenhagen School, a gap which a discursive approach does not recognise. While Copenhagen School analysts tend to focus on the speech acts of political elites and governmental theorists such as Bigo tend to focus on the techniques and operations of security professionals, a discursive analysis conceives both as central to the workings of exclusionary politics. Indeed, linguistic (narrative) and non-linguistic (technical) processes of securitisation are both approached here as discursive practices that coalesce around a deterrent rationality and a logic of selective opposition (see Chapter 8). Discourse is thus defined in relatively broad terms in this book as a 'meaningful totality that transcends the distinction between the linguistic and extra-linguistic' (Laclau, 1993:435). This book does not consider governmental techniques and speech acts to exist in separation, nor does it consider the linguistic and non-linguistic processes of securitisation to be distinct. Rather, it critically analyses both the linguistic and non-linguistic (or narrative and technical) operations through which asylum seekers are constructed as 'threatening' or 'culpable' subjects. Indeed, a discursive theory of securitisation is particularly well placed to undertake a critique of such processes, because it is able to examine the depoliticising effects and that emerge through the exclusionary interaction of technical or technological processes of securitisation, and linguistic or narrative processes of securitisation (Balzacq, 2008).

There are, then, two ways in which a discursive theory of securitisation bridges the gap that has opened up between the speech act and governmental theories of securitisation. First, a discursive analysis shows how linguistic (narrative) and non-linguistic (technical) processes of securitisation come together in terms that legitimise the exclusionary extension of restrictive regulations. From this direction, the book approaches restrictive governmental techniques as effects of the linguistic operations of securitisation. This clearly does not exhaust the meaning or relevance of governmental techniques of control, but it is one way of examining their workings. Indeed, it is a critical one from a discursive perspective, because it enables us to examine the exclusionary processes by which restrictive regulations are legitimised. This draws on an important insight of the speech act theory of securitisation, which focuses attention on the ways in which exclusionary narratives or statements legitimise 'exceptional' policy initiatives. In this book, an analysis of the exclusionary linguistic renderings of political elites is thus critically important in showing how the development of restrictive regulations over selected groups of individuals is legitimised in exclusionary terms (see Part II).

There is also a second way in which a discursive approach critically bridges the speech act and governmental theories of securitisation, which can be conceived of as working in the opposite direction. Namely, a discursive theory of securitisation draws attention to the way in which the governmental techniques of security professionals reduce the scope for the contestation or restrictive controls. From this direction, governmental regulations can be conceived of as having an exclusionary effect in terms of their movement of restrictive control out of the sphere of political debate and into the technocratic sphere of experts. As we will see in Part III of the book, this is a key dimension of a managerial approach that lends itself to the extension and diffusion of exclusionary technical operations. An analysis of the operations and effects of exclusionary politics thus requires that we examine the interactions between the technical or technological practices of security professionals and the linguistic or narrative practices of political elites. It is through a critical analysis of such processes that we can further understand how the exclusionary politics of asylum become caught in a self-fulfilling cycle of securitisation (Parts II and III).

A discursive methodology

As discussed above, this book does not strictly follow either a speech act or a governmental approach to the analysis of securitisation, but rather it develops a discursive approach that challenges the distinction between the two. Conceptualising securitisation as related to criminalisation in terms of the exclusionary logic of selective opposition, the book considers how narratives of control and regulatory practices of control come together in constructing asylum as a 'problem' or a 'threat' to the territorial order. In so doing, it approaches the 'speech acts' of political elites and the technocratic regulatory practices of security professionals (broadly defined) as mutually constituting the exclusionary politics of asylum. Such an approach is of critical purchase because it is able to explore how exclusionary linguistic and non-linguistic processes of securitisation come together in terms that legitimise the extension of restrictive regulations, while limiting the scope for their political contestation.

The book takes as its opening focus political debates, before going on to consider how exclusionary politics are enacted through various technologies of control. The analysis of political debates considers how a discourse of the asylum 'problem' has become dominant over recent years. It does this by further developing a historical analysis of the emergence of exclusionary politics of asylum, and by drawing out exclusionary narratives of control that emerge both in domestic and European political discourse, as well as in party political and popular discourse surrounding asylum. Specifically, it analyses political documents and the statements of prominent EU and domestic politicians, as well popular press cuttings. The media has played an important role in constructing asylum as a 'problem' or 'threat', and in this respect the analysis focuses on the popular press as well as on political discourse. This relatively wide-reaching analysis of linguistic processes of securitisation and criminalisation is important in drawing attention to the dominance of exclusionary narratives of asylum in, and beyond, the UK today.

The analysis of the dominance of exclusionary asylum discourse is also developed through a consideration of technical processes of securitisation. While Part II of the book primarily focuses on the justificatory narratives by which territorial referent objects such as the nation and the state are constructed in opposition to asylum, Part III of the book examines the restrictive techniques that address the 'problem' or 'threat' of asylum. In so doing, it draws on textual and technical documentation, as well as on a series of semi-structured individual and group interviews. Chapter 5 draws on documentation and on a series of interviews with immigration officers involved with an 'external' control initiative of interception (see Appendix 1), while Chapter 6 draws on documentation and on interviews with asylum seekers, community and support workers involved with the 'internal' control initiative of dispersal (see Appendix 2). An analysis of the material in Part III in relation to that of the material in Part II is important in showing how exclusionary practices of restrictive control are put beyond the sphere of political contestation through the presumption of their legitimacy.

Conclusion

This chapter has developed a discursive theory of securitisation in the attempt to create critical distance between the approach developed in this book and the objectivism of managerialism. Specifically, it has suggested that this critical distance is important in order that the exclusionary operations of managed migration can be subjected to an effective critique. A theorisation of securitisation according to the 'threatening supplement' is, it has argued, important to the development of such a critique, because it enables us to theorise exclusionary politics as a specifically reactive ideological strategy in which dislocations of a territorial order are projected onto a scapegoat other. Indeed, it enables us to conceive how state governance and national belonging are reaffirmed and put beyond question in the identification of the asylum seeker as a 'threatening' or 'culpable' subject, thus precariously reconstructing a territorial political community in the face of its dislocation. The chapter has argued that a critical analysis of this exclusionary politics requires a discursive theoretical approach that is able to bridge some of the gaps that have opened up between a speech act and a governmental theory of securitisation. Specifically, it has claimed that a discursive approach is important in developing a critique of the exclusionary interrelation between technical and linguistic processes of securitisation and criminalisation, through which exclusionary politics become caught in a self-fulfilling cycle that is increasingly difficult to contest.

It is in analysing the exclusionary interactions between these linguistic and non-linguistic discursive practices that this book develops a two-pronged critique of restrictive regulations of control. First, it critically assesses the effectiveness of restrictive controls in relation to the exclusionary narratives through which they are legitimised and, second, it critically examines their exclusionary processes and effects. It is in relation to this latter dimension that the book develops a more far-reaching critique of the exclusionary politics of asylum as a strategy that projects the failures of a territorial order onto the figure of the asylum-seeker-cum-illegal-immigrant. This occurs when various actors respond reactively to cover over the dislocations that emerge where disruptions that are internal or inherent to the territorial order meet with turbulences that come from 'outside'. It is in thinking about alternative relations that can be forged in the face of such dislocations that Part IV of the book discusses the potential for a movement beyond exclusionary politics. This more inclusionary rendering of asylum requires a rethinking of citizenship in terms that open up a political space that is not skewed against asylum seekers. Before moving in this decidedly interruptive direction, however, let us first undertake a more detailed examination of the exclusionary politics which stand in our way.

Part II The Development of the Exclusionary Politics of Asylum: Political, Public and Popular Narratives of Control

3
Moving to Europe: Charting the Emergence of Exclusionary Asylum Discourse

Chapter 1 charted various events and processes that serve as the conditions of emergence for the exclusionary politics of asylum. This chapter adds to this historical contextualisation of asylum discourse both by situating it within a longer history of exclusionary post-war immigration discourse, and also by further examining the exclusionary processes through which restrictive controls have been legitimised at the UK and EU levels. This dual focus on the exclusionary reverberations of domestic discourse and on the exclusionary commonalities of EU and domestic discourse is important for two reasons. First, it enables us to consider how exclusionary politics have a broader significance beyond our specific case study and, second, it allows us to explore how the exclusionary framing of asylum emerges even where 'post-national' or 'post-statal' citizenship potentially breaks with state governance and national belonging (Soysal, 1994; Weiner, 1998). Indeed, the analysis in this chapter suggests that it is *precisely* in a context whereby state governance and national belonging are subject to heightened dislocation that the exclusionary politics of asylum emerge.

Although exclusionary politics of the type examined here are often conceptualised as a racist politics, this book does not suggest that racism serves as an explanation for restrictive controls. Indeed, it does not claim to say anything about the motivations or reasoning of those who identify which migrants need to be restricted, prohibited or punished (see Part III). What it does claim to say something about, however, are the exclusionary operations and effects of processes of securitisation and criminalisation. It is in this regard that this analysis is influenced by an anti-racist literature, since it conceives processes of securitisation, criminalisation *and* racialisation as related through a logic of selective opposition (see Chapter 2). Thus, it conceives the identification of 'threatening' or 'culpable' subjects as an exclusionary process in which 'undesirable' migrants are marked as different, regardless of their skin colour (Balibar and Wallerstein, 1991; Doty, 1996a, b, 2003). In rejecting an analytical focus on racism (i.e. discrimination according to skin colour or ethnicity) in favour of an analytical focus on racialisation (i.e. divisions which certain groups or individuals are marked as 'different'), the analysis avoids getting caught up in a debate as to whether immigration and asylum policy can primarily be conceived of as liberal or racist (Hansen, 2000; Hansen and King, 2000; Hayter, 2000). As the discussion of 'managed migration' in Chapter 2 suggested, liberal and illiberal dimensions often coexist in a relation of constitutive tension within a broader exclusionary frame of differential inclusion. An analysis of exclusionary asylum discourse does not thus imply the absence of a liberal politics, nor does it necessarily imply the establishment of a racist politics. Rather, it points to a more complex situation in which inclusions and exclusions come together in exclusionary terms.

In drawing attention to the logical affinity of processes of racialisation and processes of securitisation and criminalisation, this chapter examines the reiterations and legitimisations that are central to the operation of exclusionary asylum discourse. The first part of this chapter reads contemporary asylum discourse as a reiteration of the exclusionary post-war response to 'new' Commonwealth immigrants. While the 'new' Commonwealth immigrant was primarily articulated as a 'threatening supplement' of a dislocated imperial order through processes of racialisation, it suggests that that the asylum-seeker-cum-illegal-immigrant is primarily articulated as a 'threatening supplement' of a dislocated territorial order through processes of securitisation and criminalisation. Situating exclusionary asylum discourse in relation to European integration, the analysis shows how the tensions and dislocations that emerge between European and domestic articulations of political community are in part covered over or mediated by exclusionary asylum discourse at both the domestic and European levels. Focusing attention on the processes of securitisation and criminalisation through which such developments are legitimised, the second part of the chapter shows how the construction of asylum-seekers-cum-illegal-immigrants as 'threatening' or 'culpable' subjects has the dual effect of naturalising and normalising the extension of restrictive controls. Drawing on European Council conclusions, Commission speeches and statements, and on UK government speeches and statements, the chapter concludes that exclusionary politics serve to precariously reconstruct political community in the face of its dislocation by bringing the EU and the UK together in a relation of mutual opposition against asylum-cum-illegal-immigration.

Exclusionary reiterations: From 'new' Commonwealth immigration to asylum

Many analysts suggest that exclusionary immigration discourse is a relatively recent development, which can be traced in the UK to the institution of immigration controls targeting 'alien' Jews in the first part of the twentieth century. For example, David Cesarani argues that the 1905 Aliens Act targeted Jewish refugees fleeing pogroms in Russia and Eastern Europe, and was characterised by a 'provoked and heightened sense of Britishness' which had a 'sharp, exclusivist edge' (1996:62). Developing this reading of 'exclusivist' discourse further, this chapter argues that an exclusionary politics is similarly evident during the 1950s and the 1960s with regard to 'new' Commonwealth immigration, as well as during the contemporary period with regard to asylum-seeking-cum-illegal-immigration. The analysis draws on primary and secondary material, and explores immigration and asylum discourse during four periods: (a) the 1950s–1960s; (b) the 1970s–early 1980s; (c) the mid-1980s–mid-1990s; and (d) 1997 onwards. Showing how processes of racialisation, criminalisation and securitisation tend to predominate where there is a dislocation of governance and belonging, it suggests that the exclusionary politics of asylum needs to be understood in part as a reactive reconstruction of the territorial political community within a broader context of European integration. Thus, while the 'new' Commonwealth immigrant was primarily articulated as a 'threatening supplement' of a dislocated imperial order through processes of racialisation, the analysis shows that the asylum seeker is primarily articulated as a 'threatening supplement' of a dislocated territorial order through processes of securitisation and criminalisation.

Between liberal and exclusionary politics: The 1950s and 1960s

The 1950s and the 1960s are often seen as a crucial juncture in the development of racialised immigration controls. Theresa Hayter (2000), for example, draws on existing analyses in arguing that UK governments during the early post-war period recruited workers from the colonies and ex-colonies on a small scale, while recruiting from Europe and Ireland on a large scale (Foot, 1965; Layton-Henry, 1992). Stephen Castles and Mark Miller (1998) implicitly contest this interpretation of migratory figures, yet they agree with Hayter on at least two issues.[1]

First, they concur that the UK's response during the early post-war period was marked, at least to some extent, by an attempt to actively encourage immigration from *both* the Commonwealth and from Europe. Second, they agree that there was a shift during 1962 specifically towards restricting immigration from the 'new' Commonwealth. This suggests that immigration policy developments were marked by a logic of selective opposition during the early post-war period, in which immigrants from the 'new' Commonwealth were marked for restriction.

Nevertheless, immigration was fiercely debated in parliament during the 1950s and 1960s, and restrictive or illiberal developments were by no means left uncontested. This is indicative of a strong liberal tradition within the UK context, which many have suggested have impeded the development of 'racist' policies (Hansen, 2000). For example, Ian Spencer's (1997) analysis of governmental debate during the 1950s and 1960s shows that, although Cabinet ministers privately displayed panic (and often hostility) regarding the immigration of British subjects from Asia and Africa during the 1960s, they simultaneously voiced concerns regarding the way in which restrictive measures might be interpreted in the public sphere. Spencer's reading of the impromptu development of restrictive immigration legislation thus draws attention to the on-going resonance of a relatively 'inclusive' imperial citizenship tradition within the UK. This was historically characterised by the institutionalisation of equal rights for British subjects of the UK, for British subjects of the colonies and for British subjects of those dominions without citizenship laws (Diez and Squire, 2008). Nevertheless, this relatively inclusive citizenship tradition needs to be conceived of in terms of a broader logic of selective opposition which, in the 1950s and 1960s excluded 'new' Commonwealth immigrants – primarily those who were not white (Hampshire, 2005).

While Spencer's analysis suggests that the formal institution of controls over 'new' Commonwealth immigrants were delayed because of tensions between a liberal and an illiberal politics, these restrictions began to take effect once the 1962 Commonwealth Immigration Act was passed under a Conservative government.[2] Indeed, such restrictions were further consolidated by developments in the mid- to late 1960s. On coming into power in 1964, the Labour Party shifted from a position of opposition to a position in favour of restriction, and promptly tightened up the implementation of the 1962 legislation. Moreover, Labour formalised controls over 'new' Commonwealth immigration both in the 1968 Commonwealth Immigration Act as well as in the 1969 Immigration Appeals Act.[3] In targeting restrictions at those who were not born, adopted, or naturalised in the UK, the 1968 legislation constructed a political community in racial terms through an opposition to 'new' Commonwealth immigrants (Doty, 1996b; Gilroy, 1987).

Indeed, it is in relation to this reconstruction of political community that we can observe the movement to a specifically exclusionary politics, which is marked by a construction of the 'new' Commonwealth immigrant as a 'problem' or 'threat'. The Commonwealth Immigration Act of 1968 was rushed through Parliament in response to populist pressure surrounding the so-called Kenyan Asians 'crisis' (Hampshire, 2005:34). This 'crisis' was conceived as such after the declaration of independence, which led to concerns that many Asian Citizens of the UK and Commonwealth (CUKC) would try to enter the UK (Hansen, 2000). That this process of racialisation emerged in a context marked by the 'aftershocks' of a dissolution of imperial governance and belonging is indicative of an exclusionary politics in which imperial dislocations were blamed on racialised 'others' (Smith, 1994). This exclusionary politics is no more evident than in Enoch Powell's infamous anti-immigrant campaign. On purportedly speaking 'for the people', Powell's notorious 1968 'Rivers of Blood' speech pronounced national decline to be a result of the 'dilution of homogenous stock by "alien strains"' (cited in Cohen, 1994:202). While government ministers publicly distanced themselves from Powell's rhetoric at the time, this analysis suggests that the distance may not have been as great as a liberal reading would have us assume. After all, 'new' Commonwealth immigration was not only articulated as a 'threatening supplement' to a racial order of governance and belonging in Powell's populist rhetoric, it was articulated as such in the development of restrictive controls that selectively opposed immigrants from the 'new' Commonwealth. It is, thus, in relation to this exclusionary reconstruction of political community and against the backdrop of imperial dislocation that we need to situate the UK's early movement towards Europe.

Moving from the Commonwealth to Europe: The 1970s and early 1980s

While the question of European integration was initially dominated by economic concerns, it could be said in retrospect that the crisis that decolonisation posed to the Britain's imperial identity was one factor related to its hesitant movement towards Europe in the early 1970s. During the post-war period the impermanence of Britain's colonial glory would seem to have been only too apparent, and the dislocatory effects of a progressive disintegration of Empire thus arguably necessitated a geopolitical repositioning. While a detailed consideration of the UK's move towards Europe is clearly beyond the scope of this book, a focus on this repositioning would seem to be important in analysing the reconstruction of political community during the 1970s. This process as characterised by two separate processes. On the one hand, the UK's cautious movement towards Europe reconstructed political community in terms that potentially disrupted a territorial order of state governance and national belonging. On the other hand, an ongoing opposition to 'coloured' immigration reconstructed political community in the racialised terms discussed above. It is, this analysis suggests, in relation to the tensions that emerge between these two re-articulations of governance and belonging that we need to interpret the exclusionary politics of asylum with which we are familiar today.

If we retrospectively read the UK as located at crossroads between the Commonwealth and Europe during the post-war period, a movement towards the latter would appear to be inseparable from an ongoing opposition to 'new' Commonwealth immigration. Needless to say, this does not stand as an explanation for the UK's alignment with Europe, but it is to say that the opposition to 'new' Commonwealth immigration coincided with such a movement. The UK's alignment with Europe was formalised during the early part of the 1970s, with membership of the European Economic Community (EEC) becoming effective from 1 January 1973. Membership entailed a commitment to the 1957 Treaty of Rome, which allowed workers of the member states the freedom to move throughout the EEC. Theresa Hayter (2000:55) suggests that this meant that 'an additional 200 million people were to have the right freely to enter and to settle in Britain', to which, notably, there was virtually no opposition. This lack of opposition is perhaps unsurprising, because European immigration was not subject to processes of racialisation during the post-war period. Indeed, in retrospect we could perhaps say that a racialised articulation of political community ran alongside its European reconstruction without significant disruption during this period.

At a European level the liberalisation of migration was more disruptive, with a new rationale for control beginning to take shape during the 1970s. A range of *ad hoc* measures emerged during the 1970s, which can be interpreted as institutionally embedding migration or free movement within the field of security (Huysmans, 2006). For example, measures such as carrier's liability were introduced by the Trevi group of Interior Ministers, which was founded in 1976 in order to enable European countries to cooperate on issues of terrorism. Immigration officials sat on Trevi working groups and, in this respect, the association of migration and terrorism that is often discussed today was already being institutionalised during the late 1970s (Geddes, 2003:130–1). Even if the 1970s can be described as characterised by a liberalisation of European immigration, it is thus important to note that we can identify a process of securitisation emerging at the European level in relation to free movement at this time. While it may be going too far to say that migration was inscribed as a threatening supplement, it would nevertheless seem to have emerged during the 1970s as a feature against which the European community was defined.

Although there were incremental changes through which the definition of illegality 'progressively embraced more people who thought they had become settled in the UK' (Sondhi, 1983:263), there is no evidence of an association of migration and terrorism at the domestic level during the 1970s. Rather, the primary operations of an exclusionary politics throughout the 1970s and early 1980s remain related to the racialisation of 'new' Commonwealth immigration. Indeed, this exclusionary discourse is evident even in the face of 'laudable' liberal reiterations (Hansen, 2000:204).[4] For example, political community was constructed against 'new' Commonwealth immigration in the 1971 Immigration Act, which introduced the concept of patriality in terms that restricted the right of abode for British subjects from non-UK areas of the Commonwealth.[5] This meant that Commonwealth citizens were only granted the right of abode in the UK if they, their parents or grandparents were born in the UK and islands (the Channel Islands and Isle of Man). The 1971 legislation thus consolidated an exclusionary politics through processes of racialisation that emerged the 1960s.[6] Indeed, before coming into office in 1979, the Conservative leader Margaret Thatcher proclaimed her sympathy with those who felt 'really rather afraid that this country might be swamped by people with a different culture' (quoted in Hayter, 2000:55–6). On coming into power, the Conservatives brought citizenship rights in line with immigration rights in the 1981 British Nationality Act, which replaced the *ius soli* principle (citizenship based on place of birth) with the *ius sanguinis* principle (citizenship based on blood). In this regard, the ongoing opposition to 'new' Commonwealth immigration can be seen as inseparable from the racialised rearticulation of citizenship and belonging.

While political community was reconstructed in exclusionary terms during the 1970s and the early 1980s, it is important to note that an emerging European order rendered the picture more complex. On the one hand, political community was domestically articulated in racial terms through an ongoing opposition to 'new' Commonwealth immigration. On the other hand, a territorial articulation of political community was partly challenged at the European level by the opening up of migration routes within the union. The 1970s were thus a critical juncture where the beginnings of a discursive transition might be identified, with two distinct discourses emerging alongside one another. The racialised reconstruction of political community at the domestic level is not necessarily at odds with a European alternative, and this is in part reflected in the relative lack of opposition to the liberalisation of European migration at the time. However, tensions between the domestic and European articulation of governance and belonging remained inherent to the UK's repositioning as a European, rather than as an imperial, state. Indeed, this analysis suggests that these tensions became increasingly dislocatory after the mid- to late 1980s.

From caution to hostility: The mid-1980s to the mid-1990s

From the mid-1980s there was a dramatic intensification of migration-related security concerns at the European level. These largely emerged as a result of the 1985 Schengen Agreement (Schengen I), whereby France, Germany, Belgium, the Netherlands and Luxembourg committed to removing internal border controls. With the majority of EEC Member states signing up to what was initially an administrative agreement requiring no parliamentary involvement, Schengen became a Convention (Schengen II) requiring parliamentary ratification in 1990. On its entry into force during 1995, Schengen thus saw the extended implementation of free movement across much of the European community. It is in relation to these developments that the rapid expansion of the Trevi group's brief during the mid-1980s needs to be understood. As police forces and security agencies extended their remit across the Schengen area, the Trevi group focused on all policing and security aspects of free movement, including illegal immigration, visas, asylum seekers and border controls.[7] Indeed, such a focus had become increasingly central since the 1986 Single European Act came into force, reflected both in the attempt to develop external borders provisions and in the development of the 1990 Dublin Convention.[8] At the EU or EC level at least, it would thus seem that a European order of governance and belonging was in part constructed against asylum-cum-illegal-immigration.

The UK's response to the opening up of internal borders was cautious, to say the least. This cautiousness can be interpreted as reflecting the centrality of a territorial order of state governance and national belonging, which was in part articulated at the domestic level through an opposition to European integration. For example, on signing up to the Single Europe Act, the former Prime Minister Margaret Thatcher was accused by Labour as having ceded sovereignty. The Tories responded by arguing that she had won an 'opt-out' from any concessions on frontiers in the very name of sovereignty (Hayter, 2000:60). The heightened cautiousness associated with the attempt to maintain a territorial order of governance and belonging can also be conceived in terms of the UK's refusal to sign the Schengen Convention.[9] When the Schengen Agreements were legally instituted after absorption into the Maastricht Treaty, a protocol was drawn up enabling the UK to opt into its provisions at a later date. In this context, the 1992 Maastricht Treaty of the European Union could be conceived of as *dislocatory* of a territorial articulation of governance and belonging. Taking force from November 1993, the Treaty for the first time granted the EU legal competence to deal with visa controls, immigration, asylum, policing, internal security, law and conventions under the Treaty's third (intergovernmental co-operation) pillar of justice and home affairs. One could say that the UK's stance towards Europe moved from one marked by caution to one marked by hostility in response to this development. Indeed, the analysis here suggests that the tensions between the domestic and a European order of governance and belonging became increasingly dislocatory at this time.

In spite of the UK's cautiousness regarding European integration, asylum and immigration policy developments moved in a similarly restrictive manner at both the domestic and intergovernmental levels. For example, the 1987 Immigration (Carriers Liability) Act imposed financial sanctions on carriers bringing passengers to the UK who were not in possession of the necessary entry documents. These proposals were developed at the intergovernmental level before they were adopted by the UK. Indeed, restrictive developments would seem to have become increasingly far-reaching at the domestic level, as well as at the European level, during this period. The 1988 Immigration Act made it easier to deport illegal immigrants; restrict rights of appeal; and reduce the rights of the dependents. This was followed in the early 1990s by the raising of the carrier liability fine and the detention of larger numbers of asylum seekers as well as by a significant increase in the asylum refusal rate, which was initiated by the 1993 Asylum and Immigration Appeals Act. The 1996 Asylum and Immigration Act cut welfare support for asylum seekers; introduced a 'white list' of safe countries; and introduced employer sanctions for those employing undocumented workers. Restrictive developments thus characterise the late 1980s and early 1990s, on this reading of UK immigration and asylum policy.

Despite tensions dominating the UK's relation to Europe throughout this period, a restrictive discourse of control would seem to have emerged at both levels during the late 1980s and early and mid-1990s. It is precisely in a context when these tensions begin to become dislocatory that a discourse of the asylum 'problem' or 'threat' emerges with such restrictive force. Indeed, the heightened tensions between domestic and European renderings of political community played an important role, among various events and processes, in creating the conditions of emergence for exclusionary asylum discourse in the UK. Such dislocations were not effectively covered over by exclusionary politics during the late 1980s and early 1990s, but rather they would seem to have been played out within the ranks of the Conservative Party. According to this analysis, it was not until there was a change of government in 1997 that an exclusionary politics of asylum emerged with full force. New under Labour, one might thus say, was that territorial governance and belonging were reconstructed in terms that brought the UK and the EU into an exclusionary relation of mutual equivalence against the 'threatening supplement' of asylum.

Exclusionary mediations: 1997 and beyond

While tensions between domestic and European constructions of governance and belonging were heightened in the UK during the late 1980s and the early to mid-1990s, this analysis suggests that one way in which such tensions have been mediated in recent years is through the articulation of the UK and the EU in a relation of mutual opposition to the 'threat' or 'problem' of asylum-cum-illegal-immigration. Indeed, Labour governments could be said to have restrictively aligned the UK with the EU in areas of asylum and immigration over recent years. For example, the UK opted into the non-free movement aspects of Schengen II in 1999 (namely Europol and the Schengen Information System), on the grounds that such a development would allow the UK to maintain strong frontier controls.[10] Such an alignment clearly does not signal the end of tensions either between or within domestic and European constructions of governance and belonging. Political community in the EU context could be described as a complex formation that is differentially inscribed (depending on the level and focus of analysis) and continuously deferred (Přibáň, 2005). Nevertheless, it would seem that the restrictive alignment of the UK and the EU contributes to the reactive masking of such tensions by articulating asylum-cum-illegal-immigration as a 'threatening supplement' against which the territorial political community is precariously reconstructed.

An exclusionary reconstruction of territorial political community is evident in an extensive range of restrictive policy developments at the domestic level. Various rafts of primary legislation have been passed since Labour has been in office, all of which could be said to have moved in a broadly restrictive direction (Squire, 2008). First, the Immigration and Asylum Act of 1999 extended external controls such as carrier liability, while it gave immigration officers new powers to arrest and detain. It also introduced forced dispersal, replaced the benefit entitlements of asylum seekers with a central National Asylum Support Service and limited appeal rights through introducing the category of 'manifestly unfounded' cases. Following soon after, the Nationality, Immigration and Asylum Act of 2002 introduced regular reporting and biometric registration cards for asylum seekers, withdrew support for 'failed' asylum seekers, limited appeal rights and introduced statutory review as an alternative to judicial review. The legislation also reintroduced a list of 'safe countries', denying applicants from these countries the right to in-country appeal, while making it an offence to enter the UK without a passport.

The Asylum and Immigration (Treatment of Claimants) Act of 2004 further limited and revised the asylum appeals system and created a single-tiered tribunal for the assessment of claims. It increased penalties on those arriving in the UK without legal documents, expanded safe third country provisions and curtailed the provision of support to asylum seeking families. In 2005 the Labour government produced a five-year plan for immigration and asylum, *Controlling Our Borders*, which emphasised the need for removal of 'failed' asylum seekers and the need for visa controls to prevent 'abuse' of the asylum system. The plan also focused on limiting the provision of protection to a temporary, rather than a permanent status, and introduced the New Asylum Model as a means to streamline the application process. Soon after, the Immigration, Asylum and Nationality Act of 2006 imposed further limitations on the right to appeal against Home Office asylum decisions, gave the Secretary of State the power to deny refugee protection on national security grounds and extended the powers of immigration officers by introducing measures to check an individuals' identity. The UK Borders Act of 2007 similarly extended the powers of immigration officers by enabling them to search and arrest without warrant, on reasonable grounds of suspicion, those suspected of offence in relation to obtaining asylum support. It also included provisions related to biometric immigration cards.[11]

What these restrictive developments suggest is that asylum seeking has been a key target of exclusionary politics in the UK over recent years.

A huge range of restrictive controls have been developed under recent governments in terms that identify asylum seekers as 'culpable' subjects in association with 'illegal immigrants'. Asylum seekers have also been identified, among others, as 'threatening' subjects that necessitate the development of extensive measures of surveillance and control, such as ID cards (Huysmans and Buonfino, 2008). Asylum seeking has thus been subject to various processes of securitisation and criminalisation, indicative of an exclusionary rearticulation of state governance and national belonging in a context marked by the dislocation of a territorial order. There are clear differences between this articulation and that which emerged during the early post-war period. While there is increasing evidence of the racial rearticulation of political community against those of the Islamic religion, the exclusionary politics of asylum differ from the exclusionary post-war politics of immigration because they emerge both within a broad frame of multiculturalism as well as in the face of territorial, rather than imperial, dislocations (Squire, 2005). Nevertheless, the analysis in this book suggests that the exclusionary politics of immigration also have a logical affinity with the exclusionary politics of asylum in terms of the reactive masking of dislocation. Going further, it also suggests that this logical affinity can be identified between domestic and EU discourse.

The exclusionary reconstruction of territorial political community is not only evident in an extensive range of restrictive policy developments at the domestic level. It is also evident in many restrictive policy developments at the EU level. These need to be understood in relation to the common EU immigration and asylum policy, which were introduced by the Amsterdam Treaty post-Maastricht. The Amsterdam Treaty came into force in May 1999, granting the EU competency in interrelated areas of asylum and immigration by moving them from the 'third pillar' of intergovernmental co-operation to the 'first pillar' of Community Law.[12] Amsterdam marked the beginning of a process aimed at the development of common European asylum and immigration policies. While substantial developments in this regard have taken place, there have been significant delays in the development of common EU asylum and immigration policies, as well as in the institutional shift of control over asylum and immigration to the European Commission. The Amsterdam amendments to the Maastricht Treaty stipulated a need for agreement over legislation by 1 May 2004, but there were significant delays in the development of this legislation in the run up to the May 2004 deadline (Peers, 2003).[13] Indeed, at the time of writing, common asylum and immigration policies still have significant gaps. In this book, such gaps and delays in the development of common policy are conceived as indicative of significant tensions in the domestic and European articulation of political community.

Despite gaps and delays, a common approach has been gradually developed in the EU context in terms that put these significant tensions to the background. This book suggests that such developments can be understood in relation to the exclusionary logic of selective opposition, which is also evident at the domestic level. While a thoroughgoing analysis of EU legislative developments clearly remains beyond the scope of this book, a critical consideration of the 'externalisation' of immigration control potentially facilitates an understanding of the exclusionary dimensions of EU political discourse. The externalisation of immigration and asylum policy can be analysed in various ways and from various directions (see Chapter 5). The next part of the chapter focuses specifically on the way in which developments such as compulsory readmission, regional or transit processing and regional protection have been legitimised by the EU Council through various processes of securitisation and criminalisation. Going further, the chapter explores how such legitimisations similarly emerge in EU Commission and UK political discourse in terms that cover over the tensions between the European and domestic renderings of political community. There are, of course, differences between EU and UK discourse, which should not be overlooked. Most notably, an analysis of EU discourse suggests that illegal immigration, rather than asylum, has tended to form the primary focus of an exclusionary politics. Nevertheless, there remains a logical affinity and significant overlap between domestic and EU discourse, through which asylum-seekers-cum-illegal-immigrants are constructed as 'threatening' or 'culpable' subjects by exceptional and routine means.

Exclusionary legitimisations: Mutually opposing asylum

By situating exclusionary asylum discourse in relation to European integration, the first part of this chapter has suggested that restrictive developments targeting asylum-seekers-cum-illegal-immigrants can be conceived of as covering over tensions and dislocations that emerge between European and domestic articulations of political community. While the analysis thus far has primarily focused on the way that such exclusionary reiterations and mediations are evident in restrictive domestic controls, this part of the chapter is more concerned with exploring the legitimisation of restrictions in EU, as well as UK governmental, discourse. Specifically, it shows how restrictive controls have been legitimised through an opposition to asylum-cum-illegal-immigration at both the European and domestic levels. Suggesting that this process masks the tensions in political community through reactively drawing the EU and the UK in a mutual relation of equivalence, the analysis is divided into three parts. The first part examines European Council conclusions in which asylum and immigration formed a key focus of debate, and shows how the extension of restrictive policies has been articulated as necessary in relation to the 'threat' posed by asylum-cum-illegal-immigration. The second part shows how a similar logic emerges in speeches and statements produced by the European Commission in terms that routinise exceptional measures of control over asylum-seekers-cum-illegal-immigrants. By complementing this with an analysis of UK political discourse, the third part suggests that the EU and the UK are drawn in an exclusionary relation of equivalence through the exclusionary politics of asylum. The chapter thus concludes that the exclusionary politics of asylum have covered over the tensions in diverging articulations of political community while at the same time it has legitimised the extension of restrictive controls.

Naturalising restriction: European Council discourse

The previous part of this chapter suggested that EU discourse is more adequately conceived of as characterised by an opposition to illegal immigration than to asylum, and that this is suggestive of a divergence between European and UK discourse. However, this divergence may be less marked than it initially appears. This part of the analysis draws on European Council conclusions produced since the Amsterdam Treaty in order to show that asylum and 'illegal immigration' have been conflated in EU political discourse since Amsterdam, as they have in domestic discourse. The exclusionary leanings of European Council discourse may be tempered by EU institutions such as the Parliament or Commission, as well as by its more inclusive internal renderings (such as the commitment to asylum on the part of the individual presidencies). However, the analysis here suggests that European Council discourse remains primarily exclusionary in its extension of restrictive controls against illegal-immigrants-cum-asylum-seekers. This is no more evident than where restrictive controls are naturalised in their articulation as *necessary* in light of the 'threat' of illegal-immigration-cum-asylum.

In retrospect, one could describe the conclusions of the Tampere meeting of the European Council in 1999 as relatively liberal, because there is a clear commitment to maintaining the right of asylum. Reasserting a commitment to the 'full and inclusive application of the Geneva Convention', the Tampere Conclusions emphasise the importance of maintaining 'the principle of non-refoulement'[14] and 'the importance [that] the Union and member states attach to absolute respect of the right to seek asylum' (European Council, 1999:Section A.II.13). Yet, after the New York terrorist attacks of 9/11 a more restrictive discourse would seem to be evident. The Laeken meeting in 2001, for example, is marked by a concern regarding the reception capacities of EU and by the indirect association of illegal immigration and asylum. Thus, proposals for a 'true common asylum policy' are directly followed by proposals for the 'more effective control of external borders' and for 'judicial and police co-operation in criminal matters' (European Council, 2001:Section IV.38–43). Indeed, illegal immigration is clearly associated with terrorism within the conclusions, in the call to 'fight against terrorism, illegal immigration networks and the traffic in human beings' (Section IV.42). The indirect association of 'illegal immigration' and asylum, along with the direct association of terrorism and 'illegal immigration' is evidence of the criminalisation and securitisation of asylum at a time of heightened sensitivity regarding cross-border mobilities.

This securitisation and criminalisation of illegal-immigration-cum-asylum can be seen as an important factor conditioning the extension of restrictive controls beyond the EU territory. The Seville Council meeting of June 2002 is a key juncture in this regard, because it is here that the Council considered how the EU might use the entirety of its relationship with countries of origin and transit in order to resolve the 'problem' or 'threat' of 'illegal immigration'. The logic of selective opposition would seem to emerge in both an eliminative and a preventative form here, with the emphasis on returning 'illegal immigrants' coupled with an emphasis on managing flows 'at a distance'. Thus, the conclusions state that 'any future cooperation, association or equivalent agreement which the European Union or the European Community concludes with any country should include a clause on joint management of migration flows and on compulsory readmission in the event of illegal immigration' (European Council, 2002:Section III.33).

It was not until the Thessaloniki Summit in 2003 that the European Council's attention was directed to the 'problem' or 'threat' of asylum-seeking more specifically. Indeed, it was the UK that brought the issue of regional protection to the table at Thessaloniki. Focusing on the development of transit processing centres (TPCs) and regional processing zones (RPZs), the UK proposal was strongly resisted by Sweden, Germany and France, particularly in relation to TPCs. Despite these internal tensions, however, the Thessaloniki Conclusions display a tentative interest in the idea of regional protection, and invite the Commission to further explore regional protection (European Council, 2002:Section II.26). This would suggest that a preventative approach to asylum has become increasingly dominant at the EU level. Indeed, the interest in regional protection flourished following Thessaloniki, with the Hague programme of November 2004 incorporating a focus on 'enhancing the protection capacity of regions of origin' in the EU's five-year immigration and asylum plans (Europa, 2004).

So does this suggest that asylum is securitised at the EU level? Clearly we cannot generalise from this analysis beyond the institution of the European Council, and it is important to note that there remain internal contestations of a restrictive approach even within the Council itself. However, there is clear evidence of a securitisation and criminalisation of asylum in European Council discourse, specifically in terms of the association of asylum with 'illegal immigration'. Moreover, one can see that 'illegal immigration' more specifically has been subject to direct processes of securitisation in European Council texts. For example, the word 'combat' features no less than eight times within the four and a half pages of the Seville Conclusions relating to immigration and asylum. It is in this articulation of the externalisation or extension of restrictive European controls to third countries as necessary dimensions in the wider war against 'illegal immigration' that enables us to see how processes of securitisation naturalise restrictive controls. Specifically, it is through the identification of illegal-immigrants-cum-asylum-seekers as 'threatening' or 'culpable' subjects that restrictions are put beyond political debate.

Normalising exceptional measures: European Commission discourse

In putting restrictive controls beyond political debate, exclusionary processes of securitisation not only legitimise restrictions but so also do they normalise exceptional measures. This is evident in an analysis of EU Commission discourse. The analysis in this section draws on speeches presented by recent Commission presidents Romano Prodi (1999–2004) and Josè Barroso (2004–9); on press releases and memos produced by the Commission; and on speeches presented by the former Commissioner for Justice, Freedom and Security (JFS) Franco Frattini (2004–8)[15] and by the former Commissioner for Justice and Home Affairs (JHA) Antonio Vitorino (1999–2004). It is important to note that the articulation of political community in Commission discourse tends to be more mixed than that of the European Council, which arguably reflects the way in which the Commission is faced with the task of treading a fine line between representing the 'European people' and placating concerns regarding the potential loss of democratic legitimacy or national sovereignty. This section considers how these tensions have been mediated in part within Commission discourse through a securitisation of asylum-cum-illegal-immigration. In so doing, the analysis shows how the exclusionary masking of tensions in political community runs parallel with a routinisation or normalisation of exceptional measures of control over illegal-immigrants-cum-asylum-seekers.

If we look at EU discourse more widely, there are clear tensions in the way in which European governance and belonging is articulated in relation to asylum and immigration. Specifically, there is ambiguity as to whether the European approach might be articulated as *common* (European) approach for a European *demos* or a *cooperative* (intergovernmental) approach for nationals of member states. The latter articulation is one that tends to predominate in European Council discourse, which is composed of representatives of the member states, while the former articulation is one that tends to predominate in Commission discourse, which serves as the 'supranational' institution within the Union.

The Commission's focus on common governance for a common European people is particularly evident in the former Commission President's speeches at the Seville meeting of the European Council. Here, Romano Prodi suggests that a common approach is both beneficial and necessary in light of increased 'illegal immigration'. Claiming that cross-border movements of people 'overwhelm the capacity and scope for action of individual states', Prodi suggests that 'illegal immigration' can 'be tackled and managed only at the EU level' (Prodi, 2002a). As such, he calls for 'courageous, farsighted policies and decisions at [the] EU level', and he poses a specifically 'European people' in relation of opposition to 'illegal immigration' (Prodi, 2002b). In so doing, he claims that the development of 'common' EU policies is a 'big' and a 'burning' issue that cannot be put 'on the back burner' (Prodi, 2002a, 2002c). We can clearly see here how Prodi makes the case for a European order of governance and belonging through pointing to its necessity in the face of the 'threat' of 'illegal immigration'.

Nevertheless, a more careful examination of Commission discourse allows us to see how the two diverging discourses of political community are mediated through an emphasis on convergence. Such a mediation is evident, for example, in the former JHA Commissioner Antonio Vitorino's discussion of the development of European immigration and asylum policy, in which he calls for a 'balanced middle way, which aims at providing added value at Community level while respecting that core decisions on admission and integration are to be left to member states' (Vitorino, 2003). Indeed, this approach is evident in relation to asylum more specifically in the following quote by the JFS Commissioner Franco Frattini who claims that a convergence of legislation and practice is 'vital' for 'member states' and 'EU citizens' who are faced with 'mass arrivals of asylum seekers':

> As we look towards a future Common European Asylum System, it is essential that we develop greater convergence, not only of legislation, but also of practice. It is vital that asylum authorities of the member states have at their disposal a 'common tool box' to answer their daily and operational needs. With such a toolbox member states can share information, improve the quality of procedures and jointly find solutions to emergency situations such as mass arrivals of asylum seekers. EU citizens in countries most affected can now see how the notion of solidarity between EU member states can work in practice.
>
> (Frattini, 2006)

Frattini's focus on convergence here signifies a concern with the gradual progression towards a 'common' European approach to asylum. Presenting this as mutually beneficial to member states *and* European citizens, the JFS Commissioner opposes asylum in terms that bring Europe and its member states into a relation of equivalence. Specifically, he does so through undertaking a classic securitising move in which 'mass arrivals' of asylum seekers are defined as requiring an 'emergency solution'.

The securitisation of asylum-cum-illegal-immigration plays an important role in the Commission's mediation of tensions in the struggle to construct a European political community. Indeed, a managerial articulation of asylum as a 'problem' or 'threat' associated with increased numbers of unauthorised entrants is clearly evident in Frattini's statement, which we contend serves to mask tensions within political community in highly exclusionary terms. Moreover, Frattini's quote draws attention to the way in which the securitisation of asylum entails a routinisation of 'exceptional' or 'emergency' measures. Rather than responding to mass arrivals of asylum seekers as an emergency in the very real sense of which it might be interpreted as such from the perspective of new arrivals, Frattini is concerned with developing more efficient operational routines in order that mass arrivals do not provoke instability for receiving states. Such, this analysis suggests, are the exclusionary managerial politics in which exceptional measures are routinised in the attempt to prevent destabilisations from the disruptive 'outside'.

Indeed, the normalisation or routinisation of exceptional measures is inseparable from the exclusionary process by which tensions in the articulation of political community are mediated through an opposition to asylum-seekers-cum-illegal-immigrants. In the above statement, Frattini takes for granted the assumption that asylum seeking, like 'illegal immigration' poses a 'problem' or 'threat' to receiving states. In the face of 'a global problem that calls for global responses', he claims that various states are 'rel[iant] on each other to create and maintain a high level of national security' (Frattini, 2005). This articulation would effectively seem to render the tensions between domestic and European conceptions of governance and belonging of secondary importance in a situation conceived of as marked by the 'threat' of asylum-cum-illegal-immigration. This is indicative of an exclusionary politics in which dislocations of governance and belonging are projected onto asylum seekers, who are rendered as 'culpable' and 'threatening' subjects and are held up as necessitating the extension of restrictive controls. Indeed, such exclusionary operations are similarly evident at the domestic level.

Exclusionary relations of equivalence: The discourse of a UK within the EU

As we saw in the first part of this chapter, the UK has seen a notable shift in its relation to Europe since Labour came into power in 1997. This is evident in the former Prime Minister Tony Blair's (1997–2007) explicit development of a pro-European philosophy, in which he responds to concerns over the loss of UK sovereignty that EU integration might raise:

> My answer is this: I see sovereignty not merely as the ability of a single country to say no, but also as the power to maximise our national strength ... Britain gains from sharing sovereignty so that Europe has a strong, single voice.
>
> (Blair, 2001)

In this speech Blair portrays Europe as beneficial to state governance, suggesting that the UK is stronger and more powerful as a 'wholehearted, not half-hearted partner in Europe' (Blair, 2001). This is not to say that tensions do not exist in this articulation of political community. For example, elsewhere Blair portrays the European project as a battle over sovereignty in which there are 'debates that have to be won'

(Blair, 2002a). With the EU conceived as undergoing 'profound change' through processes of enlargement, Blair urges that the UK does not consign itself to 'the back of the file'. Nevertheless, one could say that the UK has been a strong voice within Europe since Labour came into power in 1997, particularly in relation to the issues of asylum and immigration whereby a UK within Europe has played an important role.

As the above analysis of European discourse suggests, the Seville meeting of the European Council was an important juncture in the domestic construction of the EU as strengthening the UK's ability to develop an effective response to asylum and immigration. Responding to his critics in Parliament after this event, Blair argues:

> On immigration and asylum policy ... precisely what was asked for [by the UK] was what was achieved. It is correct to say that we would have gone further in respect of existing agreements, but it is also the case that, in respect of those agreements that we now conclude with any third country, [our proposals are] ... at the heart of the agenda – and that, with respect, is a substantial step forward.
>
> (Blair, 2002b)

In this statement Blair suggests that the UK's response to asylum and immigration is strengthened through its engagement with Europe, with the UK empowered in its ability to shape the European agenda. A similar conception of the UK as a powerful force in the development of EU policy is invoked by the former Home Secretary (2001–04) David Blunkett who in 2002 portrayed the UK as driving the EU to 'crack down hard' on smuggling and trafficking, where 'progress has been too slow' (Blunkett, 2002). Likewise, the former Home Secretary (1997–2001) Jack Straw claims that the UK is 'at the forefront in driving forward European action' on the Common European Asylum System. In this respect European cooperation has been articulated as empowering the UK, with a strong position within Europe perceived as central to the UK's ability to defend itself effectively against various 'threats' associated with asylum-cum-illegal-immigration.

The positioning of the UK within Europe is not only conceived of as beneficial in terms of the effectiveness of state governance in the face of increased cross-border mobilities, but it is also conceived of as *necessary* to the maintenance of a territorial order of governance and belonging. For example, in his 2001 speech on Europe, Blair implies that a common European-level response is necessary in a context where the 'events of 11 September have shown the vulnerability of our democratic way of life' (Blair, 2001). Going on, he suggests that 'we cannot allow

21st century criminals the benefit of 20th century national police and justice systems', with 'our national interest demand[ing] an effectively policed common EU border'. In claiming that 'we can tackle issues such as organised crime and illegal immigration only through policies shared on a Union-wide basis', Blair articulates the 'national interest' and the 'democratic way of life' as complementary equivalents within a broader European order of member states. It is thus through processes of securitisation and criminalisation that the UK and the EU become drawn in line as complementary equivalents in domestic debate, just as we have seen to occur at the EU level. Thus, the tensions between and within a domestic and European rendering of political community would seem to be of secondary importance in a context whereby cross-border transgressions are conceived of as 'threatening' the very existence of both the national and European 'way of life'.

Exclusionary politics frequently re-emerge in domestic articulations of the importance of European cooperation, and it is as part of this process that asylum seeking is associated with illegal immigration (and various other cross-border 'threats'). For example, in introducing the aims of the UK's 2005 rotating EU Presidency it was claimed that

> Many of the issues faced by governments today, such as terrorism, asylum and immigration, and organised crime can be tackled most effectively through increased cooperation between member states. In particular, priority will be given to implementing the commitments in the counter terrorism action plan agreed by the European Council. The EU will also focus on working more closely with third countries to deliver its objectives, particularly in the field of asylum and immigration. Work to strengthen the EU's external borders, and measures to manage migration flows better will be considered.
>
> (European Union, 2005)

Associating asylum with illegal immigration and terrorism as issues to be 'tackled' in this statement, increased European cooperation is again justified in terms of its effectiveness in dealing with the emergent 'threat' of asylum-cum-illegal-immigration. It remains to be seen how the UK develops this approach under a new leadership in a post-Lisbon context. What this analysis suggests, however, is that an exclusionary politics is likely to retain resonance unless there is a radical rethinking of asylum and, indeed, political community more generally. After all, if the construction of asylum seekers as 'threatening' or 'culpable' subjects (among others) brings together the EU Council, the European

Commission and the UK government in a relation of mutual equiva-lence, then it would seem to serve as a strategy that, whether inten-tional or not, has powerful political effects.

Conclusion

This chapter has argued that the exclusionary politics of asylum play an important role in mediating tensions that emerge within and between European domestic articulations of governance and belonging. Opening with a historical analysis of post-war UK immigration and asylum policy, the first part of this chapter suggested that the exclusionary politics of asylum might be conceived of as a reiteration of an exclusion-ary politics of immigration during the post-war period. This is not to suggest that there is anything more than a logical affinity between the articulation of the 'new' Commonwealth immigrant and the asylum-seeker-cum-illegal-immigration as a 'threatening supplement'. However, one could perhaps deduce from this analysis of exclusionary reiterations that the UK has a longer-standing tradition of governance and belong-ing that is articulated according to a logic of selective opposition. The analysis has also suggested that a logical affinity can be conceived at a wider level, in terms of the way in which exclusionary politics emerge at both the UK and the EU levels. Despite notable tensions both within and between the European and domestic renderings of governance and belonging, the analysis suggests that exclusionary processes of securiti-sation and criminalisation emerge across European Council, European Commission and UK governmental discourse. While such processes are by no means uniform or uncontested, the predominance of exclusion-ary politics across each of these levels is indicative of the political effec-tiveness of a reactive strategy. Specifically, the analysis has shown how an opposition to asylum-cum-illegal-immigration renders tensions in the construction of governance and belonging of secondary concern.

If the exclusionary politics of asylum bring European and domestic renderings of political community in line with one another, questions emerge as to whether or not the territorial order of political commu-nity that is constructed through an opposition to asylum-cum-illegal-immigration is properly territorial. Could it not rather be seen as post-territorial? The analysis in this chapter suggests that political com-munity remains primarily bound within a territorial frame in domestic and EU political discourse, even though this frame of the member state is subject to significant disruption. Indeed, the analysis suggests that it is in part through the exclusionary politics of asylum that a territorial order is precariously reconstructed in terms that divert attention from its dislocation. The analysis in Chapter 4 goes on to further develop this reading of exclusionary asylum discourse by considering how state governance and national belonging are precariously reconstructed in opposition to asylum-cum-illegal-immigration at a wider political and popular level. Indeed, this analysis aims to further our understanding of the ongoing dominance of exclusionary politics, in the face of various disruptions and contestations of its exclusionary frame of reference. On this reading, exclusionary politics are by no means a necessary outcome of the articulation of governance and belonging. While exclusions are constitutive of political community, this book suggests that exclusionary politics are more adequately conceived of as a tendency or strategy that always rears its head, but that never fully saturates political space. The analysis thus strives to develop a detailed understanding of the operations of exclusionary politics in order to open the political space for a movement in an inclusionary direction (see Part IV). This requires a thorough critical understanding of the operations through which exclusionary politics have become dominant, in order that their naturalising and normalising effects can begin to be undone.

4
Restricting Contestations: Exclusionary Narratives and the Dominance of Restriction

The last chapter examined how the extension of restrictive controls over asylum-seeking-cum-illegal-immigration is effectively naturalised and normalised across both UK and EU political discourse through various exclusionary operations. These operations, along with their effective naturalisations and normalisations are central to understanding the dominance of the exclusionary politics of asylum. This chapter further examines the process by which exclusionary asylum discourse has become dominant in the domestic context. Specifically, it considers how contestations of restrictive controls have been limited or marginalised, how the limitation of contestation is reflected in the increased dominance of restriction across the political spectrum and how the dominance of restriction reflects the dominance of exclusionary narratives of asylum. This entails a wider examination of public, political and popular discourse so that the limited scope of contestation can be further explored. Specifically, the chapter examines public, party political and press discourse in order to explore how the 'central ground' of domestic political debate has been occupied by an exclusionary discourse of asylum 'problem' or 'threat' over recent years. This enables us to explore the ways in which restrictive controls are naturalised through of a range of exclusionary narratives in which asylum is constructed as a 'problem' or 'threat' to political community.

A growing body of research has shown how recent policy developments have restricted the rights of asylum seekers who reside in or seek to enter contemporary Britain in order to claim refuge (e.g. Dobrowolsky with Lister, 2006; Flynn, 2005; Pirouet, 2001; Sales, 2002, 2005, 2007; Schuster and Solomos, 2004). This literature generally supports Alice Bloch's (2000) claim that New Labour's asylum policies have continued a restrictive agenda that was initiated by the Conservatives in the 1990s

(Bloch and Schuster, 2005). Working from the assumption that this development is not a simple reflection of the intentions of New Labour politicians, the analysis in this chapter contributes to a discussion about how a restrictive approach has become dominant in the UK today. There are various ways in which the consolidation of a restrictive asylum agenda under recent Labour governments can be explained. Some analysts point to the importance of government style (Lister, 2001), others point to the influential role of popular debate or press discourse (Kaye, 1998), while others stress the significance of interparty dynamics (Squire, 2008). This chapter provides a multifaceted answer to the question of how a restrictive approach has become dominant in the UK today by drawing together these various explanations as part of a broader argument that shows how restrictions are naturalised through the decontestation of exclusionary narratives.

In undertaking this analysis, the chapter is divided into two parts. The first part of the chapter draws on policy documents and independent reports, on parliamentary statements and committee reports, on parliamentary documents, on the reports and statements of key lobby groups and on media reports. It broadly maps policy developments around which contestations have emerged under recent Labour governments. Drawing attention to the wide range of challenges that have been posed to restrictive asylum policy and practice, the analysis suggests that the populist style of recent Labour governments has contributed to the limited scope and effect of such contestations. Going further, it claims that there is also evidence of an exceptional politics in which asylum seeking is articulated as an 'emergency' issue requiring executive control. This style of government both reflects and reinforces popular anti-asylum sentiment at large. Indeed, the right-wing press has been highly influential in framing the issue of asylum in the UK, while parties on the Right have often pushed for restrictive developments in the area of asylum (Frost, 2007). The importance of analysing governmental discourse in relation to wider party political and popular asylum discourse is reflected in the second part of the chapter, which draws on speeches, statements, policy documents and press releases generated by major and minor political parties in the run up to the 2001 and 2005 elections, as well as on press cuttings during the same period.[1] Suggesting that there is evidence of convergence towards restriction across the party political spectrum,[2] the analysis draws out a range of exclusionary narratives that emerge in the texts produced by political parties and the popular press. It claims that political community is constructed in opposition to asylum across the political spectrum, and shows how the ongoing division of migration into its 'desirable' and 'undesirable' elements is central to such a process. In so doing, the analysis suggests that the dominance of restrictive control needs to be understood in relation to the dominance of exclusionary narratives in which asylum is constructed as a 'problem' or 'threat' to the integrity of borders and to social stability.

Exceptional politics: The proliferation and limitation of contestations

For those analysts who envisaged the election of a social democratic party as potentially shifting the direction of asylum policy in a less restrictive direction, Labour has been disappointing, to say the least. As Alice Bloch suggests, the 1997 Labour government followed earlier Conservative administrations in introducing legislation 'that restricts entry to Britain and legislation that reduces the social citizenship rights of asylum seekers in the UK' (2000:41). Labour inherited a situation in which those seeking asylum in the UK faced increasing restrictions. For example, practices of detention and deportation were already in place, appeal rights had already been limited and in-country applicants were no longer entitled to benefits. Maintaining a commitment to detention and deportation and replacing all benefit entitlements with a system of support under the National Asylum Support Service (NASS), Labour quickly consolidated earlier moves by the Conservatives. Yet the 1999 Immigration and Asylum Act was only the beginning of the party's restrictive response to asylum. As we saw in the last chapter, there have been frequent restrictive developments in asylum policy since 1997. This part of the chapter explores how such developments have been coupled with an escalation of contestations. Focusing in particular on the way in which Labour governments have managed challenges from the judiciary and from the refugee and welfare sectors, it suggests that an exceptional style of government has emerged over recent years in terms that limit the scope and effect of such contestations.

Proliferating contestations

A wide range of actors have been involved in the contestation of restrictive asylum policy over recent years, with particular concerns emerging in relation to practices of detention and deportation. In relation to detention, there have been various criticisms of conditions within the centres. For example, concerns have been raised in relation to the racism of officers and the mistreatment of asylum seekers (BBC, 2005), as well as regarding the detrimental effects of detention on those held within such centres. Thus, the Prisons Inspectorate has been particularly critical of the ill effects of detention on the health and well-being of children, while a campaign entitled 'no place for a child' has been launched by various charities and welfare groups.[3] In addition, concerns have been raised regarding the welfare of deported asylum applicants, with contestation often focused on the removal of specific families or nationalities.

Local campaigns regarding the removal of families have become increasingly frequent; charities and voluntary sector organisations such as the Refugee Council have participated in protests against returns to Iraq; and the deportation of Zimbabweans has been widely condemned by MPs and peers, the judiciary, human rights groups and refugee organisations alike. This has been met by contestation from the Right regarding the government's 'incompetence' in relation to removals (Migration Watch UK, 2003). Indeed, a significant debate surrounding removals has been evident over recent years, as we will see below.

These proliferating contestations in part reflect the increased politicisation of asylum since the 1990s (see Chapter 1). This is perhaps most evident in the politicisation of agents who were not previously politicised in relation to asylum but have now come to the fore in criticising policy developments. The health sector is a good case in point here, with the British Medical Association criticising the negative effect of the asylum support system on the health of asylum seekers, and with healthcare professionals widely critical of the government's moves to terminate free healthcare for asylum seekers whose claims are unsuccessful (BMA, 2002). In addition, various religious and community organisations have come together in developing the 'strangers into citizens' campaign, which calls for the regularisation of those without status. Despite these frequent and intensified contestations of policy developments, however, Labour governments have often responded to the issue in highly populist terms (Lister, 2001). For example, it has widely publicised its restrictive focus on returning failed asylum seekers, thus playing to wider popular anxiety regarding the 'influx' of 'bogus' asylum seekers (most evident in right-wing tabloids such as the *Daily Mail*). Such a populist style, it would seem, contributes to a process in which the effectiveness and scope of contestation is increasingly limited. Indeed, this is particularly the case where executive control becomes paramount.

Executive control

In this book, an important factor limiting contemporary contestations of restrictive controls is Labour's 'exceptionalist' style of government in relation to asylum. According to Copenhagen School analysts, an exceptionalist style of government is conceived as a central dimension of securitisation, in which an issue is articulated as a societal 'threat' necessitating 'emergency measures' and executive control (see Chapter 2). In the Copenhagen School's Schmittian formulation of exceptionalism it is specifically when the executive works beyond the law that this process occurs. In a more mundane form, however, this process could also be seen in the former Prime Minister Tony Blair's acceptance of 'personal responsibility' in the area of asylum.[4] This displays an exceptionalism of sorts, because the issue of asylum is re-articulated as a critical issue worthy of executive control. It is important to stress here that Labour's governmental style in relation to asylum has not been characterised by exceptionalism across the board, nor has the securitisation of asylum or migration been a blanket occurrence (see Boswell, 2007). However, there is evidence of exceptionalism in Labour's approach to asylum, which contributes to the wider securitisation of asylum. Securitising moves do not, this analysis suggests, need to be continuous to be of political effect, nor do exceptional politics need to be anything more than sporadic to limit the scope of contestation over more routine restrictions. In this regard, Labour's articulation of asylum as an issue worthy of executive control is a move that is important in understanding the dominance of exclusionary politics.

That Labour's style of government leans towards exceptionalism is perhaps most evident on examining the government's relations with the judiciary, which have become increasingly tense more broadly, as well as in relation to the issue of asylum. In relation to asylum, these tensions need to be conceived in relation to the increased role that the judiciary have played in challenging restrictive policies under the European Convention of Human Rights (ECHR). The ECHR was incorporated into British law under the 1998 Human Rights Act, and a range of challenges have emerged since this time in relation to the government's breaching of the human rights of asylum seekers. We could examine numerous examples here, but a particularly interesting one for our purposes is the government's battle to deport nine 'Afghan hijackers' who were granted temporary admission when their asylum applications were refused. Under Article 3 of the European Convention of Human Rights, a panel of adjudicators ruled that these individuals could not be sent back to Afghanistan because it would endanger their life to do so.[5] Although the individuals in question entered the UK in February 2000, the case took on increased symbolic significance in a post-9/11 context because the applicants had hijacked a plane on an internal Afghan flight and forced it to land at Stansted airport before lodging their claims in the UK. The highly exclusionary discourse surrounding this case needs to be understood in this broader context.

What is notable in this case is the way in which the government's opposition to the individuals in question is extended to the judiciary. This is evident, for example, in the former Home Secretary John Reid's response to a Court of Appeal ruling that challenged the provision of 'temporary admission' status to these individuals. He says,

> The court has ruled that it is not open to me to deny leave to enter the United Kingdom to the Afghan hijackers, or people like them, whose presence we regard as undesirable. I continue to believe that those whose actions have undermined any legitimate claim to asylum should not be granted leave to remain in the UK.
>
> (cited in Gordon, 2006)

In holding up the individuals as exemplary 'undesirables' whose deportation the judiciary impedes, Reid here implicitly defines the 'Afghan hijackers' in a relation of equivalence with the 'people like them' *and* 'the court'. In so doing, he constructs an oppositional relation between the government and the court, as well as between the government and 'undesirable' asylum seekers (cum hijackers). 'Undesirable' asylum seekers, criminal 'hijackers' and the judiciary are all thus drawn into an exclusionary relation of equivalence in this statement.

The government's opposition to the judiciary is perhaps no more evident than in the attack on the appeal rights of asylum seekers. As we saw in the last chapter, appeal rights have been significantly curtailed since 1997. They formed a focus of Labour's first raft of legislation in 1999, whereby Labour consolidated the Conservative's 1993 and 1996 legislation through further challenging appeal rights. The 2002 Nationality, Immigration and Asylum Act further consolidated these moves by limiting the judicial review process and by allowing for the removal of applicants to their country of origin or to a safe third country prior to appeal. However, it was in relation to provisions in the 2003 Asylum and Immigration (Treatment of Claimants) Bill and the 2004 Asylum and Immigration Act that tensions between the government and the judiciary became particularly heightened. Specifically, contestation emerged both in relation to the government's proposed replacement of the two-tier system of appeals with an Asylum and Immigration Tribunal (AIT), whose decisions could not be challenged by judicial review, as well as in relation to the proposed removal of legal aid from asylum seekers. These reforms were criticised by a range of human rights groups and joint committees (e.g. JCHR, 2004), as well as by influential members of the House of Lords such as the Lord Chief Justice, Lord Woolf (HOL, 2006). In light of such criticisms the government partially backed down in March 2004 by allowing the High Court a role in judging whether or not the AIT should review particular decisions.

Despite the government backing down in this case, it has nevertheless succeeded in decreasing the role of the judiciary, in removing legal aid, and in limiting further the appeal rights of asylum seekers. In this respect, the government's opposition both to asylum seekers and the judiciary has generally facilitated a restrictive extension of executive control. Our concern here is less with the extension of executive control *per se* as it is with the way in which such a process closes down the scope for critical debate surrounding restrictive developments in the area of asylum. The case of the 'Afghan hijackers' is telling in this regard, and a second look at John Reid's statement allows us to see how processes of securitisation and criminalisation close down the scope for critical debate. In defining the individuals in question as 'threatening' and 'culpable' subjects, Reid makes a leap to suggest that asylum seeking, at least in its 'illegitimate' form, is 'undesirable' and, in so doing, closes off the opportunity for debate surrounding the definition of asylum seeking as such. Indeed, he goes further to close off all avenues for debate regarding the decision made by the government to deny refugee status to those whose lives are endangered in their country of origin – a country that is deemed to be dangerous in spite (or because) of the military 'intervention' of the UK and its allies. It is, instead, left to the judiciary and human rights groups to struggle to open up such lines of debate. This is highly problematic, however, because the judiciary and human rights groups primarily work to ameliorate restrictive developments initiated by the government. Indeed, this is particularly the case in a context marked by the extension of executive control. An exceptional style of government, it would thus seem, significantly reduces the scope for a contestation of restrictive developments in the area of asylum.

Limited contestations

It has not only been the human rights lobby that has faced an uphill struggle in its contestation of government policy, but so too have the welfare and refugee sectors been considerably impeded in their challenge of the government's oppositional approach to asylum. Perhaps the most notorious example in which welfare organisations have contested government policy under Labour was the campaign against the voucher system, which Labour introduced in April 2000. Under this system asylum seekers received most of their support in vouchers, which were only accepted in certain stores to buy certain products and in exchange for which, no change could be given. Particularly vocal in challenging vouchers were Oxfam, the Refugee Council and the Trade and General Workers Union (TGWU), who jointly produced the report 'Token Gestures' in December 2000 (Oxfam, 2006). Supporting the findings of a government review regarding the damaging effects of vouchers and endorsed by a network of over 80 refugee organisations, the findings of this report preceded a government announcement in November 2001 that the system would be scrapped. Nevertheless, vouchers continued to be distributed to some asylum seekers (such as those supported by local authorities due to ill health), and were subsequently reintroduced for those considered as 'hard cases' who could not be removed due to safety concerns in their country of origin.[6] Labour thus displayed an ongoing opposition both to asylum seekers and to welfare groups in this case, despite having conceded significant ground over vouchers.

We have already seen how the 2002 Nationality, Immigration and Asylum Act revised the asylum process by limiting rights of appeal. In addition, the 2002 Act focused on revising the asylum support system by setting up reception and accommodation centres, and on withdrawing support from in-country asylum seekers. In relation to accommodation centres, the government faced significant opposition from welfare groups, as well as from MPs and peers.[7] Indeed, the Lords ruled against the development of accommodation centres in isolated areas in October 2002, and the government backed down from its plans in June 2005 in part due to a lack of local support.[8] The withdrawal of state support from asylum seekers applying in-country also faced significant opposition, with refugee, welfare and housing groups, as well as the judiciary, MPs and peers raising concerns about the detrimental effects on the well-being of asylum seekers of Section 55 of the Act.[9] Let us examine the course of this challenge in further detail in order to consider how, despite the eventual success of the government's various critics, the government's executive leanings could said to have impeded the scope and effectiveness of such contestations.

The battle against Section 55 was long and protracted. Following High Court and Court of Appeal judgements in February and March 2003, the former Home Secretary David Blunkett announced that Section 55 would be revised in order to allow in-country applicants three days to apply for asylum, so long as a credible explanation was given to prove that the application was made as soon as was 'reasonably practicable'. Despite this concession, however, Section 55 continued to be challenged by the refugee and welfare sector. In April 2004, the Refugee Council and Oxfam produced a report claiming that Section 55 forced many asylum seekers into destitution and placed an unsustainable burden on the voluntary sector and refugee community (Refugee Council, 2006). This was followed by a Court of Appeal ruling (in May 2004) that ruled that Section 55 breached the human rights of destitute asylum seekers in May 2004. The Law Lord's acceptance of this ruling in November 2005 forced the government to ensure that asylum seekers would not be left homeless and destitute on the withdrawal of its support. Those who criticised Section 55 legislation were thus eventually successful in their challenge.

Despite this eventual success, it was a considerable battle for those contesting Section 55 to halt the development of this highly restrictive (many would say draconian) development. What this would seem to suggest is that, although contestations of restrictive controls are by no means hopeless, they are highly limited in terms of their ability to turn the tide of a restrictive policy agenda. There are clearly a range of factors conditioning the government's ongoing commitment to restriction in relation to asylum, and this analysis should not be taken to suggest that governmental style is anything more than one mediating factor. Nevertheless, it is an important mediating factor that contributes to our understanding of the way that restrictive controls have become dominant over recent years. This dominance is evident when we consider the battle surrounding Section 9 of the 2004 Asylum and Immigration Act, which followed that surrounding Section 55. Section 9 removed financial and housing support from unsuccessful asylum-seeking families who fail to take 'reasonable steps' to leave the UK. It was particularly controversial because it paved the way for children from asylum-seeking families without support to be taken into care.[10] In August 2005, local councils that had piloted Section 9 demanded its urgent review, while in October 2005 Barnardos (2005) published a report in which the legality of Section 9 and its effect on child-centred practice were raised as a concern. Reports were also produced by the Refugee Council and Refugee Action (2006) and the Church of England (2006) in which concerns were raised about the detrimental effect of the measure on asylum-seeking families. The limitations of these contestations are most evident, paradoxically, in the government's dropping of Section 9 in June 2007. Announcing that the measure was being dropped because it had not had any significant impact in terms of increasing the removal rate of unsuccessful asylum-seeking families, the government effectively paved the way for the future development of restrictions. Whether or not the extensive contestations of Section 9 played an effective role in impeding its development, they would thus seem to have been ineffective in challenging its exclusionary articulation.

Exclusionary politics: Narratives of legitimisation

Perhaps one of the most worrying dimensions of Labour's populist and exceptionalist tendencies is that such a style of government would seem to both reflect and reinforce anti-asylum sentiment at a wider popular level. It is largely accepted that public opinion surrounding asylum is generally negative, if not hostile (e.g. MORI, 2003; Jennings, 2005). Indeed, this analysis suggests that the dominance of restriction in the UK needs to be understood in relation to a wider exclusionary discourse of asylum that crosses the political and the popular levels. This part of the chapter further explores the exclusionary operations of such a discourse by analysing party political texts during the 2001 and 2005 election campaigns and popular press texts during the 2005 campaign. The first part shows how a convergence in political party responses to asylum between the 2001 and 2005 campaigns is suggestive of the growing dominance of a restrictive approach. This needs to be understood in relation to a broader shift towards restriction that has emerged under recent Labour governments, which is as much to do with inter-party dynamics as it has to do with government style (Squire, 2008). Nevertheless, this analysis also suggests that a proper understanding of the restrictive movement in the party political spectrum requires that we go beyond party politics in order to look at popular asylum discourse more widely. Coupling the analysis of party political texts with an analysis of press cuttings, the final part of the chapter thus goes on to show how exclusionary narratives of asylum largely dominate political and popular discourse across the political spectrum. The analysis shows how this contributes to the naturalisation of restriction while, ironically, reconstructing the territorial political community as socially stable, economically productive and morally benevolent by highly exclusionary means.

Converging towards restriction

The 2001 election campaign was fought in a context whereby asylum had become of increasing concern to policymakers and the public alike, and where concerns regarding increased numbers of applicants and regarding 'abuse' of the asylum system by 'clandestine' migrants were heightened. Application figures had risen from 46,015 in 1998 to 80,315 in 2000 (Home Office, 2005:41), while the discovery of 58 dead Chinese migrants in the back of a lorry in Dover during 2000 had inflated concerns surrounding unauthorised entrance from the Sangatte camp in northern France. In this context, right-wing parties such as the Conservatives and United Kingdom Independence Party (UKIP) emphasised the need for intensified immigration controls and for a more effective asylum system. The Conservative manifesto (The Conservative Party, 2001) defined the asylum system as in 'chaos', with 'Labour's mismanagement ... encourag[ing] unfounded asylum claims' and with the UK having 'gained a reputation as a soft touch for bogus asylum seekers'. Focusing on developing policies to deal with unfounded asylum claimants, the Conservative party outlined proposals for housing new asylum applicants in secure reception centres and for creating a Removals Agency to 'rapidly' remove unsuccessful applicants. In this respect, the Conservatives primarily focused on developing a restrictive approach to asylum during the 2001 campaign through extending the initiatives of detention and deportation.

Opposition parties of the centre and the Left explicitly challenged the policies of deportation and detention in 2001. They also challenged the voucher system discussed above (in which asylum seekers are supported through vouchers rather than cash), as well as the dispersal system (in which asylum seekers are dispersed to accommodation in various regions). For example, the Liberal Democrats (2001) stressed the need for a more humanitarian approach to refugee protection, and in so doing it promised to replace the voucher system and to review 'the failing dispersal system'. Going further, the Green Party (2001) manifesto promised to 'abolish' the voucher system, to end detention and to 'abandon' the dispersal system. In contrast, the UKIP (2001) supported detention and deportation while criticising the current system as 'afford[ing] the opportunity [for asylum seekers] to "disappear"'. The Labour Party (2001) was somewhat quiet regarding its alignment with the Right in relation to its ongoing commitment to the policies of detention and deportation. Instead, its focus of attack was the 1951 Geneva Convention.

In challenging the 1951 Convention during the run up to the 2001 election campaign, the Labour Party worked from the key managerial assumptions that were outlined in Chapter 2. These assumptions are evident, for example, in the former Home Secretary, Jack Straw's introduction of Labour's 'Effective Protection Regime for the Twenty-First

Century' to the Institute for Public Policy Research (IPPR), in which he challenges the Convention as 'no longer working as its framers intended'. Going on, he claims that 'thousands of would-be migrants are taking advantage of one aspect of the Convention – namely, that it places an obligation on States to consider any application for asylum made on their territory, however ill-founded' (Straw, 2001). By focusing on 'would-be migrants' with 'ill-founded' applications and by suggesting that 'thousands' of applicants were 'abusing' the asylum system, Straw goes one managerial step further in assuming that restriction (in this case withdrawal from the 1951 Convention) will solve the 'problem' of asylum. It is important to step back and critically question these assumptions, which are problematic both in terms of their accuracy and in terms of its likely effect on wider public perceptions of asylum. While it may be fair to suggest that not all asylum claimants require protection with the same urgency, it is another matter entirely to imply that many asylum applicants purposefully lie in order to enter Britain. Indeed, to claim that 'thousands' of migrants 'take advantage' of international refugee law in terms that has a negative impact on the UK is highly contentious, and contributes to a reactionary managerial discourse that potentially produces fear at a wider level. Labour's approach in 2001, it thus seems, was highly exclusionary.

Needless to say, Labour's critique of the 1951 Convention provoked significant criticism by other parties from across the political spectrum. On the Left, the Greens (2001) explicitly stated their commitment to the 1951 Refugee Convention and the right of refugees to seek asylum while, on the Right, the UKIP (2001) explicitly supported the Convention against what it described as 'dictatorial, insensitive and dogmatic' EU law. It was the Green Party, however, that posed the greatest challenge to Labour's restrictive agenda in 2001. Challenging control at large (in contrast to UKIP's call for intensified domestic control), the Greens called for the 'root causes' of migration to be addressed through international effort. Thus, the manifesto claimed that 'immigration controls should be progressively reduced as common security increases' (Green Party, 2001).

In contrast to 2001, the election campaign of 2005 was fought in a context whereby political and popular concerns regarding asylum were less intense than they were during 2001. Asylum applications had significantly dropped from a peak of 84,130 in 2002 (Home Office, 2005:41) to 40,620 in 2004 (European Council on Refugees and Exiles, 2008), while the recent enlargement of the EU to 15 member states had led to an emphasis on immigration from accession states, over an emphasis on asylum. In addition, a range of developments at the European and domestic levels had shifted the terms of asylum debate. For example, resettlement had been introduced domestically, while at the EU level programmes such as regional protection (designed to protect refugees in regions of origin and transit) and regulations such as Dublin II (designed to ensure that the asylum seeker makes his or her claim in the first country of entrance) had already been initiated. These developments had effectively begun the process of limiting asylum seekers' rights to claim refuge in Britain, both through displacing the provision of protection elsewhere and also through developing alternative routes to protection for (limited numbers of) refugees.

In this context, the Labour Party's position was significantly less hostile to asylum than it was prior to the 2001 election. Shifting from its position of opposition to the 1951 Convention, Labour explicitly affirmed its commitment to international refugee law during the 2005 campaign.[11] Thus, the former Prime Minister, Tony Blair, states that 'the problem with asylum is not the UN Convention. There is nothing in the Convention which stops us rejecting unfounded asylum claims' (Blair, 2005). Indeed, Labour's restrictive approach was presented more subtly during 2005. Drawing on the five-year plan that was published in February 2005, the Labour Party (Labour, 2005a) emphasised the need to limit the protection of refugees who take the asylum route to a temporary, rather than a permanent, status. Labour's relative subtlety in presenting its proposals in the area of asylum should not divert attention from their content, however. Labour's differentiation of protection provisions for refugees claiming refuge at port or in-country and those seeking resettlement from a distance signals a clear opposition to asylum seeking, as does Blair's statement regarding 'unfounded' claims. While Labour's approach in 2005 stands in contrast to its more far-reaching questioning of the 1951 Refugee Convention in 2001, it thus remains marked by a clear opposition to asylum seeking in particular.

Indeed, this opposition to asylum is also evident in the Conservative Party's position, which was far from subtle in its presentation. The party's campaign began with an advertisement that the then party leader, Michael Howard, placed in the *Telegraph*, in which he claimed that the Conservatives would set an 'annual limit on immigration and a quota for asylum seekers' (Howard, 2005a). Rearticulating this focus on quotas in relation to refugees, rather than asylum seekers, the former Shadow Home Secretary David Davis (2005) promised that the party would (a) 'pull out of the 1951 Convention'; (b) 'sanction the immediate removal of unfounded cases'; (c) 'detain … claimants who have no documents'; and (d) 'break the link between claiming asylum and coming to Britain'. Describing the asylum system as a 'chaotic shambles', the Conservative Party (2005) thus challenged the right to asylum embodied within the 1951 Convention and claimed instead that it would take 'genuine refugees in the care of the UNHCR' through a 'quota-system'. Both the main parties thus moved to break the link between asylum and refugee protection in 2005.

While minor parties of the centre and the Left remained critical of the restrictive approaches of the two main parties during the 2005 campaign, we contend that these challenges were limited. Indeed, this is reflected in what appears to be a convergence towards restriction across the party political spectrum. Most critical of restriction in 2005 was the RESPECT coalition (2005a), as we will see. However, RESPECT emerged out of the anti-war movement and in this respect its platform with regard to asylum remained limited. The Liberal Democrats (2005a) were critical of both the Labour and the Conservative approach to asylum. Thus, the party affirmed its commitment to the 1951 Convention, stated its commitment to the development of an independent asylum agency for the processing of asylum claims and called for asylum seekers to have the right to work while their claims are processed. Similarly, the Green Party (2005a) was critical of exclusionary framing of asylum. Nevertheless, the challenge posed by these parties was less far-reaching in 2005 than it was in the 2001 campaign in two key ways. First, contestations regarding deportation and detention were limited to a focus on their implementation, rather than their existence and, second, there was no evidence of a progressive alternative to restriction, as was the case in 2001.

The only party that explicitly opposed detention and deportation in 2005 was the RESPECT coalition, which claimed that detention was an attack on civil liberties and that deportation was problematic in terms of its violent effects (RESPECT Coalition, 2005a). The Green Party offered qualified support of deportation in 2005, claiming that returns should be implemented on a 'mainly voluntary' basis (Green Party, 2005b). The Liberal Democrat Party similarly claimed that returns should be conducted in a way 'more supportive' of returnees and that detention should be rendered more humane through keeping children out of adult detention centres and detaining adults in detention centres rather than prisons (Liberal Democrats, 2005b). This, albeit qualified, support of deportation and detention is arguably suggestive of party political convergence towards restrictive controls.

This convergence regarding detention and deportation needs to be considered in relation to the virtual consensus that became apparent in 2005 regarding the positive effects of controlled economic migration.

This would seem to contribute to a process in which the scope for a more progressive alternative to restriction with regard to asylum is significantly reduced. The three main parties were more open to the benefits of economic immigration to Britain during 2005, and this represents a significant shift from the 2001 campaign in which only the Liberal Democrats, the Greens and UKIP maintained such a focus.[12] Nevertheless, this openness towards immigration, like an openness to refugee resettlement, runs in parallel to a more exclusionary discourse of asylum (see Chapter 2). This is evident, for example, in the former Home Secretary Charles Clarke's introduction to the five-year plan, whereby the selectivity of an exclusionary logic of opposition comes to the fore. Claiming that 'migration is vital for our economy', Clarke contends that it is 'essential that we enforce the rules rigorously and fairly'. Continuing to 'welcome economic migration', he reassures that the 'system will be supported by new measures to ensure that it is not abused'. Similarly, while extending a 'welcome [to] genuine refugees' he pledges that Labour will 'continue to root out abuse of the system' (Clarke, 2005:7). This is indicative of a logic of selective opposition, which is central to the exclusionary politics of asylum and which effectively entails the incorporation of a liberal discourse of managed migration and a humanitarian discourse of refugee protection (see Chapter 8). Indeed, it is in relation to these restrictive 'inclusions' that we need to understand the Green Party's movement towards an acceptance of 'minimal' controls (Green Party, 2005b).[13] In contrast to the party's emphasis in 2001 on gradually doing away with restrictive controls, the Green Party implicitly conceded in 2005 that a movement away from control might not be possible after all. This is not only indicative of convergence towards restriction, but is also indicative of the increased dominance of a wider exclusionary discourse of asylum.

Exclusionary narratives of asylum

Thus far the analysis in this chapter has suggested that, despite significant contestations, a restrictive approach has become increasingly dominant in the UK since the Labour came into power in 1997. Although the Labour Party and its ministers have clearly played a central role in extending restrictions over asylum seekers, it is not appropriate to blame Labour for the emergence and consolidation of exclusionary politics. Such a move would imply an intentionality that this analysis perceives to be impossible either to prove or properly achieve. It would also contravene the critical claim that blaming 'others' is an unproductive and highly problematic form of engagement. Nevertheless, recent Labour

governments do need to be held responsible for restrictive developments in the area of asylum, as the first part of this chapter implies.
Indeed, they need to be held responsible alongside other political parties (most notably the Conservatives) for a shift in the party political
spectrum that has rendered restriction the norm (Hansen and King,
2000; Squire, 2008). That said, party political dynamics do not occur in
a vacuum, nor are restrictive policy developments isolated from their
wider discursive legitimisation. For this reason, a more detailed analysis
of the exclusionary narratives through which restriction is (implicitly or
explicitly) legitimised is critical to our understanding of the dominance
of a restrictive approach to asylum in the UK today. It is to an analysis
of the ways in which these exclusionary narratives reconstruct political
community against asylum-cum-illegal-immigration that the analysis
now turns.[14]

We have already seen how restrictive policy initiatives such as detention and deportation are legitimised as necessary to the development
of a liberal approach to economic migration and to a humanitarian
approach to refugee protection. This is clearly demonstrated in the
Labour Party's summary of its approach to asylum and immigration:

> Labour believes in a firm, fast and fair asylum and immigration
> system together with controlled economic migration, fulfilling the
> needs of our economy. Britain has a valuable tradition of offering a
> safe haven to those genuinely fleeing persecution. We are proud of
> that tradition but we cannot tolerate abuse of the system.
>
> (Labour Party, 2005b)

In this statement, migration is divided into its 'desirable' and 'undesirable' elements in terms that define intensified restrictions as necessary for the development of a liberal and humanitarian approach to
immigration and refugee protection. It is the reference to 'abuse' that
is indicative of the exclusionary dimension inherent to this approach,
in which political community is defined against the asylum seeker *qua*
'culpable' or 'threatening' subject.

Indeed, this exclusionary articulation of asylum is more explicit in the
former prime minister Tony Blair's introduction to the five-year plan in
2005. Opening with the claim that immigration is 'vital to our economy
and prosperity', Blair challenges a conception of immigration as a 'burden' on public services, and characterises the British people in terms of
their 'generosity and tolerance'. However, halfway through the text there
is a significant shift in emphasis and tone, with Blair claiming that 'this

traditional tolerance is under threat from those who come and live here illegally by breaking our rules and abusing our hospitality' (Blair, 2005:5). In articulating asylum as a 'threat' that is indistinguishable from illegal immigration, this statement demonstrates well how the legitimisation and naturalisation of restrictive policy developments runs parallel with a reconstruction of political community in opposition to asylum. Ironically, it is through this exclusionary articulation that the moral benevolence of the British political community is (precariously) inscribed.

Before we go on to consider in more detail the specific ways in which political community is constructed through an opposition to asylum-cum-illegal-immigration, let us further explore the way in which this exclusionary logic of selective opposition emerges at the wider level of political and popular discourse. As we will see, a selectively oppositional discourse in which asylum is articulated as a 'threat' to political community is not limited to the discourse of the Labour Party, but emerges in its most exclusionary form across the right wing of the party political spectrum. Moreover, it is also evident within popular press texts. One of the striking points of convergence in 2005 is the widespread, if limited, support within the popular press for an increased openness towards immigration, particularly from Europe. For example, the left-wing broadsheet *The Independent* describes migrant workers as 'filling the void in factories and farms left by a British workforce either unwilling or unable to work' (Independent, 2005a). In addition, the left-wing tabloid *The Mirror* includes a leading article that says: 'don't let's pretend Britain doesn't need some immigrants' (Mirror, 2005a). The right-wing broadsheet *The Daily Telegraph* grudgingly accepts that some immigrants have 'a positive effect on the economy' in one of its news reports (Daily Telegraph, 2005a). Even the right-wing tabloid *The Daily Mail* includes an article that suggests the 'mass importation of migrant workers seems to be born of economic necessity' (Daily Mail, 2005a).

Nevertheless, this relatively widespread acknowledgement of a more liberal approach to immigration is significantly qualified across the popular press. The selective inclusion of 'desirable' (read: economically productive European) immigrants is qualified in all of the articles introduced above, other than in the *Independent* leader. For example, the *Telegraph* qualifies its suggestion that immigration may have a positive effect on the economy through linking 'spiralling immigration' with 'the pressure on public services', while the *Mirror* notes that the economic need for immigration 'doesn't mean that numbers should not be controlled'. Considerable opposition to European immigration is evident in the right-wing press specifically, such as in the *Daily Mail's* contention that a 'trickle' has turned into a 'torrent' (Daily Mail, 2005b). Even papers on the Left are marked by an exclusionary approach to asylum. Thus, while the *Mirror* (2005a) claims that immigrants must be accepted 'for the sake of our economy' and that 'this country has always thrown open its doors to people who face death and torture', it goes on to oppose 'those who falsely claim asylum'.

Moreover, exclusionary articulations of asylum are widespread within popular media discourse. The *Mail* is renowned for its anti-asylum stance, and this is reflected in a more quantitative summary of its coverage. In a total of 20 articles, reports and letters that were analysed, the paper uses exclusionary terms such as 'bogus refugees' twice, 'bogus asylum seekers' twice, 'frauds' twice and 'would-be refugees' once. Asylum-seekers-cum-illegal-immigrants are described as 'abusive' once, and are associated with 'hijackers' once, 'fake husbands/wives' once, 'bogus students' once, and (believe it or not) 'one-legged roofers' once. Moreover, oppositional narratives are frequent and wide-ranging in the *Mail*'s coverage. A concern with 'rising numbers' is stressed five times, and this is reflected in metaphors regarding the 'influx' once, the 'invasion' once and the 'pouring in' of immigrants to the UK once. The (unspecified) 'problem' of asylum-cum-illegal-immigration is articulated in terms of its 'strain on public services' twice, a 'dilution of culture' twice, as contributing to 'community tension' twice, and as having a 'negative effect on schooling' once. In this respect, the *Mail* constructs a community of 'taxpayers' (nine times) and 'homeowners' (twice) through an opposition to asylum-cum-illegal-immigration.

These exclusionary narratives are not unique to the *Mail* however. Even in a left-wing broadsheet, such as the *Independent*, an analysis of a total of 21 articles, letters and reports found reference to a 'deluge' once, and to 'large numbers' of illegal immigrants once. This is narrated as putting a 'strain on the infrastructure' once and as posing a 'cost to the taxpayer' three times.[15] A similar narrative is evident in an article in the *Mail*. Posing 'council tax payers' in opposition to asylum seekers, the latter are portrayed as costing 'millions to councils which have to deal with new arrivals and provide education and social services for asylum seeker's families' (Daily Mail, 2005c). Similarly, the *Telegraph* suggests that Labour's five-year plan would see 'no upper limit to the number of economic migrants or refugees' who are 'a burden on the public purse' (Daily Telegraph, 2005b). In developing these exclusionary narratives, the right-wing papers tend to naturalise the association between asylum and illegal immigration by opposing them to a socially stable and economically productive political community.

The exclusionary narration of asylum is similarly evident in right-wing party political discourse. While the Conservatives (2005a) claim to be open to limited numbers of 'genuine refugees' and 'hard workers', they primarily emphasise the importance of dealing with those who do not have a 'genuine claim'. The Conservative's securitisation and criminalisation of asylum seeking is particularly evident, for example, in the former Shadow Home Secretary David Davis' focus on the importance of removing

> those who are shown to have destroyed their documents ... who the Home Secretary considers to be a potential threat to public order or a person likely to incite racial hatred, [as well as] people who are not persecuted by a State, or people who have committed a serious offence abroad or in Britain after arrival, including involvement in terrorism (including hijacking), drugs or prostitution'.
>
> (Davis, 2005)

In this statement, asylum is articulated as a 'threat' of unauthorised entrance that is associated with both criminality, and terrorism, while the scope of those worthy of protection is significantly reduced. Such a narrative is developed in highly exclusionary terms by the former Conservative leader Michael Howard who injected a sense of urgency into the debate. He says 'there are literally millions of people in other countries who want to come and live here. Britain cannot take them all' (Howard, 2005a). In this statement the articulation of asylum-cum-illegal-immigration as a 'threat' requiring emergency action is indicative of an exceptional politics similar to the type examined in the first part of this chapter.

Indeed, the Conservatives legitimise this emergency action as necessary for the protection of the 'British people' in the face of the asylum 'problem' or 'threat'. Howard says,

> The British are decent, tolerant people. They always have been willing to help those in genuine need. Tolerance and respect for others run in the bloodstream of British values. But many people now feel that their tolerance, their sense of fair play, and their desire to help others are being abused ... The British people want a government that shares their values ... the values of the forgotten majority – the people who make up the backbone of our country. They have been forgotten, neglected and taken for granted by Mr. Blair.
>
> (Howard, 2005b)

Howard undertakes a classic populist move in reconstructing a unified 'British people' in opposition to the government elite in this statement. More to the point, he undertakes a classic exclusionary move. Dividing refugees into their 'desirable' and 'undesirable' opposites, Howard welcomes limited numbers of refugees in 'genuine need' as members of the 'tolerant' British people, while at which he rejects asylum seekers who 'abuse' the British sense of 'fair play'. In other words, asylum is inscribed as a threatening supplement against which a morally benevolent political community is defined. It is this *exclusionary* reconstruction of political community as morally benevolent that we conceive as highlighting a tension at the heart of contemporary asylum discourse – a tension that would seem to be highly effective in covering over the dislocations of a territorial order.

There are two sets of exclusionary narratives that are important in this exclusionary reconstruction of the territorial political community; the first relates to the integrity of the nation state's external borders and the second relates to the stability of the nation state's internal social relations (Squire, 2005). These narratives are evident, for example, in the Conservatives' legitimisation of restrictive controls where Howard (2005a) defends the party's restrictive proposals as necessary in order that 'good community relations, national security, and the management of public services' can be successfully maintained. These dimensions are central to the exclusionary politics of asylum, for it is primarily with regard to border integrity (here: national security) and social stability (here: good community relations and the management of public services) that restrictive controls are legitimised. Indeed, these legitimisations emerge across right-wing party political discourse. For example, the UKIP focuses its concern on 'the strains placed upon our transport, health, education and housing resources' (UKIP, 2005), while former Veritas leader, Robert Kilroy-Silk, claimed that 'the people who pay, who lose out, who have to pay the social cost of the increased pressure on their housing, on their social services, on their hospitals and schools are the poor bloody British, as always' (Veritas, 2005). Supporting a conception of the socially stable political community as under threat, the marginal parties of the Right thus join the Conservatives in constructing political community against asylum-cum-illegal-immigration. In so doing, exclusionary narratives regarding the pressure posed to public services become central to a definition of asylum as a 'problem' marked by 'abuse' of increasing numbers of unauthorised entrants.

These legitimisations of restriction are important for the analysis in Part III of this book, which examines the effects of restrictive policy initiatives in relation to the exclusionary narratives that frame their development. Before we go onto examine the exclusionary interrelation between narratives and technologies of control, however, let us briefly return to the question of contestation. If the analysis in this section has shown exclusionary narratives to be widespread, does this mean to say that there are no alternative narratives evident in political or popular discourse? This analysis suggests that alternatives are evident. For example, the Liberal Democrats strongly challenged asylum discourse during the 2005 campaign, with this particularly evident in the party's care not to present asylum seekers as 'abusive'. Indeed, the party implicitly challenges such a conception, manifest in the claim that the party will

> Protect people fleeing from persecution by dealing with asylum applications fairly and more quickly, which will also minimise any opportunities for anyone to exploit either the system or asylum seekers.
>
> (Liberal Democrats, 2005a)

In this statement the Liberals implicitly criticise a discourse of the asylum 'problem' through articulating 'abuse' (or exploitation) as a broader problem in which the asylum seeker can play a role as victim *or* perpetrator. Nevertheless, it would seem that this alternative rendering of the asylum seekers as a victim remains of limited critical effect, because it remains caught within a humanitarian frame of reference that is central to an exclusionary frame of managed migration that effectively depoliticises asylum seekers (see Chapter 8).

Indeed, while both the Greens and the Liberal Democrats are careful not to oppose asylum in nationalistic terms, it is only the Greens that develop a more critical account of asylum that is entirely free of exclusionary narratives. The 2005 Green Party manifesto discusses asylum and migration in relation to 'peace, security and international policy', thus linking the issue to arms sales and unfair trade practices. It also suggests that 'greater public understanding is key to a sustainable long term solution'. Clearly this is important in opening up debate about the role that countries such as the UK play in contributing to the production of forced migrants, whether such individuals are primarily forced to move for economic, political or, indeed, environmental reasons. Nevertheless, in the party political texts that were analysed very few positive representations of asylum seeking are developed as an alternative to the negative representation of the asylum seeker as a threatening, criminal figure. Although a concern with the rights of the genuinely persecuted and with migrant rights are evident, and although a naturalised association of asylum and illegal immigration is challenged through the use of the (not unproblematic) term 'genuine asylum seeker' (Green Party, 2005b), the reach of the Green's challenge remains limited.

Similarly the RESPECT coalition fails to develop alternative narratives or representations of asylum, despite the party's claim that 'vulnerable' asylum seekers should not be exploited in the 'racist bidding war over immigration' (RESPECT Coalition, 2005b). This suggests that those parties of the Left do not so much present a critical alternative to exclusionary asylum discourse, as they do neutralise, tame or criticise a discourse in which asylum seekers are defined as 'threatening' or 'culpable' subjects.

Similarly, there are limited alternative articulations of asylum in the popular press. The most critical rearticulation of asylum evident at this level is, perhaps unsurprisingly, in *The Independent*, where a negative conception of asylum seekers is challenged by the suggestion that asylum seekers are 'brave and enduring' (Independent, 2005b). Nevertheless, this articulation of asylum seekers as political subjects quickly slips into a humanitarian articulation of asylum seekers as depoliticised victims. For example, a news report documenting the seizure of three boatloads of African migrants in the Canary Islands opens by saying, 'YOU MIGHT call it an invasion', and goes on to challenge such a conception by suggesting that 'if this is an invasion it's one of the weak, the desperate, those for whom home has become a place of terminal hopelessness' (Ibid.). While the paper develops a critical rereading of asylum in terms that challenge many of the dominant articulations of asylum 'abuse' here, it also falls back into a humanitarian discourse that this book suggests is incorporated within an exclusionary approach. Indeed, the *Independent's* failure to include the voices of asylum seekers within any of the articles that were analysed weakens the effective reach of the left-wing broadsheet's challenge. In this respect, one could conclude that a critical alternative to an exclusionary asylum discourse is absent from mainstream political and popular discourse.

Conclusion

The analysis in this chapter has argued that contestations of a restrictive asylum agenda are highly limited both in terms of their scope and also in terms of their effectiveness. It has developed a multifaceted explanation of this limitation of contestations by examining the exclusionary operations of the Labour government, of political parties and of the popular press. Specifically, it has suggested that the proliferation of contestations surrounding restrictive asylum policy developments have been limited by the exceptionalist style of recent Labour governments, and that this style needs to be understood both in terms of a broader shift towards restriction in party political discourse and also in relation to a wider dominance of exclusionary narratives that cross party political and press texts. This, it seems, is crucial in understanding the naturalisation of restriction that occurs through the articulation of asylum as a 'problem' or 'threat'. Indeed, it is also critical in understanding how political community is constructed as socially stable, economically productive and morally benevolent through the very opposition to asylum-cum-illegal-immigration. This, the analysis suggests, brings contradiction to the very heart of an exclusionary politics; a contradiction that is productive in the sense that it facilitates a covering over of territorial dislocation through the construction of a selective and exclusionary distinction between 'desirables' and 'undesirables'.

Throughout the course of this chapter the analysis has moved from a consideration of restrictive policy to a consideration of exclusionary narratives and back again. This movement has been critical in showing how an understanding of the dominance of restriction needs to be considered in relation to a dominance of exclusionary narratives that cross the political and popular levels. The next part of the book will further develop the analysis of this exclusionary interaction from the opposite direction, by looking at the way in which exclusionary narratives regarding unauthorised entrance and social instability frame restrictive practices, which in turn feed back into exclusionary narratives. An analysis of the two-way interaction between linguistic and non-linguistic processes of securitisation and criminalisation is critical to understanding the way in which a discourse of the asylum 'problem' or 'threat' has become naturalised or dominant in the UK today (a UK that we approach as positioned within the EU). Indeed, it enables us to critically disentangle the self-fulfilling cycle in which the securitisation and criminalisation of asylum becomes caught, in order that the scope for contestation might be effectively reopened.

Part III The Extension and Diffusion of the Exclusionary Politics of Asylum: Deterrent Technologies of 'Internal' and 'External' Control

5
Interception as Criminalisation: The Extension of Interdictive 'external' Controls

The analysis thus far has shown that asylum policy has become increasingly restrictive in the UK since Labour came into power, and that it is in relation to the UK's movement towards Europe that we can, in part, understand the development of the exclusionary politics of asylum. While Part II of the analysis focused on the exclusionary operations through which restrictive policy developments are naturalised, normalised and decontested in domestic and European debates, this part considers the exclusionary operations through which oppositional narratives of asylum-cum-illegal-immigration are consolidated by 'internal' and 'external' technologies of control. Specifically, this rests on the observation that any analysis of the exclusionary operations of managed migration requires a two-way consideration both of the way in which the logic of selective opposition is embedded in the technical practices of professionals who work across the broad field of migration control, as well as of the way in which such a logic is embedded in political and popular debate (see Chapter 2). Indeed, a proper consideration of the dominance or decontestation of restrictive developments in the area of asylum requires an analysis of the ways in which the administration of human mobility is extended and dispersed through technical practices of migration control that are selectively applied according to a rationality of deterrence. Such technical or governmental practices are central to the exclusionary and depoliticising processes through which 'undesirable' migrants are transformed into 'culpable' and 'threatening' subjects who are denied political agency (see Part IV).

It has become increasingly evident that the securitisation of migration entails governmental technologies of surveillance and control that are embedded at a technical level (Bigo, 2005; Huysmans, 2006).

For example, Thierry Balzacq (2008) suggests that migration is securitised through capacity sharing instruments such as information databases, and that a speech act approach cannot capture the securitising effects of these techniques. From another angle, Huysmans and Buonfino (2008) contend that migration is not so much directly articulated as a security 'threat' in political debate as it is securitised by its association with multiple 'threats' through the development of security technologies such as ID cards. These analyses all offer support to Didier Bigo's suggestion that an analysis of the routine technical and governmental practices of security experts is critical in understanding the contemporary production of 'threats' (see Chapter 2). The analysis in this chapter also supports the claim that securitisation, like criminalisation, is a process that works by technical and governmental means, and that a consideration of the routine activities of experts in the field of migration control is important to our analysis of the exclusionary politics of asylum. Indeed, it conceives an analysis of the interrelation between technical and linguistic or narrative processes of securitisation and criminalisation as critical in furthering our understanding of the way in which exclusionary politics become dominant, decontested and depoliticised through the selective extension and diffusion of restrictive controls that work according to a complex rationality of deterrence. It is only through a careful examination of such interactions, the analysis suggests, that we can engage from a position of critical distance with an exclusionary politics that becomes caught in a self-fulfilling cycle of securitisation and criminalisation.

The analysis in this chapter critically examines the exclusionary interaction of narratives and techniques by showing how the managerial articulation of asylum as a 'problem' of increased numbers of unauthorised entrants is effectively produced through the deterrent technology of interdiction (De Genova, 2004). Focusing on a UK-led EU initiative, Project IMMpact, in Bosnia Herzegovina, the analysis draws on a range of texts and interviews with immigration officers (see Appendix 1) in order to critically examine the exclusionary techniques through which interdictive 'external' controls are extended against 'undesirables' such as asylum seekers. In so doing, two main lines of argument are developed, both of which are critical to the broader claim that exclusionary politics become increasingly dominant by constituting asylum seekers as scapegoats for the dislocation of a territorial order. The first part of the chapter develops this argument regarding the dominance or decontestation of restriction by showing how techniques of interception, which have been central to the development of European border control, are better conceived of in terms of a selectively deterrent and criminalising technology of interdiction. Situating interception in relation to externalised control and exploring the institutional and technical processes of securitisation and criminalisation through which interception is developed as interdiction, it introduces Project IMMpact as emerging in a field of migration control that is marked both by the extension of restrictive controls beyond territorial borderlines, and also by the managerial or technical collaboration of policing and military agencies. Such processes contribute to the decontestation of restrictive controls by moving them into the technical realm and out of the public realm where they are open to wider scrutiny and debate.

In the exclusionary politics of asylum, it is not *simply* because the extension of interdictive techniques is depoliticising in a technical sense that they are problematic. Technical processes of depoliticisation are highly troubling wherever they emerge. Nevertheless, the central concern of this book is with the *exclusionary* operations and effects of restrictive techniques of control, which are conceived of as entailing a selectively oppositional rationality of deterrence that is depoliticising on several counts. It is with regard to the processes by which governmental techniques of professionals in the field of migration control embed a specifically *exclusionary* politics that the analysis in this chapter is developed. Specifically, it critically examines how an exclusionary politics masks the dislocations of a territorial order by reactively projecting them onto 'undesirables' such as asylum seekers through the technology of interdiction. The second part of the chapter develops this critique by considering the *effects* of a rendering of interception as interdiction, specifically in relation to the way that the exclusionary operations of migration control professionals draw on and reaffirm exclusionary narratives regarding the 'threat' or unauthorised entrance. It is here that the chapter develops a second line of argument, by showing how the 'illegality' of asylum seekers is produced as such through the very extension of interdictive controls. Challenging the managerial assumption that interception responds to a pre-existing 'threat' of unauthorised entrance, the chapter thus argues that interdiction effectively criminalises asylum seekers through *constituting* them as 'culpable' and 'threatening' subjects. This has the effect of both shrinking the space of asylum while at the same time projecting 'internal disruptions' of a territorial order onto 'external turbulence'.

From interception to interdiction: Introducing Project IMMpact

The importance of governmental practices *qua* professional techniques for any analysis of the exclusionary construction of political community is clearly evident in relation to migration control. There is a growing literature on the proliferation of border control technologies, which focus attention on the governmental techniques that are employed both by state and non-state (or private) actors in the management of human mobility (Epstein, 2007; Muller, 2005; Zureik and Salter, 2005). These analyses of the governmental techniques enacted by migration control professionals importantly draw attention to the technical and technological processes through which the state is constituted as an actor with authority. This is important, because it highlights one of the central claims in this book: that the territorial political community (*qua* state or nation) is not a pre-given 'referent object' with an authority that is incontestable, but rather it is constructed as such through a wide range of practices. In examining the specifically *exclusionary* technical construction of political community in this part of the chapter, the analysis suggests that the governmental practices in the field of migration control are increasingly organised around a complex rationality of deterrence. Specifically, it suggests that this rationality is characterised by the selective extension of restrictive and preventative controls beyond traditional territorial borderlines (Lavenex 2004, 2006). The first part of the analysis introduces Project IMMpact in relation to the wider extension of preventative migration controls, and shows how technical interceptions and externalised policies are similarly designed and articulated according to a rationality of selective deterrence. The second part of the analysis examines the operational techniques enacted by migration control professionals, and shows how interception *qua* interdiction entails both institutional and technical processes of criminalisation and securitisation. Such developments, the chapter concludes, are indicative of exclusionary technical and managerial operations that selectively extend the reach of restrictive controls while simultaneously reducing the scope for their contestation.

Project IMMpact and the extension of restrictive controls

Chapter 3 suggested that the externalisation of European immigration and asylum policy entails processes of criminalisation and securitisation that are central to an exclusionary politics. Interception – namely the prevention of migrants and refugees from entering and settling in the European territory – would seem to demonstrate a similar rationality or logic. Thus, it is not only regional protection and transit processing that are conceived as caught up in an exclusionary politics (see Chapter 3). A range of externalised immigration and asylum policies also take on a new light on the basis of this analysis (see Lavenex, 1999, 2004; Lavenex and Uçarer, 2004). For example, the integration of readmission clauses into development agreements with third countries of origin or transit (Samers, 2004), like the integration of migration control requirements into accession agreements as part of the European Neighbourhood Policy (Smith, 2005), are suggestive of the exclusionary extension of migration control beyond the territorial borderline. If it is in the shifting of asylum and immigration policy out to third countries and to countries that serve as a 'buffer zone' between the EU and third countries that the extension of an exclusionary politics can be conceived at the level of policy development, it is in the development of interception that we can see a parallel development at the level of technical practice. It is the latter dimension that forms the focus of the analysis here.

Before we go on to further examine the exclusionary technical operations that are central to the extension of migration control through interception, let us first introduce Project IMMpact as an exemplary interceptive initiative in which controls are extended by preventative means. As a UK-led EU initiative developed in the 'transit' region of Bosnia Herzegovina (BiH), Project IMMpact can be conceived of as a restrictive migration control initiative that prevents the unauthorised entrance of 'undesirables' onto the legal and geographical territory of EU states such as the UK.[1] Project IMMpact ran from September 2001 until August 2002, and had the explicit aim of training BiH State Border Service (SBS) officers in techniques of border control. While its was initially located at Sarajevo airport, the initiative was rapidly extended to other airports such as Mostar, Tuzla and Banja Luka, before being developed as a mobile training programme for officers in SBS units located across BiH (UNMIBH, 2002).[2] The name of the project refers to its development of an <u>imm</u>igration <u>pact</u> 'between the newly deployed State Border Service [SBS] of BiH and participating EU countries' (South East Europe Security Cooperation Steering Group, 2002). Project IMMpact thus serves as an early example through which we can examine the UK's extension of restrictive controls beyond its territorial borders through an engagement within Europe (see Chapter 3).

The European, rather than the strictly domestic, relevance of Project IMMpact is evident in its origination as a response to concerns raised by the French Presidency during 2000 over the role of the Balkans as a transit route for migration to northern European states. Initiated by the UK and Italy, Project IMMpact is described as 'one result of the Blair/Amato initiative early in 2001, seeking to stem flows of irregular migration through Bosnia Herzegovina and Croatia into the EU' (INDIS, 2003). The UK's concern with this route is evident in the Home Office's (2003) suggestion that 'the Balkans have become the main gateway to Europe of a multi-million pound business in illegal immigration, drug smuggling and people trafficking'. Similarly, the former British Immigration Minister, Beverley Hughes (2002), describes the Balkans as a region composed of 'transit countries', while the Special Representative of the Secretary-General and Coordinator of the UN Operations in BiH estimates that '10 per cent of all illegal entrants to Western Europe pass through the "BiH route"' (Klein, 2001). The importance of the Balkans as a transit region is also highlighted by the manager of Project IMMpact, who claims that the initiative is important in dealing with 'the problem of increased flows of illegal migrants passing through the Balkans into the EU' (Interview 1, Appendix 1). In this respect Project IMMpact can be categorised as an exemplary case in the interceptive development of restrictive European and UK border or migration controls.

It is important to note that those involved in the implementation of the initiative do not always present IMMpact as an interceptive migration control project that prevents the entrance of 'undesirables' *en route* to the UK and the EU. For example, the project manager contests what he describes as 'cynical journalistic' interpretations of the project as developed solely in the interests of the UK and the EU (Interview 1, Appendix 1). He suggests that IMMpact is less a police and military project of prevention than it is a development project by which the UK has contributed to the border enhancement of the new BiH state. In this respect, Project IMMpact might be categorised as one of a growing number of projects that simultaneously address development and migration control concerns.[3] Nevertheless, a critical reading of this articulation of IMMpact as a development initiative might point to the way that a developmental agenda serves as one way in which exclusionary European migration controls are effectively extended beyond traditional territorial borderlines. Indeed, the United Nations Mission in Bosnia Herzegovina describes the project's assistance of the SBS in terms of its facilitation of the 'fight against organised crime and illegal immigration' (UNMIBH, 2001). It thus would seem to be fair to interpret Project IMMpact as an interceptive UK and EU initiative that extends restrictive migration control in preventative terms.

The preventative extension of interceptive migration controls is by no means particular to the UK or EU context, and has been developed most notoriously by states such as Australia and Canada (Hyndman and Mountz, 2008; Kernerman, 2008; McMaster, 2001). Nevertheless, Europe remains a fertile ground for the examination of such techniques. Interceptive techniques range from those that prohibit the entrance of 'undesirables' to those that force their return, and from those practiced in regions of origin to those practiced in transit and reception regions. In this respect, interceptive migration controls are not simply deterrent in the sense that they stop 'undesirables' from entering the territory, although this to be one important dimension of the prohibitive or interdictive application of a deterrent rationality. They are also deterrent in the sense that they impede 'undesirables' from settling. A deterrent rationality, in other words, would seem to entail processes of elimination (e.g. return) and prevention (e.g. detention), while demonstrating a complexity that renders it more far reaching in effect yet less comprehensive in its application than a managerial interpretation would have us assume (see Chapter 6).

It is by conceptualising techniques of interception in relation to this rationality of deterrence that this book conceives *interdiction* to be critical to the managerial operations associated with the exclusionary politics of asylum. Before further developing this reading of managerial interception as exclusionary interdiction, Project IMMpact needs to be situated more firmly within a growing field of European migration control. Specifically, it needs to be situated in a field that is characterised by the selective prevention of the entrance of 'undesirables' onto the EU territory, which entails the extension of restrictive controls beyond the traditional territorial borderline. There are numerous examples that we can draw here, many of which bring the 'spectacle' of border control to the fore. During 2003, for example, the UK was a participant in Operation Ulysses, an EU initiative led by Spain that extended EU migration control off the coasts of the northern Mediterranean and the Canary Islands. In so doing, Ulysses practiced techniques of interception over migrants from Africa using armed vessels and military aircraft, with this involving 'naval, police and coast guard forces from France, Italy, Portugal, Spain and the United Kingdom' (European Security and Defence Assembly, 2005). The techniques employed by IMMpact are somewhat less spectacular than those practiced by Operation Ulysses. However, what both of these projects have in common is their development of interceptive techniques of control that are designed to prevent 'undesirable' migrants from entering the territory of EU states such as the UK.

Because preventative projects of interception such as Ulysses and IMMpact are relatively early examples of an emergent European approach to migration control, they allow us to begin the process of exploring the exclusionary reiterations that emerge in the gradual move from a cooperative to a common European border management programme (see Chapter 3). EU initiatives began as co-operative inter-governmental projects between member states, and primarily remain as 'joint operations' and as 'operational co-operations' between member states. However, in 2005 the European Agency for the Management of Operational Cooperation at the External Borders of the Member States of the European Union, Frontex, was set up in order to 'integrate national border security systems of Member States against all kind of threats that could happen at or through the external border of the Member States of the European Union' (Frontex, 2008a). The institutionalisation of Frontex thus arguably signals the development of a European border control programme that is articulated and designed in terms that prevent the unauthorised entrance of 'threatening undesirables'.[4]

While a detailed examination of Frontex remains beyond the scope of this analysis, the techniques of interception engaged by Frontex imply that exceptional and routine practises of securitisation are often intertwined in practise. Specifically, their intertwinement brings together as part of a wider exclusionary politics, in which the rationality of deterrence is framed according to a logic of selective opposition.[5] The agency promotes integrated border management through co-operation and the exchange of information, it undertakes risk assessments, and it seeks co-operation with neighbouring and third countries. It also homes BorderTechNet, which is an IT network that is designed to 'support the development of capacities and technologies facilitating cooperation between Member States in the field of border security for the management of external borders' (Frontex, 2008c). In addition, Frontex carries out joint operations on land, sea and air borders, and has recently set up Rapid Border Intervention Teams (Rabits), which are made up from a pool of experts from the member states who are trained by Frontex in order that they can be deployed in 'urgent and exceptional situations' (Frontex, 2008b). Frontex, it would seem, thus engages routinised techniques of information-gathering alongside exceptional techniques of border control and, in so doing, extends restrictive migration controls while constructing 'undesirables' as 'threatening' by technical or technological means. Specifically, it extends control through technologies of interdiction that are articulated and designed according to a selectively oppositional deterrent rationality. This, an analysis of Project IMMpact suggests, is indicative of the exclusionary reiterations of Frontex that a focus on the technical and institutional renderings of securitisation and criminalisation brings to the fore.

Project IMMpact as an interdictive technology

A consideration of the way in which an exclusionary logic of selective opposition becomes embedded in the techniques of professional migration control requires an analysis of both institutional and technical processes of securitisation and criminalisation. In particular, it requires a consideration of the agencies that become embedded within the field of migration control, as well as a consideration of the instruments or techniques that are central to the constitution of this field (Bigo, 2005; Bigo and Tsoukala, 2006). Indeed, it is only through such an examination that we can begin to consider how the institutional and technical overlap between policing and military agencies and techniques in the field of migration control interrelates with exclusionary articulations of the asylum 'problem' or 'threat' at the level of popular and political debate. One way in which this interrelation might be conceived of is in terms of the way in which 'threats' are constructed (or are not constructed) as a result of the dynamic struggle between actors and institutions seeking to gain purchase in the area of migration control (Boswell, 2007; Huysmans, 2006). Another way in which it might be conceived of is in terms of the way in which actors and institutions or agencies engage (or do not engage) exclusionary narratives in order to make sense of and give authority to the technical practices of interdiction that they enact on an everyday basis.[6]

Before developing an analysis of these interactions from the latter direction, let us further examine the institutional and technical processes of securitisation and criminalisation that are critical to the exclusionary politics of asylum. It is primarily through an analysis of the institutional and technical engagements of policing and military agencies that we can see how interceptive techniques at the professional level of migration control are more adequately characterised as deterrent technologies of interdiction. Law enforcement agencies such as Interpol and Europol have been central players in the development of interdictive migration control, as have military agencies. Thus, the manager of Project IMMpact describes how he and his colleagues 'saw ways in which we could seek help from SFOR [the NATO stabilisation force in BiH] to assist in the overall aim of tackling illegal migration flows' (Interview 1, Appendix 1). Indeed, there has been a considerable emphasis on the 'civil-military management of non-military risks' over recent years, with military technology and equipment perceived as beneficial in the development of techniques such as profiling and surveillance (South East Europe Security Cooperation Steering Group, 2002). What this technical engagement of military and policing agencies in the field of migration control would seem to suggest is that the identification of 'undesirable' migrants as 'threatening' entails much more than linguistic speech act. It also entails an institutional engagement that brings professional security and policing experts together in a managerial 'war' against 'culpable' and 'threatening' mobile subjects.

So what techniques do such institutional engagements entail, and how do they contribute to a wider exclusionary politics in which asylum seeking is both securitised and criminalised? Most notably, we can see that a range of information-gathering tools have emerged in the European context over recent years, tools that contribute to the criminalisation and securitisation of 'undesirables' such as asylum seekers. For example, the EU is developing a new image archiving system called FADO, which will allow member states to 'exchange information on EU official documents and help detect any papers that may be counterfeit' (see Bigo, 2005). Similarly, Project IMMpact incorporates intelligence and information-gathering techniques as central dimensions of its training programme for SBS officers in BiH. In particular, the initiative includes techniques such as interviewing, profiling and forgery detection (INDIS, 2003; Interview 1, Appendix 1). These developments suggest that technical processes of criminalisation and securitisation occur where policing and intelligence techniques of information gathering saturate the field of migration control.

Indeed, a more detailed focus on information gathering techniques allows us to further examine how exclusionary processes of criminalisation and securitisation are central to their operation. An example of this is the EURODAC system, which is a biometric database that became operational in 2003. Thierry Balzacq (2008) suggests that EURODAC is a good example of the 'functional creep' that characterises securitising tools. The system was originally set up as part of the Dublin Convention in order to prevent 'asylum shopping', but now includes the biometric information of third country nationals found to be irregular residents of a member state, and of third country nationals found crossing the border of a member state irregularly, as well as of asylum applicants. In this respect an analysis of EURODAC enables us to see how 'undesirables' such as asylum seekers and 'illegal migrants' become indistinguishable from one another through their association as 'threatening' equivalents to be opposed. Developing Balzacq's argument a step further, one could thus say that 'functional creep' is evidence of the embedding of a logic of selective opposition in the technical field of migration control, in which complex legal differentiations between migrants, refugees and, indeed, citizens are replaced with a less precise (but more easily operational) distinction between 'desirable' and 'undesirable' subjects.

EURODAC is not the only database that includes information on 'undesirables'. The Schengen Information System (SIS II post-enlargement) is a database that includes information on 'certain categories of persons', with the aim of facilitating the 'prevention and detection of threats to public order and security'. It captures information about migrants and non-migrants who are either suspected of, or have been found guilty of, crimes that are deemed to pose a security threat to EU member states. In so doing, it renders all those that are entered into the system as 'culpable' subjects.[7] More recently, the EU has initiated the Visa Information System (VIS), which is a biometric database designed to prevent 'visa-shopping' throughout the Union. It has also developed tools such as the Information and Co-ordination Network (ICOnet) in order to facilitate an exchange between member states of strategic, tactical and operational information concerning illegal migratory movements (Europa, 2008). These developments in the area of information gathering might all be conceived in terms of their exclusionary extension and reiteration of co-operative programmes that were developed in the 1990s.[8]

Indeed, it is precisely through an analysis of these institutional and technical processes of criminalisation and securitisation that we can see how the 'benign' managerial technique of interception is better understood as a selectively deterrent interdictive technology. This, the analysis suggests, brings to the fore questions regarding the relationship between the routine and the exceptional (see Chapter 2). Approaching such questions through the analysis of interdiction specifically, this preliminary reading of the relationship between routine and exceptional techniques of interception would seem to suggest that they are increasingly intertwined as two dimensions within a single, selectively oppositional, logic. Specifically, this analysis suggests that it is in the exclusionary intertwinement of routinised techniques of information gathering and 'exceptional' practices of border control that interception is practiced as interdiction. A consideration of the Immigration Liaison Officers (ILOs) network that has emerged in the EU context is telling in this regard (see Bigo, 2000b). Posted in countries of origin and transit, ILOs bring information-gathering techniques to border controls in terms that prohibit the entrance of 'undesirables' through interdiction.[9] It is this extension of routine information-gathering into the 'spectacular' realm of border control (and vice versa) that effectively moves interdictive technologies beyond political debate and public scrutiny. This exclusionary interaction is no more evident than where the 'benign' managerial movement of information gathering extends its reach into biometrics, for it is here that an exclusionary politics of securitisation and criminalisation moves in the direction of abjectification (see Chapters 6 and 7). This is what renders so troubling the deterrent technology of interdiction that is professionally applied in the field of migration control.

Producing illegality: The exclusionary effects of interdiction

The first part of this chapter argued that the extension of interdictive controls by technical means entails a depoliticisation of exclusionary operations through the removal of restrictive control from public scrutiny. This is a highly problematic development that renders it increasingly difficult to contest restrictive controls at the level of public or political debate. Indeed, it brings to light the critical limitations of a linguistic theorisation of securitisation that remains caught in an analysis of the speech acts of political elites, as well as the difficulties that all of us face in our attempt to think about and act upon asylum in terms that move us beyond an exclusionary politics. Before we go on to consider how such a critical rethinking of asylum might proceed (see Part IV), it is important to further explore the exclusionary interrelation of technical and narrative processes of securitisation and criminalisation, specifically through a consideration of their effects. This task is approached in the first part of the analysis by exploring how actors engage exclusionary narratives regarding the 'threat' of unauthorised entrance in order to make sense of and give authority to the technical practices of interdiction that they enact on an everyday basis. This leads to the second part of the analysis, which goes on to develop a dual-pronged critique of the interrelation of technical and narrative processes of interdiction through a consideration of their exclusionary effects. Specifically, the analysis develops a critique of interdiction in its 'own terms' by showing how Project IMMpact effectively produces 'illegality' or unauthorised entrance as a 'problem' that it is designed to resolve. Going further, the analysis develops a critique of interdiction from a position of critical distance by showing how Project IMMpact effectively shrinks the space of asylum and, in the process, projects 'internal disruptions' of a territorial order onto 'external turbulence'.

Exclusionary narrations of interdiction

What is notable from the discursive perspective developed in this book is that exclusionary processes of securitisation and criminalisation are not only evident in Project IMMpact's technical extension of interdictive control. So also do such processes emerge in the narration of the project as an initiative in a wider 'war' against criminal 'threats'. For example, the former British Home Secretary David Blunkett invokes a military metaphor in opposing his discussion of the initiative. He says: 'Criminal gangs are behind a multi-million pound business smuggling people, drugs and goods. Actions like Project Immpact [sic] in Bosnia Herzegovina have reduced illegal immigration through Sarajevo airport by 90%'. Going further, he says: 'Organised criminals co-operate across national borders and so must we ... Organised criminals must not be more organised than we are – better, more effective co-operation is the key to combating cross-border international crime'. As such, Blunkett suggests that a key aim of interdictive initiatives such as Project IMMpact is to target the organisers of cross-border crime in order to 'disrupt and dismantle criminal networks' (Home Office, 2003). While asylum is not explicitly targeted for opposition in this statement, one could perhaps say that it implicitly features in its wider technical, political and popular association with 'illegal immigration', which is placed in a relation of equivalence with the 'threat' of organised crime in Blunkett's statement.

Indeed, it is not only at the level of political debate that IMMpact is articulated as part of a wider 'war' against asylum-cum-illegal-immigration (or illegal-immigration-cum-asylum). It is similarly articulated as such at the technical level, where migration control professionals make sense of and give authority to the technical practices of interdiction that they enact on an everyday basis. It is here that the closing words of the manager of Project IMMpact are telling. Drawing BiH and the UK together in a relation of mutual opposition to illegal-immigration-cum-asylum, the manager of IMMpact undertakes a classic managerial move in authorising interdictive controls in terms of their *necessity*:

> Perhaps I should conclude by saying that this is a global problem that needs to be tackled at a global level. In this sense my answer to the cynical journalists would be that it is not just an EU problem but also a global problem, which is why we need to include those at the margins such as the Balkans.
>
> (Individual interview 1, Appendix 2)

In narrating unauthorised entrance as a 'global problem' requiring global co-operation, the manager here draws the EU, the UK, BiH and, indeed, the *entire globe*, in a relation of opposition to asylum-seekers-cum-illegal-immigrants. In so doing, he gives authority to the daily practice of interdiction in terms that reconstruct a territorial order against 'threatening' and 'culpable' subjects.

Military and development personnel, like immigration officers, similarly authorise Project IMMpact in terms that reconstruct a territorial order of governance and belonging against asylum-cum-illegal-immigration. While the initiative has primarily been conceptualised as an example of interceptive UK and EU border control here, it also needs to be considered in relation to wider stabilisation efforts within Bosnia Herzegovina (BiH) through which the new state and its borders have been constructed by the 'international community'. The BiH State Border Service (SBS) was officially activated on 6 June 2000, with the NATO stabilisation force (SFOR) and the International Police Force (IPTF) joining Project IMMpact within the history of the service's development through their early provision of training to its officers (SFOR Informer, 2002b).[10] In addition, the United Nations Mission in Bosnia Herzegovina (UNMIBH) played a central role in the reconstruction of BiH. The SBS is described with pride by the UNMIBH co-ordinator Jacques Paul Klein (2001) as 'symbolic of BiH sovereignty and identity' because of its status as 'the first multi-ethnic law enforcement institution'. Describing criminal smuggling and trafficking of persons as 'undermin[ing] BiH' through 'contributing BiH KM 250 million every year to criminal syndicates', he presents Project IMMpact as potentially increasing state revenues through combating cross-border crime. This authorisation of the initiative is one that, in some senses quite literally, reconstructs a territorial order in opposition to its 'anarchical outside'. In so doing, the newly formed BiH is narrated as a socially stable, culturally integrative and economically productive nation state alongside morally benevolent EU states such as the UK.

It is not only in opposition to cross-border crime that the authorisation of the interdictive techniques of Project IMMpact entails a reconstruction of the territorial order of state governance and national belonging. As we have already seen, Project IMMpact is authorised according to its benefits in preventing 'illegal immigration' to EU states such as the UK. SFOR describes BiH as being 'used as a springboard to Western Europe' (SFOR Informer, 2002b), while the UNMIBH co-ordinator claims that 'BiH has already become not just the springboard, but also a magnet, for continued illegal migration to European destinations' (Klein, 2001).

This authorisation of IMMpact reflects that which emerges at the level of political debate, in which the initiative is presented as mutually beneficial to BiH and to EU states such as the UK. Thus, in discussing the initiative the former Foreign Secretary Jack Straw claims that co-operation in 'tackling organised crime' can foster 'stability and prosperity of Europe and the wider world', as the Balkans moves towards 'full Euro-Atlantic integration' (cited in Home Office, 2003). This reconstruction of a territorial order engages the UK, the EU and BiH in an exclusionary relation of mutuality against asylum-cum-illegal-immigration-cum-organised-crime-cum .... The list goes on. Indeed, an exclusionary politics is an expansive politics in various senses of the word. It is expansive in the sense that it facilitates an extension of migration controls beyond traditional territorial borderlines, and it is expansive in the sense that it can bring various territorial equivalents in a relation of opposition to a generalised list of mobile 'threats' that are related through association. Thus, in working alongside various international partners through interdictive initiatives such as Project IMMpact, the UK extends migration controls against 'international terrorist networks' as well as against asylum-seekers-cum-illegal-immigrants (Blunkett cited in Home Office, 2003). It is here that we can see how the exclusionary reconstruction of a territorial order has a wider relevance than the specific focus on asylum that is developed in this book.

Constituting asylum seekers as 'culpable' subjects

Any critique of the depoliticising interrelations of technical and narrative processes of securitisation and criminalisation requires a movement beyond the analysis of its exclusionary operations to a consideration of its exclusionary effects. It is this movement that is central to the first part of the critique of Project IMMpact developed here, in which the effectiveness of the initiative in preventing the unauthorised entrance of 'undesirables' such as asylum seekers is critically assessed. Specifically, the analysis shows how interdiction effectively produces 'illegality' or unauthorised entrance as a 'problem' that managerial interception is designed to resolve. While Project IMMpact was explicitly articulated and designed in order to prevent 'illegal immigration', the immigration officers interviewed largely identified cross-border migrants in relation to their national attributes and 'undesirable' behaviours. For example, one interviewee described Sarajevo airport as a 'backdoor' for 'Turks and Iraqis' to reach the UK, while another raised concerns regarding 'abuse of the Bosnian visa regime' by Indian, Chinese, Pakistani and Bangladeshi migrants (Interview 2, Appendix 1). This would seem to suggest that migration control professionals distinguish between migrants in relatively simplistic terms, working from the division between 'desirable' and 'undesirable' rather than in terms of the complex legal distinctions that have emerged in relation to economic migration and refugee protection over recent years (see Chapter 1).

It is important to note that, during the period when Project IMMpact was running, four out of six of the groups highlighted by immigration officers were categorised in the top ten nationalities claiming asylum in the UK (Refugee Council, 2001).[11] Whether or not these nationalities were successful in claiming asylum would seem to be superfluous to the claim that Project IMMpact most likely interdicted those *en route* to EU states such as the UK in order to seek asylum, if we work from the position of the asylum seeker. However, even if we work from the position of UK officials, it would seem that Project IMMpact most likely interdicted refugees, because 36 per cent of Iraqi asylum applicants, seven per cent of Turkish asylum applicants, 11 per cent of Pakistani asylum applicants and six per cent of Chinese asylum applicants received positive decisions on their claims in 2001 (Ibid.). This would suggest that a simplistic operational distinction between 'desirables' and 'undesirables' is highly problematic in terms of its effect on the provision of refugee protection.

Questions emerge here regarding whether it is possible for immigration officers to distinguish those seeking protection from those who are not, and whether such migration control professionals are authorised in making judgements regarding the 'desirability' of individual migrants. These questions are difficult to answer, and only some suggestive comments can be made here. What we know is that various migrants take unauthorised routes to protection in a context whereby legal routes to protection have been selectively closed down through visa impositions and intensified border controls (Castles and Miller, 1998). We also know that the legal process of judging whether or not an individual can be categorised as a refugee is complex, contested and ambiguous (Puumala, 2008; Bohmer and Shuman, 2007). What is particularly concerning, then, is that immigration officers involved in the implementation of interdictive initiatives such as Project IMMpact hastily make decisions on a daily basis regarding who should be targeted for prohibition. Perhaps most concerning is that these decisions are not publicly scrutinised, nor are the implications of making such decisions openly debated. Indeed, they do not appear to be carefully considered by migration control professionals, on this (albeit limited) analysis. Thus, on being asked what provisions are made for asylum seekers intercepted by the initiative, the IMMpact project manager claimed that 'there is ample opportunity for claims to be made en route'. Going on, he drew attention to the difficulty that states such as the UK have in 'absorbing large numbers' of asylum seekers (Interview 1, Appendix 1). This not only suggests that those involved in applying technologies of interdiction do not see it as necessary to consider whether those whose entrance is prohibited are in need of protection, it also suggests that immigration officers draw on exclusionary narratives regarding the 'threat' that asylum poses in order to authorise their everyday practices of interdictive control.

These findings have important implications in terms of the criminalisation of asylum seeking. What the analysis suggests is that, in the attempt to manage cross-border mobilities, migration control professionals who apply interdictive techniques play a key role in *constituting* the asylum seeker as an 'illegal' or 'culpable' subject. In other words, interdiction consolidates legal processes of 'illegalisation' (such as visa regulations) by effectively producing 'illegality' or unauthorised entrance as a 'problem' that it is designed to resolve (De Genova, 2002, 2004, 2007). Paradoxically, it is thus in the very 'failure' (or inability) of such initiatives to impose total control over what Nikos Papastergiadis (2000) calls the 'turbulence' of cross-border mobilities that interdiction would seem to achieve its authority. Thus, the imperative of initiatives such as Project IMMpact to measure this immeasurable and 'govern the ungovernable' essentially become stories of failing success that require just that *little bit more* effort (Aradau and van Munster, 2007). This is evident in the project appraisal which, in emphasising the successes of Project IMMpact, also draws attention to its inevitable failures:

- The number of potential irregular migrants passing through Sarajevo airport en route to the EU has been reduced by 95% in comparison with the first 8 months of 2001
- The number of irregular migrants detected on the Croatian side of the border and returned to BiH has been reduced by 70%
- The number of irregular migrants detected in Slovenia has also fallen by 70%

(INDIS, 2003)

If the appraisal of Project IMMpact is to be summarised in a sentence, one could say that the story it tells is of interdictive techniques that work well, but that are in need of further development. This is indicative of a self-fulfilling cycle in which exclusionary politics become caught where technical and narrative interrelations are mediated through a logic of selective opposition.

The exclusionary politics of preemptive *refoulement*

A critical reading of Project IMMpact enables us to see how technical and narrative processes of securitisation, criminalisation and interdiction come together as part of a selective and depoliticising rationality of deterrence that effectively produces 'illegality' or unauthorised entrance as a 'problem' that extended migration controls are designed to resolve. To leave our critique here, however, would risk reinforcing the exclusionary cycle that this book strives to critically intercede. Indeed, it would risk reaffirming a managerial narrative that assumes that there *really are* increasing numbers of illegal immigrants that take advantage of our generous asylum system, and that *we really do* have to stop them before – well, before something very frightening that we *naturally do not* want to happen actually *does* happen. The aim is not to be provocative here, but rather it is to demonstrate how easy it is to be drawn back into a seemingly benign managerial discourse in which asylum seekers are presumed to be 'culpable' and 'threatening' subjects that necessitate the extension of restrictive controls. It is in the attempt to maintain critical distance from this mangeralism that the critique moves to a second level in this part of the chapter, by suggesting that interdiction can be conceived as a form of pre-emptive *refoulement*.[12] Taking seriously the claim of EU states such as the UK to be 'morally benevolent' and committed to the provision of refugee protection (see Chapter 4), the analysis of interdiction thus goes one step further here in order to show how an exclusionary politics in which territorial dislocations are projected onto asylum seekers effectively reduces the scope of refugee protection to the select few. This, the analysis shows, is indicative of an exclusionary politics that is selectively inclusive, as well as selectively exclusive, in its operations.

The analysis of Project IMMpact has already shown how the extended application of interdictive migration controls entails a shrinking of the space of asylum by technical means. By taking as a starting point exclusionary narratives of unauthorised entrance and reading the effects of technical interdiction back into these narratives, the analysis has shown how narratives and techniques of migration control reaffirm one another in their mutual opposition to 'undesirables' such as asylum seekers. Indeed, the shrinking space of asylum is also evident if we move back to the level of political debate, in which there is a notable absence of refugee protection considerations in the exclusionary articulation of interdictive migration control initiatives such as Project IMMpact. In the texts analysed, the primary managerial concern was with the organised smuggling of consenting migrants, while humanitarian concerns were largely absent or diverted to the organised trafficking of exploited migrants. A telling example in this regard is the UK government's legitimising narrative of Project IMMpact, which is indicative of the securitisation and criminalisation of illegal-immigration(-cum-asylum). Specifically, it is suggested that 'the Balkans have become the main gateway to Europe of a multi-million pound business in illegal immigration, drug smuggling and people trafficking' (Home Office, 2003). It is this criminalisation and securitisation of asylum in its implicit association with 'illegal immigration', the analysis suggests, that is critical to our understanding of the shrinking space of asylum.

What may be worth dwelling on a little longer here is the notable exclusion of the *human* dimension of smuggling within the statement. Both smuggling and trafficking are posed alongside illegal immigration, but only trafficking is directly conceived in human terms. The way in which this managerial articulation of 'illegal immigration' removes its human element is highly significant. The official distinction between smuggling and trafficking has shifted slightly over time, but what has remained an ongoing distinguishing factor is exploitation. While smuggling refers to the movement of migrants across borders by criminals who receive payment for their 'services' by smuggled migrants, trafficking entails the movement of migrants (not necessarily across borders and not necessarily with payment) in terms that set up a relation of exploitation between the trafficked and the trafficker. This suggests that smuggling is critical to the managerial articulation of asylum as a 'problem' of 'abuse' because it is according to this framework that the unauthorised entrance of asylum seekers is assumed to be a transgressive act of 'illegal immigration' in complicity with those of organised criminals. Whether deliberate or not, the preclusion of the human dimension of smuggling in the above statement thus effectively reflects and consolidates an exclusionary process in which those seeking asylum 'at port' or 'in-country' are dehumanised and depoliticised through their equivalential association with 'illegal immigration' and organised crime. The production of 'culpable' subjects, in other words, reduces the space of asylum in terms that works against the political engagement of people seeking asylum (see Part IV).

A shrinkage of the space of asylum is reflected in the movement of humanitarian concern into the realm of human trafficking. This process entails two interrelated discursive moves. First, it entails a move in which asylum *qua* refugee protection is rendered invisible – both are, quite literally, removed from the above statement, as well as from the discussion of IMMpact at large. Second, it entails a move in which the human dimension is relocated alongside trafficking in specifically humanitarian terms. Again, this can be seen as a broader discursive shift in the framing of interdiction, through which 'threatening' subjects are criminalised and 'vulnerable' or abject subjects are depoliticised at the same time (Aradau, 2004b, 2008). More to the point, the articulation of those who are trafficked as vulnerable victims is relevant for this critique of pre-emptive *refoulment* because it enables us to see how humanitarian concerns are diverted from asylum and refugee protection towards the exploitation of (primarily female) sex workers (see Andrijasevic, forthcoming). Thus, even in a situation where interceptive controls prohibit the passage of those seeking refuge, interdiction is presented as humanitarian in nature in terms of its ability to challenge the 'evil' and 'heinous' crime of human trafficking (McShane, 2003). Interdiction, it would seem, is thus effectively authorised by humanitarian means. It is here that we can see how exclusionary narratives and exclusionary techniques of migration control come together to effectively reduce the space of asylum. Such a shrinkage of the space is evident in the very commitment of EU states such as the UK to refugee resettlement, which is problematic because it affirms exclusionary distinctions between the 'desirable' and 'undesirable' and between 'genuine' refugees and 'bogus' asylum seekers. Such developments are all indicative of a process of pre-emptive *refoulement*.

Indeed, by focusing on pre-emptive *refoulement* we can observe how the complex play of inclusion and exclusion within the exclusionary politics of asylum effectively mediates the internal contradictions or disruptions of a territorial order in highly reactive, ideological terms (see Chapter 2). There are various ways in which we can see these internal contradictions at work in contemporary asylum discourse, the most obvious of which would seem to be the articulation of highly restrictive migration controls as necessary to the maintenance of a 'morally benevolent' political community. Contradictory as this articulation clearly is, a discursive approach mitigates against a simplistic reading of contradictory articulations in terms of 'rhetoric' versus 'reality'. Instead, it allows us to question what the *effects* of such a contradictory articulation might be in relation to the wider construction of meaning and identity. Considering this in relation to the book's thesis regarding the dislocation of territorial governance and belonging (see Chapter 1), the analysis suggests that the contradictory articulation of benevolent interdiction is indicative of a wider deterrent rationality that operates according to the exclusionary logic of selective opposition. This, it seems, effectively reconstructs a territorial order of governance and belonging (in the face of the dissolution of such an order) in distinctly exclusionary terms. Pre-emptive *refoulement* is a classic example in this regard.

Indeed, this reading of exclusionary politics perhaps allows us to begin the process of critically interceding the contradictory processes that emerge in contemporary (de)territorialised reworkings of governance and belonging (see Walters, 2004). These contradictory processes are no more evident than in extended migration controls, which effectively produce borderzones that further disrupt the internal workings of a territorial order. These borderzones emerge in terms that disrupt the existence of territorial borderlines. That borderlines do not exist can be conceived of in two directions. On the one hand, territorial borderlines do not exist because they are continuously traversed by the 'external turbulence' of cross-border mobilities (Mezzadra and Nielson, 2003). On the other hand, territorial borderlines to not exist because they are continuously traversed by 'internal disruptions' of state governance and national belonging, such as those transnational relations constituted through the process of interdiction (Bigo, 2005). It is where the latter are masked and the former are highlighted that the reactively ideological form of an exclusionary politics would seem to emerge. Specifically, such a politics emerges where dislocations are projected onto 'external turbulence' without any acknowledgement of 'internal disruptions'. The analysis in this chapter has shown this exclusionary process to be marked by the constitution of 'undesirables' as threatening supplements of a territorial order that, for various reasons, faces its own dissolution. This entails a technical and narrative decontestation of pre-emptive *refoulement* as well as a depoliticisation of political subjects in terms that remove the exclusionary operations of managed migration away from the sphere of public debate.

Conclusion

This chapter has shifted our attention from the sphere of political debate to the professional field of migration control in order to explore the exclusionary interactions of narratives and techniques of migration control through the lens of interdiction. Specifically, it has shown that an analysis of these two dimensions enables us to see how securitisation and criminalisation become caught in a self-fulfilling cycle that reduces the scope for public scrutiny and critical debate. The analysis has suggested that this depoliticising process occurs at two levels. The first part of the chapter suggested that decontestation or depoliticisation primarily occurs where the exclusionary operations of securitisation and criminalisation shift to the technical or managerial level. Thus, the development of information-gathering tools and the involvement of the police and the military in the field of migration control entail a movement of restrictive controls beyond the sphere of public scrutiny. In the second part of the chapter the analysis went on to suggest that this depoliticising process mirrors, and is mirrored in, similar processes of decontestation at the levels of political debate and professional self-authorisation. Specifically, it occurs where the reduced space for asylum is articulated as *necessary* to the managerial development of a humanitarian approach to migration. These depoliticising tendencies come together in exclusionary terms against asylum seekers through the extension of interdictive technologies of control beyond territorial borderlines. This contradictory process, the analysis suggests, paradoxically reconstructs a territorial order in deterritorialised terms while simultaneously constituting an exclusionary politics in which the territorial dislocation of political community is projected on 'turbulent' mobile subjects who transgress territorial borderlines.

There are several important effects of these exclusionary interactions that come to the fore in this analysis. The most obvious effect that the analysis has drawn attention to is the way in which it effectively produces 'illegality' or unauthorised entrance as a 'problem' that interdiction is designed to resolve. Rather than responding 'naturally' to a pre-existing 'threat' of asylum-cum-illegal-immigration, policymakers and migration control professionals might thus better be conceived of as authorising the extension of restrictive migration controls through interdiction. On this reading, interdiction becomes increasingly necessary in its very failure. Indeed, this points to a more fundamental political effect of the exclusionary operations of interdiction, in reconstructing a territorial order that faces its own dissolution. The analysis has suggested that this is a contradictory process that serves to divert attention or ideologically mask the dislocations that emerge in historical conditions where both 'internal disruptions' and 'external turbulences' are intensified. It is in masking such processes in specifically reactive terms that asylum seekers are constructed as 'culpable' and 'threatening' subjects necessitating the extension of restrictive control.

There is not only a clear political effectiveness to this exclusionary politics. So also, it would seem, is there a certain economic effectiveness to this process, to which the analysis can only begin to point to here. Drawing on the work of Nicholas De Genova (2002, 2004, 2007), one could say that the production of 'illegality' entails a process of abjectification or 'illegalisation' in which asylum-seekers-cum-illegal-immigrants are potentially constituted as exploitable workers. Indeed, this insight comes out of the suggestion that a deterrent rationality works according to a logic of opposition that is both selective *and* depoliticising. The next chapter will show how this selective rationality of deterrence is manifest in the punitive technology of dispersal, like it is in the preventative technology of interdiction. It is in the punitive movement through processes of securitisation and criminalisation towards abjectification that this book conceives the potential transformation of asylum seekers from political subjects, through 'culpable' and 'threatening' subjects, to 'abject' subjects that are exploitable as legally vulnerable, cheap and flexible workers (see Part IV). This requires a second critical examination of the depoliticisations of a deterrent rationality that is inscribed according to a logic of selective opposition, this time through the abjectifying lens of diffuse punitive controls.

6
Dispersal as Abjectification: The Diffusion of Punitive 'Internal' Controls

In the last chapter we saw how the articulation of asylum as a 'threat' associated with unauthorised entrance entails an extension of interdictive 'external' controls in terms that feed into an exclusionary cycle of securitisation and criminalisation. This process, it was argued, effectively extends migration controls in terms that shrink the political space of asylum through pre-emptive *refoulement*. Indeed, this process is reflected in the analysis of 'reception' provisions in this chapter, which are better approached as 'internal' migration controls. The development of criminalising and securitising interdictive technologies at the 'external' level has important implications when it comes to a consideration of the position of those who enter the territory of the UK to claim asylum. While the 1951 Convention legally permits asylum seekers to enter a 'host' country without authorisation, the interdictive state is less permissive. New arrivals that apply for asylum either 'in-country' or 'at port' are already discursively inscribed as 'threatening' transgressors who are in cohorts with criminal smugglers, despite their having committed a crime against nobody (see Chapter 5). Where exclusionary managerial assumptions regarding the culpability of asylum seekers are entrenched across the political, popular and technical levels, 'internal' migration controls thus move in a punitive direction. In developing a dual-pronged critique of such exclusionary operations, this chapter examines the punitive technology of dispersal as part of the wider revision of asylum 'support' in the UK. Rather than providing a support service for asylum seekers in the UK, the analysis shows how dispersal entails a rendering of asylum support as a technology of punishment. This, it is argued, can be conceptualised as part of a wider rationality of deterrence that selectively moves through processes of criminalisation and securitisation towards abjectification.

The punitive nature of UK asylum reception practices is relatively widely charted in the literature, including that of academics and researchers (e.g. Bloch and Schuster, 2005; Flynn, 2005; Sales, 2002, 2007; Schuster, 2003a, 2005b) as well as that of agencies involved in the provision of support to those seeking asylum (e.g. Independent Asylum Commission, 2008). Critical attention has often been focused on detention and deportation, which are of particular importance in relation to processes of securitisation and criminalisation. Deportation is central in understanding processes of 'illegalisation', because it is in becoming subject to deportation that an asylum seeker's status shifts to one of irregularity (see De Genova, 2002, 2004; Gibney, 2008). Even where the deportability of an individual is not legally founded, however, his or her culpability can be produced through the technology of detention (see De Genova, 2007; Welch and Schuster, 2005). Migrant detention targets a range of individuals, and has been significantly increased over recent years. As well as those who have overstayed beyond their visa entitlements, individuals are often detained at the end of the asylum process in preparation for their removal. In addition, asylum seekers are detained immediately on arrival or during the course of their asylum claim being assessed. This occurs where their claim is deemed clearly unfounded or if it is deemed likely that they will abscond (Savage, 2005:227), although evidence suggests that detention is often practiced in more arbitrary terms (BID, 2008). The detention of asylum seekers, in this respect, is similar to deportation; it is a criminalising technology that inscribes asylum seekers as 'culpable' subjects. As a technology that is increasingly used for both security and for immigration purposes, detention can also be seen as a securitising tool by which migration and terrorism are institutionally and technically associated as 'threats'.

Dispersal sits alongside the exclusionary technologies of deportation and detention in constructing asylum seekers as 'culpable' subjects. In this respect, an analysis of the punitive technology of dispersal allows us to show how asylum seekers become subjects of criminalisation and securitisation even prior to, or in the absence of, their actual detention and deportation. Nicholas De Genova (2002, 2005, 2007) suggests that deportation and detention gain their effectiveness as much in their potentiality as in their actuality, with deportability and detainability producing 'culpable' subjects that become vulnerable to both economic and political exploitation. If we take this emphasis on detain*ability* and deport*ability* as our starting point, dispersal can be read as a punitive technology that produces asylum seekers as 'culpable' subjects even before their guilt is officially established. What a focus on dispersal thus adds to the analysis of deportation and detention is an understanding of the way in which routine techniques of punitive control permeate the daily experiences of those asylum seekers within the UK, even where they are not identified as requiring 'exceptional' treatment in the form of detention and deportation.

This chapter develops a dual-pronged critique of dispersal, first by assessing its effects in relation to the specified goals of the initiative in resolving the 'problem' of service strain and social instability and, second, by challenging its exclusionary and abjectifying operations. The analysis draws on a range of policy documents, as well as on a series of semistructured individual and group interviews carried out with practitioners involved in the implementation of dispersal, with asylum seekers subject to the practices of dispersal, and with members of an established local community from a key dispersal region in the city of Birmingham (see Appendix 2 for individual and group interviews). Charting the punitive techniques that dispersal brings to asylum support in the UK, the first part of the chapter suggests that dispersal is not only a managerial operation designed to resolve the problem of service 'strain', but it can also be conceived of as part of a wider deterrent rationality that precariously reconstructs political community against asylum-seekers-cum-illegal-immigrants. It argues that this reading of dispersal enables us to see how exclusionary operations of securitisation and criminalisation become embedded at a much more diffuse level throughout the UK, as asylum 'support' is engaged as asylum policing. The second part of the chapter goes on to consider the effects of such a process from the position of the asylum seeker. It is here that the critique of dispersal is further developed. Showing how dispersal tends to aggravate service strain and social instability through the process of its implementation, the chapter argues that dispersal is better conceived of as a divisive initiative that constitutes a hostile environment in which asylum seekers are vulnerable both to physical attack and also to economic exploitation. This, the chapter concludes, is central to an exclusionary politics in which asylum seekers are blamed for failures that are the political community's 'own'; a politics that potentially moves the asylum seeker through a position of culpability into a situation of abjection.

From dilution to punishment: Everyday productions of culpability

While it is often suggested that the UK dispersal initiative can be conceived according to a rationale of deterrence or punishment (Boswell, 2003c), the precise sense in which, as well as the degree to which, it can be conceptualised as such remains unclear. This part of the chapter develops an account of dispersal that clearly locates the initiative as a punitive technology within a wider rationality of deterrence. The first part of the analysis introduces dispersal generally and in the Birmingham case specifically, which is the area in which this research was carried out. The second part then goes on to introduce dispersal in terms of its design and articulation as a managerial technique of dilution, which in the UK is legitimised according to narratives of 'service strain' and social instability. The analysis suggests that this can be conceptualised as a specifically exclusionary rendering of dispersal, and claims that dispersal can thus be conceived as a punitive technology in which political community is precariously reconstructed through its opposition to the 'problem' or 'threat' of asylum. This claim is consolidated in the third part of the analysis, which shows how dispersal entails an extension of the exclusionary logic of selective opposition through the diffuse everyday operation of processes of criminalisation and securitisation. This, it is argued, suggests that the rationality of deterrence is not simply a preventative one that strives to 'keep asylum seekers out', as is conventionally assumed, but rather it is a selective and depoliticising rationality that both prohibits and punishes 'undesirables' such as asylum seekers.

Introducing dispersal to Birmingham

To define it simply, dispersal is an initiative whereby asylum applicants are transported to various locations for the provision of their support. Although the dispersal initiative has only relatively recently been introduced as part of a comprehensive national programme of asylum support in the UK, it has both a longer history in the UK as well as a wider applicability in the European context. Dispersal was used in the UK on an *ad hoc* basis in the 1970s and 1980s in order to relieve interethnic tension, most notably where there was a sudden increase in the numbers of Ugandan Asian and Vietnemese refugees (Joly, 1996). It was also used in order to address accommodation shortages in the 1990s, when large numbers of refugees from Bosnia and Kosovo were granted temporary protection (Boswell, 2001; Schuster, 2005b). Although dispersal displays differing characteristics in each national context (see Boswell, 2003; Schuster, 2005b), managerial concerns regarding increased numbers and regarding the spatial concentration of new arrivals have been central to the development of dispersal across a range of EU states, including Germany (Boswell, 2001;

Schuster, 2005c), the Netherlands and Sweden (Robinson, Andersson and Musterd, 2003).

As we saw in Chapter 4, dispersal was introduced in the UK by the 1999 Immigration and Asylum Act, where the initiative was articulated as a key dimension of the newly formed National Asylum Support Service (NASS). The NASS was established on 3rd April 2000 in order to provide support to asylum seekers whose claims are being assessed. The service is responsible for funding the voluntary sector to provide emergency support to asylum seekers on their arrival and to provide 'one stop' advise for all asylum seekers. It is also responsible for providing a basic package of subsistence and accommodation for destitute asylum seekers, and for providing subsistence support to asylum seekers housed by alternative means. In 2003, the NASS was reorganised to form a regional structure, the stated aim of which was to increase the presence of the NASS 'at the point of service delivery' (IND, 2005a). Since this reorganisation, the NASS has been divided into 12 regional offices,[1] with the support provided to asylum seekers dispersed to Birmingham monitored by the NASS West Midlands regional office (IND, 2005b).

In this chapter the analysis draws on interviews with practitioners, asylum seekers and local community members in the city of Birmingham specifically (see Appendix 2). Birmingham has played an important role in the development of the dispersal initiative because it is one of the main areas where dispersed asylum seekers are accommodated. At the end of 2004, for example, the West Midlands accommodated 6,285 dispersed asylum seekers, with only the North West (6,410) and Yorkshire and the Humber (9,350) accommodating a higher number (The Refugee Council, 2005). At this time Birmingham accommodated 1,825 of these asylum seekers, and as such it housed more dispersed claimants than any UK city other than Glasgow (5,790) and Leeds (2,195) (Refugee Council, 2005). In quantitative terms, Birmingham is thus a key case to consider in relation to dispersal (see Griffiths, Sigona and Zetter, 2005; Zetter, Griffiths and Sigona, 2005). However, it also has specificities that differentiate it from other cities receiving asylum seekers. Birmingham has large and well-established ethnic communities and there are thus a wide range of community organisations that are able to support those newly arriving to the area. As such, one might expect the reception of dispersed asylum seekers to be less hostile than in cities such as Glasgow or Hull, where asylum seekers are often more visibly 'different' from established local communities and where existing residents are less familiar with those of diverse backgrounds. It is important to bear this in mind when we consider how dispersal contributes to the production of a hostile environment, for it would suggest that the experiences of many asylum seekers within Birmingham are likely to be less extreme than for those in some 'accommodating' regions.

Not all asylum seekers are dispersed by the NASS. Some are detained in Immigration Service removal centres and others are housed in immigration short-term holding facilities while their claims are 'fast-tracked'. The fast-track scheme was introduced in 2000, and was extended when the New Asylum Model (NAM) was implemented in 2007. NAM is a key dimension of the 2005 five-year plan for Asylum and Immigration (see Chapter 4), and was set up in order to speed asylum application processing times and in order to aid removal (Home Office, 2006). Bail for Immigration Detainees (BID, 2008) calculates that 1,605 asylum seekers had their claims assessed as part of the fast-track system at three detention centres in 2007. In March 2007, a total of 1,435 persons who had claimed asylum at some point were held in detention centres, 55 of which were in short-term holding facilities (Home Office, 2007:10). This compares to a total of 48,795 asylum seekers (including dependents) who were supported by NASS (Ibid.:8). Such figures suggest that NAM has not so much increased the numbers of those held in detention as it has extended the control and surveillance of asylum seekers more widely (BID, 2008). In a context where asylum seekers are not able to work, the majority of asylum seekers are thus supported by the NASS.

Dispersal is not a compulsory scheme, but it is the only means of support for those who are deemed destitute (see Boswell, 2003:320). Some asylum seekers supported by the NASS live with friends or family members, and are entitled to receive subsistence support at 70 per cent of current income from the post office using an application registration card (ARC) provided by the NASS. For those who qualify for accommodation as well as subsistence, the NASS identifies an accommodation space with a public, social or private provider working under a contract with the NASS in a dispersal region (Refugee Council, 2005). There have been some limitations to asylum seekers' participation in the dispersal initiative. For example, in December 2004, 40,750 asylum seekers in the UK received subsistence support in accommodation funded by the NASS while 20,875 received subsistence-only support (Heath and Jeffries, 2005). A similar pattern was evident in March 2007, with 36,785 asylum seekers supported in dispersal accommodation while 10,935 received subsistence-only support (Home Office, 2007:8). Despite these limitations, however, the majority of asylum seekers that are supported by the NASS receive both subsistence *and* accommodation, and are thus subject to dispersal. As such, an analysis of the experiences of dispersed asylum seekers is important in examining the reception of asylum seekers in the UK more generally.

Managerial dilution and exclusionary politics

Dispersal is generally conceived to be organised according to a rationale of dilution, in which new arrivals or specific groups of migrants are dispersed to avoid their excessive concentration in one area (Robinson, Andersson and Musterd, 2003). In the UK the managerial operation of dispersal is primarily articulated and designed in relation to service provision and accommodation needs. Indeed, the preliminary objective of the NASS was to spread the financial and social costs of hosting asylum seekers. In particular, the NASS was set up in order to respond to the 'financial and administrative strain' on local authorities in the South East:

> Responsibility for supporting and accommodating asylum seekers had previously been with Benefit Agencies or Local Authorities, however this had created a financial and administrative strain especially on those in London and Kent. As a direct response to this, NASS was set up and the vast majority of asylum seekers eligible for support are now supported by NASS.
>
> (IND, 2005c)

Mirroring this rationale, dispersal was designed in order to 'relieve the disproportionate burden' on housing and services on London and the South East (NASS secretariat, 2005). It was thus primarily set up according to the availability of accommodation, in order to dilute the concentration of asylum seekers in regions within the UK that were deemed to be 'overburdened' in their provision of accommodation and public services to asylum seekers (see Boswell, 2001:2–3, 2003:320).

The articulation and design of dispersal in terms of dilution is approached here as a managerial technique, which is characterised by an exclusionary logic of selective opposition in which the principle of assimilation plays a key role (Squire, 2005). Although dispersal is explicitly articulated as a 'problem' in administrative and financial terms, the analysis in Chapter 4 suggests that an articulation of asylum as 'threatening' service provision entails exclusionary processes of securitisation and criminalisation. Indeed, the analysis has suggested that such processes are related to processes of racialisation in terms of the selective logic of opposition by which they operate. In this regard, the assimilation of asylum seekers according to a rationale of service strain might be seen as only one step removed from the assimilation of asylum seekers according to a rationale of racial or cultural dilution. Indeed, Sarah Savage suggests that the lessening of racial tension is an implicit aim of the initiative, even if this is not explicitly stated (Savage, 2005:224–5).[2] While a racialised logic of selective opposition is not far removed from the managerial operations of dispersal, however, this analysis suggests that the exclusionary tendencies of dispersal fall more in line with processes of securitisation and criminalisation. This is particularly the case at the level of political and popular debate, in terms of the narration of asylum as a 'threat' to public service provision (see Chapter 4). It also seems to be the case at the level of technical or professional practice, where dispersal engages punitive techniques that constitute asylum seekers as 'culpable' subjects on an everyday basis.

What the analysis suggested in the last chapter is that technical and narrative operations of securitisation and criminalisation are often interrelated with one another in exclusionary managerial discourse. Specifically, the analysis of interception suggested that the technical rendering of an exclusionary politics is evident in the institutional engagements of the police and military in the field of migration control, as well as in the coming together of information-gathering techniques and border controls through interdictive technologies. These technical processes, it was shown, interrelate with narrative processes of securitisation in exclusionary terms, because the technical production of 'threats' serve to legitimise their ongoing development through the consolidation of exclusionary narratives at the level of political and popular debate. In this chapter dispersal is seen as becoming caught up in a similar cycle of securitisation and criminalisation, in which the 'problem' of service strain is reproduced by technical means. However, the analysis in this chapter also highlights a somewhat different rendering of the managerial operations of exclusionary politics, because dispersal does not entail policing and military agencies directly. Rather, an analysis of dispersal would seem to suggest that an alternative process is also at play in the exclusionary politics of asylum, in which the diffusion of technical practices of securitisation and criminalisation entails their emergence in new, and often unexpected, places.

Dispersal as a punitive technology

Although dispersal was explicitly set up by Labour to ease the 'financial and administrative strain' on public service provision in the South East, it can also be interpreted as a central dimension of a deterrent rationality that is developed by punitive means (Boswell, 2001:2–3). This is partially reflected in the history of the initiative's development, which can be seen as a story of reduced support for asylum seekers. Up until the Conservative government removed welfare benefits from asylum seekers in 1996, national government was responsible for supporting asylum seekers. The High Court ruled in 1996 that local authorities were responsible for the provision of care and accommodation of asylum seekers deemed to be destitute or at risk, thus the cost of support moved from state welfare system to local authority budgets. As a temporary solution designed to save money and to reduce accommodation pressures, local authorities (most notably those in Kent and London) began to institute dispersal 'by stealth' through renting cheap accommodation from private landlords in other areas (Boswell, 2001:11; Savage, 2005:222–3). In response to this, the government set up a voluntary dispersal system, before developing the no-choice dispersal system for destitute asylum seekers in 2000. The emergence of dispersal, in this regard, might be conceived of as part of a broader framework of deterrence through punishment, a central dimension of which has been the successive limitation of support for asylum seekers and their families (see Chapter 4).

That dispersal forms part of a broader rationality of deterrence is also supported in the institutional embedding of the NASS Agency within the Home Office and, in particular, within the Border Agency. The Border agency replaced the Border and Immigration Agency (BIA) in 2008, as well as the Immigration and Nationality Directorate (IND) before it. This agency plays a central role in implementing a deterrent agenda; evident in the job description provided for workers under the former IND, which claims that 'it is our job to deter illegal workers and illegal entrants, and Immigration Officers have legal powers to detain them and remove them from the country' (IND, 2005d). Although deterrence is explicitly linked to detention, deportation, 'illegal immigration' and the role of immigration officers in this statement, the fact that the NASS, dispersal and asylum seeking are located as part of this institutional structure is telling. Indeed, dispersal was explicitly articulated as a deterrent policy by the former Home Secretary Jack Straw when it was first introduced, and the political articulation of the initiative in such terms is supported through the punitive processes by which asylum reception becomes linked with compulsory relocation for the destitute (Pearl and Zetter, 2002:234–9). In this book, dispersal is conceived as a punitive technology that is related to a wider rationality of deterrence, and as running parallel to deportation and detention, as well as to interdiction, through its inscription of asylum seekers as 'culpable' subjects.

Perhaps the most obvious way in which asylum seeking is criminalised through the process of dispersal is in the policing role that the NASS officials play in implementing the initiative. Asylum seekers generally have no choice as to where they will be dispersed, and in this respect those implementing the initiative often have to enforce compliance. This is evident in the NASS policy bulletin, which gives guidance to the outreach team on what to do when an asylum seeker fails to travel to the arranged dispersal accommodation. While the emphasis is on 'encouraging asylum seekers to travel in line with the dispersal arrangements that have been made for them' (IND, 2005e), the NASS outreach team is also required to *ensure* that asylum seekers travel by reminding them of 'the likely consequences of him [sic] failing to comply with a condition of his support' (Ibid.). If no 'reasonable' reason is given for failure to comply with the dispersal order, such consequences are the termination of support. This is stated in a leaflet given to asylum seekers in the NASS emergency accommodation, which states that 'IF YOU FAIL TO TRAVEL AS ARRANGED THE OFFER OF SUPPORT MAY BE WITHDRAWN AND YOU WILL BE REQUIRED TO LEAVE YOUR CURRENT ACCOMMODATION' (Ibid.). When it comes to the implementation of dispersal, then, officials from the NASS are often required to play a policing role.

The policing role that officials from the NASS play is also evident in the techniques of surveillance and control that are used to ensure that dispersed asylum seekers are compliant with the terms of their support. The NASS requires that asylum seekers sign agreements to declare any work undertaken (Individual interview 2, Appendix 2). In addition, various additional practices of surveillance and control were described by the dispersed asylum seekers interviewed. For example, Susanne suggests that the NASS outreach team carried out a check to ensure that she maintained the hygiene and security of her dispersal accommodation (Individual interview 4, Appendix 2), while P describes a more extreme experience of his visit to the regional NASS office, which began with a fingerprint check and culminated in a cross-examination about how he had re-entered the UK (Individual interview 6, Appendix 2). These examples are suggestive of the central role that surveillance and control play in the contemporary asylum 'support' system, which is most evident in the development of electronic tagging and increased reporting requirements under the NAM. As one asylum support worker suggests:

In terms of checking that people are living in the accommodation, checking they are not working, checking they aren't letting someone else live in that accommodation, and all that sort of thing ... there are sizeable resources that NASS can put into that. But to have resources that look at whether or not someone is having financial support – to have the resources to check and see whether NASS is actually meeting its statutory obligations to feed asylum-seeking families – that doesn't actually happen.

(Individual interview 1, Appendix 2)

Despite the specification of the NASS as being a 'support service' for destitute asylum seekers, the statement of this public asylum support worker suggests that the NASS primarily plays a policing role.

The punitive nature of dispersal is not only evident in the policing role that officials from the NASS play, but so also is it evident in asylum seekers' experience of dispersal as an isolating and disruptive, if not a downright unpleasant, process. Isolation was a recurrent theme in the interviews carried out with dispersed asylum seekers (cf. Savage, 2005:229). For example, Susanne describes how she felt 'like one family' in emergency accommodation, and that her dispersal away from these initial contacts left her feeling 'like someone who's lost in a forest, like someone who's dropped from a plane in the forest and you have to learn to talk with the animals' (Individual interview 4, Appendix 2). This process of isolation is clearly exacerbated by the fact that asylum seekers generally have no choice about the region to which they are dispersed nor, indeed, the people with whom they are dispersed. Only one of the five interviewees who directly experienced dispersal was dispersed to an area close to that of their emergency accommodation, and for this P twice claims to be 'lucky' (Individual interview 6, Appendix 2). Indeed, several factors were described as exacerbating asylum seekers' experience of isolation and disruption. First, the multiple dispersals of asylum seekers (often from one dispersal region to another dispersal region) are described as disruptive by Guy, who claims that from his perspective it was as if 'life is starting and starting and starting and starting again' (Individual interview 5, Appendix 2). Second, a delay in dispersing new arrivals from one area to another is described as isolating and disruptive by David, who claims that his experience of dispersal was 'bad' and 'unhappy'. David says, 'I did five months in the hostel, [in] emergency accommodation, found some friends in the same place in the emergency accommodation, and now I have to move from Birmingham to Manchester' (Group interview 1, Appendix 2).[3] It is worth noting, at this point, that in both of these cases dispersal was practiced *between* dispersal regions rather than from the South East to a dispersal region, thus raising questions about the explicit rationale of dispersal as relieving the 'burden' on accommodation and services in the South East.

The very failure to move asylum seekers out of emergency accommodation swiftly does not only provoke isolation, but it is also described by several interviewees as a downright unpleasant experience. Emergency accommodation provides basic bed and board and limited additional subsistence, and in this respect it is inappropriate for extended periods of stay (Savage, 2005:229). Most of the asylum seekers interviewed had been housed in emergency accommodation where bedrooms were shared with up to three other people. Various concerns regarding the food and hygiene standards in this accommodation were raised, particularly by those who remained in the accommodation over an extended period of time. For example, John raised concerns regarding the food provision in emergency accommodation: 'We [are] from different backgrounds, with different culture and food, but we are mixing, we are obliged to eat the something that makes [sic] feel bad or ill in different way' (Group interview 1, Appendix 2). David agrees: 'you have rice, chicken, salad – every time. Like a cycle, only the same'. In addition, the location of three or four people in a room is a health concern for Rocky, who says that there is 'no difference if one is ill'. With 65 people in his hostel, David raises concerns about hygiene in 'sharing a bathroom' with so many people, while Rocky claims that 'during the long time the people use the same cups, the same plates'. He says: 'Someone who cleans the plate sometimes is not using the hot water' (Ibid.). For those housed in emergency accommodation for long periods of time, life within a hostel would seem to be an uncomfortable and unpleasant experience that is punitive in effect, if not in intention.

The degree to which those developing and implementing dispersal *intend* the initiative to be punitive is not a key concern here, because this analysis is concerned with the exclusionary operations and effects of dispersal rather than with the explicit or implicit purpose or intent of policy initiatives. Nevertheless, questions regarding agency and intentionality are important ones that need addressing, an engagement with which may shed some light on the way in which the securitisation and criminalisation of asylum becomes self-fulfilling through the exclusionary interactions of technical and narrative processes. There are several points that need to be made here. First, it is important to acknowledge that dispersal is largely designed to be a deterrent initiative (see Pearl and Zetter, 2003), and that some of the punitive techniques and processes outlined above are thus systemically organised as such (presumably with a greater or lesser degree of intentionality). Second, it is important to note that the NASS system, like the asylum system as a whole, has faced a range of logistical and administrative difficulties, and in this respect many of the processes that are experienced as punitive by asylum seekers are simply a result of poor administration and design (see Boswell, 2001). Nevertheless, the administrative and logistical difficulties that have emerged in the implementation of dispersal need further critical consideration. As we will see below, administrative incompetence is not only evident in a delay in dispersing many asylum seekers from emergency accommodation, but so also is it evident in terms of the chaotic provision of subsistence support by the NASS. To say that such failures are intentional would clearly go a step too far (as well as being impossible to prove or disprove definitively). However, what can be said is that these failures are likely to be of less concern where asylum seekers are assumed to be 'culpable' and 'threatening' subjects who 'abuse' the asylum system, because those who are effectively punished are not perceived as having the right to complain.

To put it simply, one could say that punitive techniques are not so much *deliberate* dimensions of dispersal as they are evidence of the technical embedding of a logic of selective opposition, which makes exclusionary marks on 'culpable' subjects at an everyday level. The managerial techniques of asylum 'support' practitioners are not formed in isolation from the exclusionary narratives of criminalisation and securitisation that we examined in Part II of the book, nor are such exclusionary narratives formed in isolation from the governmental techniques that we explored in Part III. Rather, the exclusionary inter-relations between narrative and technical securitisations and criminalisations are intertwined as part of a broader rationality of deterrence that works in accord with a logic of selective opposition. Indeed, the normalisation of punitive techniques, in such a context, may go some way in explaining the anomalous practice of multiple dispersals noted above. Reminding ourselves of the primary specified aim of dispersal, one might legitimately question how far the process of moving an asylum seeker from one dispersal region to another relieves the 'burden' on the South East. It may well be that in this case such contraventions of the explicit aim of dispersal become eclipsed by administrative practices in which bodies are moved to spaces in arbitrary terms. What this analysis suggests, however, is that such technical processes also have a meaning and authority in terms of a rationality of deterrence that entails punitive technologies. Indeed, whether or not such an approach is intended to be punitive is irrelevant to its description as effectively punitive from the position of the asylum seeker.

From asylum support to asylum police

As we have already seen, the fact that asylum seekers are inscribed on an everyday level as 'culpable' subjects without any legitimate right to complain is evident in the way in which asylum support is practiced as a form of asylum policing. What is notable in terms of the earlier suggestion that dispersal signals the technical *diffusion* of exclusionary controls is that a range of voluntary, public, private and refugee welfare agencies become incorporated as operative agents of the punitive technology of dispersal (see Griffiths, Sigona, and Zetter, 2005; Zetter, Griffiths and Sigona, 2005). Although regional officers from the NASS play a role in ensuring that the physical dispersal of asylum seekers runs smoothly and in ensuring that accommodation providers meet their contractual obligations, the NASS plays a relatively minor role in the provision of support to asylum seekers. Rather, those on the 'front line' of implementation are voluntary sector agencies such as the Refugee Council (contracted by the NASS to provide emergency accommodation and advice regarding subsistence claims with the NASS), as well as public and private housing providers (contracted by the NASS to provide accommodation and limited additional support to dispersed asylum seekers). A consideration of how these various agencies become caught up in the process of policing asylum seekers is important in drawing attention to way that technical processes of securitisation and criminalisation are diffusely extended in terms that depoliticise an exclusionary politics through processes of co-option.

In the previous section we saw how the emergency accommodation that the voluntary sector provides to new arrivals contributes to the development of dispersal as a punitive regime. Agencies such as the Refugee Council have thus directly contributed to the development of punitive techniques, which positions such agencies in a policing role as much as in a supportive role. This is not to say that such agencies do not play a critical role in challenging punitive techniques, nor is it to say that agencies such as the Refugee Council have given up on the provision of support to asylum seekers (see Chapter 4). Indeed, the voluntary sector plays an important mitigating role against some of the most punitive dimensions of dispersal. For example, David describes how the voluntary sector in Manchester (Bury) had meetings every month in order to facilitate interaction between asylum seekers in the region. He describes such meetings as offering relief from the experience of isolation that he faced through the process of dispersal: 'we met other friends, maybe your countries friend there ... to try to play together, to discuss, it was very helpful. And you know when you live alone it is no good. Here is stressful country so when we alone sometimes – depression' [*sic*] (Group interview 1, Appendix 2). Indeed, the interviewed asylum seekers unanimously described the 'one stop' advice provided by the voluntary sector as helpful in facilitating their access to support from the NASS. Nevertheless, the voluntary sector has been compromised in its supportive role through participation in the deterrent technology of dispersal, reflecting what David Griffiths, Nando Sigona and Roger Zetter suggest to be the incorporation of such organisations within a punitive dispersal regime (2005:173). Similarly, they suggest that refugee community organisations have become co-opted as part of a restrictive regime through dispersal. In this regard, an analysis of the technical operations of exclusionary politics suggests that everyday processes of securitisation and criminalisation emerge in somewhat unexpected places.

Indeed, it is not only the voluntary and refugee sectors that have been compromised in providing support to asylum seekers through their participation in the deterrent technology of dispersal. So also have a more diffuse range of agencies become practitioners of a punitive technology, most notably public and private housing providers. While those asylum seekers interviewed largely describe the support provided in dispersal accommodation in positive terms when compared to emergency accommodation, the provision of support to those housed in dispersal accommodation has a clear punitive and policing dimension. Thus, while the NASS contract specifies that a provider must 'receive somebody, induct them into the property and the area, and signpost them toward education if necessary, and to health services including the dentist, and legal services if we are asked' (Individual interview 2, Appendix 2), it also specifies that accommodation providers must develop surveillance and control mechanisms to ensure asylum seekers' compliance with restrictions on their movement. Thus, a local housing manager says:

> they [accommodated asylum seekers] shouldn't be absent more than five days ... we're supposed to notify NASS and their support would be terminated. And one of our functions is to check that they're there, we're supposed to visit once a month everybody ... and that's about checking that they're still present.
>
> (Individual interview 1, Appendix 2)

The ability of accommodation providers to challenge the punitive techniques that emerge as part of the deterrent technology of dispersal is clearly curtailed by the contractual basis on which they operate. The most obvious example of this limitation is when an asylum seeker's support from the NASS ceases and the housing provider gives an eviction notice. This primarily occurs when an asylum seeker receives a negative decision on his or her asylum application, with eviction inevitably following sooner or later. As the local authority manager goes on to explain, 'failed' asylum claimants 'just have to go, we haven't got any powers to make any provision for them so we have to evict them' (Ibid.).

Indeed, significant frustration is displayed regarding the punitive techniques that emerge as part of the dispersal technology by one public sector accommodation support worker, who describes a process in which his supportive role is compromised through his engagement with the NASS. It is worth quoting intensively here, in order to show how this situation is conceived as generating hostility between him and the asylum seeker by the support worker in question:

> the system works so badly and the people [i.e. the asylum seekers] that we work with become so brutalised as a result of not having any entitlements, of not having any food for weeks on end sometimes – they become very angry, unsurprisingly. The people [i.e. the NASS officials] actually making the decisions – or *failing* to make the decisions – they [the asylum seekers] don't have any access to. That's quite a cynical thing I think ... So the people that get shouted at are the people [i.e. the support workers] that have to phone [the] NASS and that have to get this culture of hostility and to speak to them [i.e. to the NASS] to be told, well, 'tough'. That frustration then becomes a circuit if you like, you actually start to avoid seeing people [i.e. asylum seekers] sometimes, to be honest with you, because you just know you are going to get nowhere with it, its going to drag on and on, the person that you speak to ... they're going to think you are useless ... You end up I think becoming angry sometimes with the person who you see as putting you in this situation, who is this person who comes in and is moaning to you cause they've got no food, or whatever, and you know there is nothing that you can do about it because you know you are just going to get some administrative rubbish [from the NASS] that will basically say 'they will get it when we sort it, 'tough'.
>
> (Individual interview 1, Appendix 2)

From this accommodation support worker's point of view, the frustrating job of playing 'middle man' between the NASS and individual asylum seekers at times culminates in hostility.

It is in the operational rearticulation of support as a punitive technology that such frustrations and hostilities emerge. Such a process would seem to create an ontological disjuncture between the framing of asylum seekers as people who are worthy of support, and the framing of asylum seekers as 'culpable' subjects with no right to complain. The above statement suggests that support workers can fall into the gulf that lies between these irreconcilable positions. This is particularly the case when their role in providing support becomes indistinguishable from their role in policing asylum seekers. In inhabiting such a position, asylum support workers find themselves joining the widening ranks of practitioners who are caught up in the exclusionary politics that produce asylum seekers as 'culpable' subjects by punitive, as well as interdictive, means. In this book, such a diffusion of punitive controls is conceived of as intertwined with the extension of interdictive controls within a wider deterrent rationality. This rationality cannot simply be conceived of as keeping 'undesirables' out, but rather needs to be understood in more complex terms as a selectively oppositional rationality that extends and diffuses exclusionary operations with various depoliticising effects.

Producing abject subjects? The exclusionary effects of punishment

While some analysts have implied that deterrence can be conceived as one of the goals of dispersal, this analysis suggests that deterrence is more appropriately conceived of as an organising rationality than as the policy goal. Although dispersal was initially defined as a deterrent policy by the former Home Secretary Jack Straw, the reticence of policymakers in explicitly defining the initiative as such most likely reflects the impossibility of measuring its success in deterring 'would-be' asylum seekers. After all, a range of factors come into play that have a bearing on whether or not refugees or migrants claim asylum in the UK, and it is difficult, if not impossible, to stipulate whether or not dispersal has an impact in this respect (see Schuster, 2005b). In critically assessing the success of the initiative according to its specified goals, this part of the chapter returns to the earlier reading of dispersal as a managerial operation of dilution in order to consider how far dispersal successfully spreads the financial 'burden' and social 'threat' of asylum. In drawing attention to the lack of success of dispersal on a conventional reading, it goes on to develop an alternative critique of the initiative in terms of its abjectification of asylum seekers within the UK. Specifically, it argues that the 'benign' managerial operation of dispersal is better understood as part of an exclusionary politics that effectively constitutes the asylum seeker as a scapegoat for failures that are the political community's 'own'. As such, it reduces the scope for solidaristic political engagement by moving the asylum seeker through a position of 'culpability' into a situation of abjection.

Aggravating service strain, generating hostility

A conventional analysis of the effectiveness of the dispersal initiative can begin with the exclusionary narrative of the 'problem' of service strain, which the analysis in Chapter 4 showed to be a key exclusionary narrative at both a political and popular level. Indeed, Sarah-Jane Savage interprets the focus on relieving the 'burden' on accommodation and services in the South East as one of four main policy goals of the UK dispersal initiative, the others of which are to reduce the overall financial costs of the asylum support system, to diffuse interethnic tensions and to aid refugee integration (2005:224–6). In assessing the effectiveness of the initiative in addressing these policy goals, she argues that dispersal largely fails on all four counts, as well as falling short on the goal of deterring 'would-be' asylum seekers (Ibid.:228–37). This 'failure' is supported by this analysis, as well as by additional research carried out by the Home Office, the Audit Commission and leading researchers that have examined the dispersal initiative. First, research has shown that various problems have impeded the success of dispersal in relieving the 'burden' on accommodation and services in the South East. Non-participation has been highlighted as a key issue in this regard, with many non-participants remaining in London (Boswell, 2003:322; Savage, 2005:229; Schuster, 2005:616). In addition, the delay in moving asylum seekers out of emergency accommodation has been seen as creating pressure on emergency housing in the South East (Savage, 2005:229). In terms of relieving the pressure on the South East, dispersal can thus be interpreted as relatively ineffective in practice.

Savage suggests that dispersal has not only been ineffective in relieving the 'burden' on services in the South East, but also that the initiative has been ineffective in reducing the overall financial costs of asylum (Ibid.:230–1). Specifically, she draws attention to the failure of central government to pay for the full cost of supporting asylum seekers, and draws attention to the financial implications for local authorities and service providers who have to cover costs where infrastructure and services are not adequately developed to deal with new arrivals. This claim is backed up by the analysis here. While there is limited additional money available for the education of asylum-seeking children, there is no logical pattern of resource allocation following the dispersal process. This is reflected in the experiences of those interviewed who found the process of accessing basic services difficult. For example, Susanne describes a situation where she was sent from one school to another in trying to locate a place for her daughter, before finding a sympathetic Head Teacher who was supportive:

> So I went to one [school] and they sent me to St. Augustine, I went to St. Augustine and they said they were full already ... because we were dispersed late. So they sent me to St. Patrick's, and that is where she [my daughter] goes to school now.
>
> (Individual interview 4, Appendix 2)

Similarly, Susanne experienced difficulties in accessing a doctor, describing a situation where 'the NHS had to interfere before I could get one ... because when I tried to look they told me that they were all full up' (Ibid.). These findings support those of the Audit Commission (2000), which found many asylum seekers were unable to access public services properly due to a failure on the part of national government to properly inform health and education bodies within dispersal regions regarding the needs of asylum seekers. It also supports the findings of a Home Office report examining the dispersal initiative, which suggests that the initiative has led to increased 'burdens on local services' in dispersal regions (Home Office, 2001).

One could perhaps say with irony that dispersal is successful in 'spreading the burden' of asylum, but only in terms of its spreading of asylum as a *burden*, rather than in terms of its relief of the experience of local communities in receiving asylum as such. This is not to say that asylum should be automatically interpreted in these exclusionary terms, but it is to say that asylum has tended to become constituted as a 'burden' through the 'benign' managerial operation of dispersal. This is particularly the case where asylum seekers are dispersed to areas of deprivation in which resources are relatively scarce and unemployment is relatively high, which has often occurred under the accommodation-led dispersal scheme in the UK (see Schuster, 2005b:617; Home Office, 2001). In Birmingham, asylum seekers are largely housed in deprived areas with a 'depressed' housing market and with a range of related pressures on public services. In this sense, dispersal tends to aggravate existing pressures, particularly since additional resources are not adequately injected into the area to support new arrivals.

This process goes both against the explicit policy goal of reducing interethnic tension, as well as against the explicit policy goal of aiding integration, because it tends to generate hostility towards asylum seekers by more established residents (see Boswell, 2003:324; Savage, 2005:233–4). This is evident in the statement of a longer-term resident of the Handsworth region of Birmingham, who claims that new arrivals are privileged over members of more established local communities in relation to the provision of accommodation:

> [It is] very difficult for our community at the moment in housing, because when we apply to another house the housing association refuse us because they say that they have to re-house the asylum seeker first. They have to priority right first. That's our problem at the moment.
>
> (Group interview 3, Appendix 2)

Going on, the interviewee draws a clear distinction between her own position as a refugee and that of newly arriving asylum seekers. A section of the interview serves to show this more clearly:

VS (Interviewer): Could you say something more generally about the effect on the local area that the dispersal of asylum seekers has had?

LCR: That's very difficult for us actually, because they give the refugee a very bad reputation. Because when – even now, I am a refugee, 15 years ago I arrive in England. But now, whenever I hear that some asylum seekers arrive in Birmingham I start to worry, really worry.

VS: Why are you worried?

LCR: They [do] not adjust themselves into society, into new life, and they try to ... sorry to say that, they just try to steal or burgle, something like that. Yeah. Because it happens many times around Handsworth. So we [do] not feel safe, like before. The more they arrive, the more we feel insecure.

VS: And so you feel it makes it difficult for established refugees here as well?

LCR: Yes, yes. Because when they, the English people, when they look at the oriental look like me, they don't think I am different. Different from the asylum seeker. They think I am the same. That's very difficult.

(Ibid.)

The interviewee in this quote clearly perceives her social status as a refugee as precarious, and as threatened by the arrival of new asylum seekers in the local area. Taken alongside the first quote, the interview would seem to suggest that service strain – or at least its perception – is aggravated through dispersal, while hostility is potentially generated through its exclusionary operations. Indeed, this is a claim that the majority of the interviews with dispersed asylum seekers in Birmingham support, as we will see below. In this respect, dispersal cannot be said to be successful in reducing interethnic or racial tension, nor can it be described as facilitating the integration of refugees. Rather, it potentially does precisely the opposite through dispersing new arrivals to areas that already experience pressures in relation to the provision of public services.

These concerns have been addressed in part in response to the Home Office's (2001) operational review of the dispersal initiative, which develops a range of suggestions in order that service strain and local hostility might be eased in dispersal regions. However, it is important to question whether or not developments such as the relocation of asylum seekers to more affluent regions can ever address the problem of service strain as it stands. It would seem that the critical question in this regard is not how dispersal can be implemented more effectively in order to relieve the problem of service strain. Rather, it is whether the spreading of the 'burden' of asylum can ever solve such a problem. After all, one might legitimately ask whether the problem of service strain is a 'problem' related to increased numbers of asylum seekers at all. If it is more appropriately conceived as a problem that is related to the dissolution of the welfare state (a problem that warrants investigation in its own right), then it would seem that our critical focus is more appropriately directed to questions regarding the wider *effects* of the displacement of concerns regarding service strain onto asylum seekers than it is to questions regarding the impact of dispersal on local communities. It is thus to a critique of these wider effects that we will now turn, specifically through considering the consequences of the diffusion of a punitive technology from the position of asylum seekers who are dispersed within the UK.

From culpability to abjectification (and back again)

As the analysis in the last section suggests, one of the main consequences of the displacement of concerns regarding service strain onto asylum seekers that emerges as part of the justification for dispersal is that asylum seekers face increasing hostility within dispersal regions. This has been particularly evident in cities such as Glasgow, Sunderland

and Hull, where there have been various (fatal and non-fatal) violent attacks on asylum seekers. Even in Birmingham, which the chapter has suggested may be a less hostile environment for new arrivals, many of the asylum seekers interviewed described their reception as one marked by the hostility of more established communities. For example, Susanne describes a process of intercultural struggle as causing problems for her in settling in Birmingham:

> the problem you get in Birmingham is there are too many cultures and most of them stay together to themselves. The Sikh people they want to be to themselves, the Pakistani people they want to be to themselves, Jamaicans want to be to themselves ... its like everybody wants to – Jamaicans wants to say 'Britain is mine, England is mine, this is mine, I have right to live'. Like there's a struggle ... each culture is struggling to be more prominent.
>
> (Individual interview 4, Appendix 2)

Susanne's statement here is perhaps indicative of the limited scope for solidaristic political engagement in the hostile social context that is, at least in part, generated by exclusionary politics. Indeed, several asylum seekers describe Birmingham as a 'dangerous' city. In particular, Abbas describes his experience in Birmingham as marked by hostility, claiming that some of the local residents 'hate us'. While it is not possible to generalise from our limited sample, what these findings would suggest is that hostility is a problem for large multicultural cities such as Birmingham, even if there have not been high-profile attacks in this case. From the position of asylum seekers, dispersal might thus be interpreted as a divisive initiative that creates a hostile environment in which asylum seekers are vulnerable to physical attack. This occurs precisely because they are produced as scapegoats for existing social problems such as service strain.

Dispersal does not only have the effect of rendering asylum seekers vulnerable to physical attack, but so also does it have the effect of rendering asylum seekers vulnerable to economic exploitation. This is most probable where asylum seekers opt out – or are *pushed* out – of the dispersal system of support (see Boswell, 2003:326). As we saw above, asylum seekers are subject to a range of punitive techniques under dispersal, with destitution being a key example in this regard. Where asylum seekers are denied the limited subsistence support to which they are entitled, they become vulnerable to economic exploitation. This is particularly the case where asylum seekers are denied the right to work, and where they are excluded from social and kinship networks of support through the process of dispersal. Of those asylum seekers interviewed, over half supported by the NASS found their support stopped without warning. The exception here is Susanne, who says that on several occasions when she had lost her ARC entitlement card the NASS provided her with money in advance (Individual interview 4, Appendix 2). This starkly contrasts with the experience of P, who describes an intermittent pattern of support over the five years that he was seeking asylum, whereby he only received NASS payments on taking court action against the organisation (Individual interview 6, Appendix 2).[4] In this regard, dispersal would seem to produce abject subjects that are economically exploitable, as well as 'culpable' subjects that are politically exploitable.

Indeed, various housing providers draw attention to problems with the provision of support by the NASS. For example, the local authority manager describes a situation where 'hiccups' with allowances is 'a very common problem' (Individual interview 2, Appendix 2). Going further, a public sector asylum support worker describes the NASS system as 'incompetent' and 'inaccessible'. Referring to one case where support was stopped due to an administrative error, he claims:

> So I registered the problem, days went past, she still had no money; phoned again, registered the problem, days went past again, she came back, she still had no money; phoned again, registered the problem, days went past again. Third phone call – 'oh yeah, it is coming up on the system that they cannot action that, you need to phone a particular number' – which is the public number; it takes ages to get through basically ... and all the time they are refusing to give her money even though that is money she is legally entitled to ... it took around three weeks just to get a minor thing like that sorted out.
>
> (Individual interview 1, Appendix 2)

What this statement would seem to confirm is that the NASS system forces many asylum seekers into destitution once they are dispersed. If anything, it is perhaps surprising that asylum seekers do *not* choose to work without authorisation in this context. As P claims:

> If I had gone to the black market and helped myself I would not go through all this suffering. But I am not here to hide myself. I am here to be heard about my case and to be protected.
>
> (Individual interview 6, Appendix 2)

Going further, Guy suggests that 'if people are desperate ... they can easily be recruited in the criminality system' (Individual interview 5, Appendix 2). Nevertheless, many asylum seekers interviewed describe how they have coped with destitution in alternative ways.

Among those asylum seekers interviewed that had experienced the termination of their support from the NASS, one found support with Social Services, one found support within the local community and one began working. In other words, only one out of a total of eight asylum seekers interviewed decided to work without authorisation, despite the vulnerable situation that several were forced into under the dispersal initiative. In explaining his decision to take up work, Abbas describes the limited and irregular support that he had received from the NASS (Group interview 2, Appendix 2). In his case, the punitive technology of dispersal could be described as taking Abbas full circle from his inscription as a 'culpable' subject without the right to complain, through to an abject subject without the benefit of adequate support or the permission for self-reliance, and back to 'culpable' subject through his work within the informal economy. Such, it would seem, are the exclusionary politics of asylum, which pull asylum seekers and support workers alike into a cycle of criminalisation and securitisation in which abjection seems to be the only route out.

Conclusion

Rather than relieving the 'problem' of service strain and social instability, this chapter has argued that the dispersal initiative tends to exacerbate existing problems in the provision of services through introducing new arrivals to areas that have relatively high levels of unemployment and relatively limited resources. This consolidates exclusionary narratives that legitimise the development of restrictive policy initiatives such as dispersal, while generating local hostilities to asylum seekers. In this regard asylum seekers are constituted as scapegoats for problems that are, more often than not, *nothing to do with them*. One of the central operations of this process is that asylum seekers are inscribed as 'culpable' subjects who are denied the right to complain regarding their poor treatment. Dispersal in this respect can be conceived of as a punitive technology that is selectively organised in terms of a rationality of deterrence; a rationality that both reduces the political agency of asylum seekers by moving them through 'culpability' in the direction of abjection, and also that reduces the scope of solidaristic engagement between asylum seekers and local community members through aggravating service strain and generating hostility. In this respect, the punitive technology of dispersal can be seen as central to the depoliticising tendencies of a deterrent rendering of exclusionary politics, which reconstructs political community in reactive ideological terms. This exclusionary interaction of technical and narrative processes of securitisation and criminalisation has various effects. Perhaps of most concern is the fact that exclusionary politics become caught in a self-fulfilling cycle of self-legitimisation. For those seeking asylum in the UK, the technology of dispersal entails routine punitive techniques that permeate everyday life, even where asylum seekers are not identified as requiring 'exceptional' treatment in the form of detention and deportation. Invoking the 'culpability' of asylum seekers *en masse*, the rationality of deterrence thus inscribes punitive techniques as the norm and extends the range of agencies that become caught up in the policing of asylum seekers. Asylum support thus becomes inseparable from asylum policing, while the isolation and destitution of asylum seekers becomes widespread. In this respect dispersal is not only a divisive and exclusionary initiative that has a political effect in terms of its production of a scapegoat for the dislocations of a territorial order. It also has an economic effect in terms of its production of legally vulnerable and financially destitute subjects that are easily exploited as 'flexible' workers. This, it would seem, signals a movement from culpability to abjection, a movement that ironically seems to take the abject subject straight back into the exclusionary politics of securitisation and criminalisation that is so difficult to break.

In the final part of this book we return to take a second look at this movement through securitisation and criminalisation towards abjection, this time from a critical distance. The story that the analysis in Parts II and III of this book has told is a somewhat bleak one, which signals the increasing dominance of the exclusionary politics of asylum. By showing how a logic of selective opposition is embedded across the popular, political and technical spheres, the analysis has pointed to the extension and diffusion of exclusionary linguistic and governmental operations, which incorporate a range of actors in the reactive ideological reconstruction of the territorial political community. This process signals a deterrent rationality, which leads to a shrinkage of the space for asylum and refugee protection and the correlative extension of prohibitive and punitive controls both beyond and throughout the nation and the state. The reconstruction of the 'morally benevolent' and 'socially stable' territorial order, in other words, entails both exclusionary and deterritorialising operations that continuously disrupt the ideological cover of state governance and national belonging. An exclusionary politics thus deals with internal disruptions by reactively projecting them onto 'external turbulence'. This, the analysis suggests, constitutes asylum seekers as 'threatening' and 'culpable' subjects who find that their only route out of exclusionary politics takes them in the direction of abjection.

So does this leave us in a position of abjection in developing a critique of exclusionary politics? The analysis claims that it does not. Indeed, the analysis in Part IV suggests that, whatever our position, we need not resign ourselves to abjection. After all, the exclusionary operations of a territorial order are not pregiven and ordained from 'above'. Rather, sovereign power is constructed through various practices at various levels according to a logic of selective opposition. That this logic is manifest in specific rationalities, such as deterrence, suggests that alternative rationalities might be developed that entail differing logics to the exclusionary territorial one that we have examined here. It is in the attempt to locate an alternative rationality by which the exclusionary politics is critically interceded that the analysis moves to a second level of critique in the next chapter. Rather than approaching the asylum seeker as a 'threatening' and 'culpable' subject, it considers how the shrinking space of solidaristic political engagement that an exclusionary politics entails is interrupted by 'misplaced' engagements of asylum seekers as political subjects. By approaching abjection from the position of the asylum seeker, rather than from the position of the state, Part IV thus commits itself to the more difficult task of considering how the self-fulfilling cycle of exclusionary politics might be critically interceded.

Part IV Contesting the Exclusionary Politics of Asylum: From Deterrence to Engagement

7
Sovereign Power, Abject Spaces and Resistance: Contending Accounts of Asylum

Thus far this book has told the story of an exclusionary politics of asylum that becomes caught in a self-fulfilling cycle; a cycle in which asylum seekers are interdicted and punished on the 'grounds' of their 'threatening culpability'. Thus, we have seen how a discourse in which asylum is constructed as a 'threat' or a 'problem' has emerged at both the domestic and the European levels (Chapter 3), and we have seen how this criminalising and securitising discourse has become increasingly dominant across the mainstream political spectrum (Chapter 4). Indeed, we have seen how this discourse is also extended at a more diffuse technical level, thus entailing a range of restrictive policies and deterrent technologies that often produce or aggravate the very policy 'problems' and societal 'threats' that they are designed to resolve (Chapters 5 and 6). In this respect, the analysis has entailed a two-way consideration both of the way in which the logic of selective opposition is embedded in the technical practices of professionals who work across the broad field of migration control and also of the way in which such a logic is embedded in political and popular debate. In so doing, it has shown how punitive and interdictive controls consolidate the exclusionary narratives that legitimise such technologies in the first place. The analysis might thus be read as showing how asylum seekers have become the victims of an exclusionary discourse that becomes caught in a self-fulfilling cycle, the effects of which are that the institution of asylum becomes practically eroded (Chapter 5) while the reception of asylum seekers becomes an increasingly hostile and exploitative affair (Chapter 6). This rather bleak conclusion is supported both by the suggestion that many contestations of exclusionary politics have been limited by a discourse in which asylum seekers are securitised and criminalised (Part III) and by the claim that a range of agencies have been co-opted within an exclusionary politics through the institutionalisation of a deterrent approach to asylum (Part IV). Nevertheless, if we are to engage a critical alternative as a challenge to the reactive ideological discourse that has been charted throughout the course of the book thus far, then it is important that we consider how contending accounts of asylum critically intercede in the exclusionary politics of state governance and national belonging.

The critical alternative that is introduced here can be conceived of in terms of a specifically *political* approach that challenges the depoliticisations of a rationality of deterrence by opening up engagements that run in accordance with a rationality of solidarity. This takes us beyond a rethinking of asylum to a more radical rethinking of citizenship (see Chapter 8). The research that authors such as Peter Nyers (2003, 2008) and Anne McNevin (2006) have carried out into contemporary mobilisations of refugees and migrants suggests that contestations of the exclusionary politics of asylum can be interpreted as constituting political community, governance and belonging in terms that exceed a territorial frame. As such, these works not only facilitate a reconceptualisation of asylum, but they also allow us to rethink migration and citizenship more generally. Specifically, they allow us to perceive how the very 'undesirables' that are construed as the moving targets of restrictive controls act as 'key protagonists in global struggles concerning freedom of movement, social recognition, workers rights and the right of asylum' (Nyers, 2008:160). Rather than approaching refugees and migrants as passive victims of an exclusionary politics, the work of these critical analysts of migration and citizenship thus draws attention to the various political engagements through which refugees and migrants constitute themselves as subjects with the 'right to have rights' (see Nyers and Moulins, 2007). It is in drawing attention to the political agency of refugees and migrants in this way that our analysis might move beyond a territorial frame of political community – a frame that is constituted both through and against various processes of deterritorialisation (see Part III). More specifically, such a focus can be developed in terms that exceed a *reactive* pro-territorial framing of politics, which conditions the assumption that 'undesirables' such as asylum seekers are 'threatening' transgressors of the nation state's sovereign borders. In addition, it might exceed what might be conceived to be the anti-territorial 'flip side' of this nationalistic discourse, namely a humanitarian discourse that rests on the assumption that refugees or migrants are 'threatened' victims of the global community. Rather than engaging a pro-territorial or an anti-territorial perspective along these lines, this book suggests that it is only in moving carefully beyond a territorial frame that the contending engagements of 'undesirables' can be perceived in political terms.

This chapter takes a first step beyond a territorial frame of reference by exploring how the political engagements of asylum seekers *qua* irregular migrants (see Chapter 1) critically interrupt the exclusionary operations of state governance and national belonging. It does this both through exploring the exclusionary production of abject spaces, as well as through exploring the critical inhabitation of abject spaces. The first part of the chapter discusses the notion of abject spaces with reference to Giorgio Agamben's work on sovereign power and the camp. While it acknowledges the importance of Agamben's work in showing how an exclusionary politics moves towards the reduction of asylum seekers to 'bare life', it makes the case for an approach that takes as its starting point *resistance*, rather than sovereign power. Thus, instead of showing how sovereign-bio-power produces depoliticised and dehumanised spaces of abjection, the analysis draws on the work of Engin Isin and Kim Rygiel (2006) in showing how sovereign-bio-power produces multiple abject spaces that are crossed through with contestations of abjectifying processes of dehumanisation and depoliticisation. Such a claim is further developed in the second part of the chapter, which shows how the proliferation of abject spaces is met by a proliferation of contestations surrounding the exclusionary politics of asylum. In particular, it considers how the critical inhabitation of abject spaces by the *No Borders* and *No One Is Illegal* movements serves to enact citizenship, governance and belonging in terms that exceed a territorial frame. This, it is argued, occurs through acts of solidarity that bring various citizens and irregular migrants together through the 'misplaced' claiming of rights and obligations.

The exclusionary production of abject spaces: Resisting sovereign-bio-power

The work of Giorgio Agamben has been highly influential in the discipline of international relations over recent years. This is particularly the case in the context of a 'war on terror', which has given greater credence to Agamben's (1998, 2005) rereading of Carl Schmitt's theory of the sovereignty as the power to suspend the law without its annulment. This part of the chapter considers how Agamben's notion of sovereign power facilitates a conceptualisation of the exclusionary processes of securitisation and criminalisation as related to the production of abject spaces. The first part discusses the camp, which Agamben defines in relation to the reduction of human life to 'bare life'. It suggests that Agamben's analysis of sovereign-bio-power is important in understanding the exclusionary politics of asylum, because it allows us to conceptualise how processes of securitisation and criminalisation feed into processes of dehumanisation and depoliticisation. However, it argues against Agamben's formalistic and totalising reading of sovereign-bio-power as producing abjection within the space of the camp. Instead, it shows how a more complex and contested reading of the exclusionary politics of asylum can be developed by taking as a starting point *resistance*, rather than sovereign-bio-power. The second part of the analysis develops this approach by drawing on the work of Engin Isin and Kim Rygiel (2006), and shows how the production of multiple abject spaces brings sovereign-bio-power into contact with various struggles, resistances and contestations. While the biopolitical exercise of sovereign power may be dehumanising and depoliticising in effect, the analysis thus draws attention to those dimensions that exceed or precede a sovereign power that has turned both biopolitical and extraterritorial.

Sovereign-bio-power as an exclusionary politics

A critical engagement with Agamben's theory of sovereign power is useful in developing an analysis of the exclusionary politics of asylum, even if his theorisation works at a different level and differs in its focus from the analysis developed in this book. In particular, a discussion of Agamben's theorisation of the 'zone of indistinction' and of 'the camp' is important to the development of a critique of the exclusionary politics of asylum, because it allows us to see how processes of securitisation and criminalisation move in the direction of abjection. As we saw in Chapter 2, the Copenhagen School's theory of securitisation has two key features: first, it is characterised by an exceptionalism in which an issue is removed from the sphere of normal politics and, second, it is characterised by a dichotomous relationship between friend/enemy. It is in relation to these dimensions that Agamben speaks to the theory of securitisation, although he does so indirectly through an engagement with the work of Carl Schmitt. The exceptionalism that informs Schmitt's reading of the friend/enemy relation refers to the sovereign decision, which is characterised by a suspension of the law without its abrogation (see Schmitt, 1996, 2005). For Copenhagen School analysts such as Ole Wæver (1995), this exceptionalism is problematic because it grants the sovereign a power that is beyond the law, while speeding up the process of politics in terms that precludes proper political debate. Similarly, the exceptional power of the sovereign is problematic for Agamben, though for different reasons. Specifically, he conceives the exceptionalism of sovereign power as problematic because it extends its reach into the depths of human life in terms that leave no space for an authentic political existence. Agamben's theory can thus be employed in order to focus critical attention on the way that intertwined processes of securitisation and criminalisation are played out on the physical bodies of those 'enemies' (i.e. 'threatening' and 'culpable' subjects) who are subject to the exercise of sovereign power.

While Agamben's quest for a 'new politics' founded on an authentic political existence is problematic on various counts, his theorisation of sovereign power may nonetheless be critically engaged in order to develop our understanding of the exclusionary politics of asylum. A key line of enquiry that here relates to the question of whether or not Agamben's theory of sovereign power successfully challenges a territorial framing of politics; a frame in which distinctions between inside and outside, and between friend and enemy often become normalised along nationalistic lines. It is here that Agamben's (1994) discussion of the refugee as a 'limit concept' located in a 'zone of indistinction' is of particular importance. For Agamben, the zone of indistinction is understood in terms of the structure of the exception or of the ban, which serves as the founding moment of sovereign power in which the relationship between law and politics collapses. Agamben argues that a 'zone of indistinction' or a 'threshold of undecidability' is produced through this process in which the sovereign is placed both inside and outside the juridical order (Agamben, 1998:15–29). He defines this as 'the paradox of sovereignty', in which the sovereign is constituted as a 'limit concept' at the threshold of law and politics. Similarly, he defines the refugee and *homo sacer* (i.e. sacred life, meaning that which can be killed but not sacrificed) as structurally analogous figures that are located within a zone of indistinction between the inside and the outside of the legal order. It is by being included through their very exclusion that Agamben suggests the figures of the sovereign, the refugee and *homo sacer*, demonstrate the lie of a straightforward distinction between inside and outside, or between friend and enemy.

In theorising the zone of indistinction, Agamben suggests that the figure of the refugee 'makes it possible to clear the way for a long-overdue renewal of categories in the service of a politics in which bare life is no longer separated and excepted' (1998:134). Before we engage with the question of bare life, let us consider the critical effectiveness of Agamben's focus on the refugee as a figure that is 'included through exclusion'. Agamben's discussion of the figures of the sovereign, of the refugee and of *homo sacer*, is useful in showing that the boundaries between inside and outside are never clear-cut (or in showing how processes of inclusion and exclusion are interlinked in complex ways). However, his focus on those figures that are positioned in relation to the logic of 'inclusion through exclusion' would seem to reduce the heterogeneity of processes of inclusion/exclusion (see Balibar, 2002). In overlooking those figures that are structured in relation to the logic of 'exclusion through inclusion', Agamben would seem to become locked in the territorial frame which he is so desperate to transcend. As Engin Isin and Kim Rygiel (2006:186) note, Agamben desires a new model of international relations that is organised around reciprocal relations of aterritoriality or extraterritoriality. However, in turning to the refugee in his quest to renew the categories of politics, Agamben would seem to incorporate that which potentially exceeds a territorial political frame within a totalising system of sovereign power. David Owen has argued that the modern definition of a refugee supports the territorial framing of politics by illustrating the regulative idea 'that normal states act to secure the liberty and welfare of each and every individual in their own national populations' (2005:11). Rather than turning to the refugee, which Owen suggests is a figure that serves both as an exception to the rule of interstate movement and also as a burden to the protecting state, a focus on the more ambiguous figure of the asylum-seeker-cum-illegal-immigrant would seem to leave us with a messier picture of the territorial frame. In drawing attention to a figure that is excluded through his or her inclusion, this analysis thus brings into view the turbulent dislocations that both precede and exceed the totalising impulse of sovereign power (see Mezzadra and Nielson, 2003). It would seem that Agamben risks overlooking these messy and ambiguous social processes in his focus on the refugee.

Agamben touches on this totalising impulse in his discussion of the camp. For Agamben, the camp serves as an exemplary space in which the structure of the exception or the ban can be seen at work, with the ban defined as 'the essential structure of sovereign power from the very beginning' (1998:111). This formalistic reading of the camp and the ban is one that is problematic, because it reads into Western politics, an inevitability that reifies the space of the camp. However, Agamben's formalistic reading does belie a more concrete reading that might be extrapolated from his discussion of the European concentration camp. Reading the space of exception in more historical terms, Agamben suggests that the camp emerges at a point whereby the functional nexus between the localisation (land), the order (state) and the inscription of life (birth or the nation) on which the modern nation state is based enters into 'a lasting crisis' (1997:113–4; Perera, 2002).

It is in Agamben's formalistic translation of this historical condition that the camp becomes defined as central to the entire history of Western politics and philosophy. However, if we take as our starting point the claim that there has been a rupture in the nexus of state-nation-land on which the territorial frame relies we may be able to rescue Agamben's claim that the camp serves as a 'hidden regulator of the inscription of life in the [legal] order', while remaining sensitive to those turbulent elements that exceed and precede sovereign power. This leads us down a less formalistic path than the one that Agamben ventures, while bringing attention to the many cracks that emerge in the picture that he paints of sovereign power.

Agamben's formalistic reading of the camp is reflected in his suggestion that Foucault was wrong in conceiving biopower as separate to the workings of sovereign power. Agamben (1998:104–12) develops this argument by claiming that the distinctive feature of sovereign power lies in its transformation of bare life into sacred life. In so doing, he not only suggests that sovereign power reproduces an originary zone of indistinction by drawing of lines between the inside and the outside according to the logic of 'inclusion through exclusion'. He also suggests that the sovereign's banishment of *homo sacer* reproduces an originary zone of indistinction between political existence (*zoe*) and bare life (*bios*). In Agamben's reading, the camp is thus defined as an exceptional space in which the distinctly sovereign relation of the ban can be witnessed in its originary biopolitical form. Specifically, the camp is defined as a zone of exception within which people are transformed into 'bare life' (physical or biological life) and detained under a sovereign law that is held in suspension. It is in relation to this theorisation of the camp that Agamben's reading of Foucault into Schmitt leads him to the conclusion that sovereign power and biopower are imbricated 'from the start'. How convincing or useful Agamben's formalistic reading of sovereign-bio-power is remains a matter of debate (e.g. Butler, 2006). As suggested above, this analysis approaches the intertwinement of sovereign power and biopower as a concrete, historical tendency, rather than as an originary given. From this perspective, the camp may be conceived of as an exemplary space in which the exertion of sovereign power over the physical life of detained people is most clearly evident. However, this is not to suggest that the processes of dehumanisation and depoliticisation that this exertion enacts are all-consuming. While Agamben may be correct to identify sovereign power and biopower as complexly intertwined in the current juncture, he goes a step too far in seeing the two as imbricated from the start.

In summary, a critical engagement with the work of Giorgio Agamben suggests that the exclusionary politics of asylum can be further understood in relation to processes of dehumanisation and depoliticisation, which are associated with a sovereign power that has turned biopolitical. That we could ever return the figure of the asylum-seeker-cum-illegal-immigrant to the authentic political existence that Agamben so desires is unlikely. However, what we can do is consider how the biosovereign rendering of such a figure as an inexistent subject is disrupted by resistances, struggles and contestations that exceed or precede the logic of sovereign power (see Isin and Rygiel, 2006:189; Nyers, 2003, 2008). Specifically, we can do this by drawing attention to the political (and thus the human) processes that emerge within those abject spaces where the political existence of 'threatening' and 'culpable' subjects is subject to erasure. Such a focus counteracts Agamben's totalising reading of sovereign power as reducing the human form to 'bare life', and takes as its analytical starting point resistance. Thus, while this analysis draws on Agamben's work to develop a diagnosis of the reactive nature of an exclusionary politics in which sovereign-bio-power attempts to capture or contain that which precedes and exceeds it within a (de)territorialising programme of dehumanisation and depoliticisation, it also attempts to go beyond this diagnosis in order to challenge a territorial framing of politics in which the irregular migrant is defined either as 'threatening' the nation state or as 'threatened' by his or her own inexistence. In this reading, the exclusionary politics of asylum is better conceived of as the meeting – often violent – between sovereign-bio-power and that which precedes and exceeds it. It is to these various abject spaces of contestation that we will now turn.

Resisting the exclusionary production of abject spaces

In taking as an analytical starting point resistance, rather than sovereign-bio-power, the analysis in this section takes a step beyond a reactive territorial framing of asylum in terms of threat or vulnerability and focuses attention on the creative political agency of irregular migrants. It does so by looking at various meeting points in which 'sovereign power' comes face to face with the 'turbulence of migration' (see Papastergiadis, 2000; Mezzadra and Nielson, 2003). Specifically, the analysis draws attention to alternative readings of asylum that emerge where turbulence or resistance is engaged in terms that exceed and contest the reactive processes that constitute sovereign power *qua* state governance and national belonging. In so doing, the analysis draws upon Engin Isin and Kim Rygiel's theorisation of abject spaces. Defining abject spaces 'not [as] spaces of abjection but [as] spaces of politics', Isin and Rygiel (2006:184) accept that the biopolitical exertion of sovereign power has both dehumanising and depoliticising tendencies. However, they do not accept that depoliticisation and dehumanisation is the inevitable outcome of detainment or containment. Rather, Isin and Rygiel conceive abject spaces as characterised by a range of resistances, struggles and contestations. The analysis in this book suggests that the struggles of irregular migrants both precede and exceed the operations of sovereign power, and that exclusionary politics emerges where sovereign power is reactively reconstructed against 'dislocatory turbulence' through various discursive operations at the technical, political and popular levels. While the operations of sovereign-bio-power move in the direction of transforming 'undesirables' through 'culpable' subjects (who are interdicted and punished for bringing turbulence to the territorial order) and towards 'inexistent' subjects, it thus comes face-to-face with irregular migrants who contest these violent and exclusionary processes. It is when irregular migrants come together with others to mobilise against these processes of securitisation, criminalisation and abjection that resistance becomes transformed into contestation and turbulence becomes transformed into a solidaristic political act.

In their reading of abject spaces, Isin and Rygiel identify the camp as one of several meeting points in which sovereign power detains or contains those without the right to have rights. Specifically, they define abject spaces as those in which those who have the right to have rights are transformed into abjects who do not have access to rights. Influenced by Hannah Arendt and Jacques Ranciere, they identify the frontier and the zone as abject spaces akin to the camp, in which people without the right to have rights are rendered invisible and inaudible. However, Isin and Rygiel suggest that the camp is essentially distinct from the frontier and the zone, because it serves as a space in which those political subjects with legal status are turned into those 'who have not the rights that they have' (2006:189). In contrast, the frontier and the zone come together in impeding the ability of those without rights to enact them (ibid.). While an analysis of forced migration more generally would need to address the process of transformation in which the citizen becomes redefined as a refugee within abject spaces such as the refugee camp, it is the abject spaces that come under the categories of the frontier or the zone that are particularly pertinent to this analysis. Specifically, the meeting place of resistance and sovereign power that Isin and Rygiel define as the *frontier* is useful in conceptualising the abject spaces that were highlighted in the analysis of interdiction in

Chapter 5, while meeting place of sovereign power and resistance that they define as the *zone* is useful in conceptualising the abject spaces that were highlighted in the analysis of punishment in Chapter 6.

Isin and Rygiel define frontiers as 'those spaces where the mobility of people is regulated and [where] national and international laws are suspended through the creation of buffer zones through which people can be processed' (2006:190). Specifically, frontiers emerge in transit spaces, and are characterised by a struggle to prevent the abject from exercising social, political and economic rights (ibid.:191). In their discussion, Isin and Rygiel draw attention to extraterritorial transit processing centres and regional protection areas as examples of abject spaces that are structured according to the pre-emptive logic of the frontier. Similarly, the analysis of interdiction in Chapter 5 demonstrates the depoliticising tendencies of pre-emption, in which irregular migrants who claim social, political and economic rights by crossing borders are detained, contained and/or turned back by extraterritorial means. The process of interdiction, in this respect, can be interpreted as a reactive operation against the 'turbulence of migration' – a reaction that is composed of various processes that come together as part of a broader exclusionary rationality of deterrence. This exclusionary rationality, messy and complex as it is, tends to reduce the possibility that irregular migrants will constitute themselves as political subjects. In this context, Isin and Rygiel interpret the ongoing physical struggle of irregular migrants to cross borders as political acts that 'render themselves existent and present while simultaneously exposing the web of strategies and technologies of otherness that [emerge through the] attempt to render them inexistent' (2006:193). It is in this respect that the turbulence that precedes state governance and national belonging *at the same time* can be seen as that exceeding the restrictive controls through which the territorial order is in part constructed. After all, in crossing borders without authorisation irregular migrants refuse to conform to the exclusionary operations of sovereign-bio-power (see Owen, 2005). Even where irregular migrants become caught as asylum seekers within a self-fulfilling cycle of securitisation, criminalisation and abjection, their constitution as 'threatening' and, subsequently, 'inexistent' subjects is always open to contestation, specifically because it is founded on a prior resistance to the (extra)territorial dictates of a sovereign-bio-power that constitutes itself precisely through an opposition to illegal immigrants.

While frontiers regulate the mobility of people by extraterritorial means, zones are defined as 'spaces where abjects live under suspended rules of freedom' (Isin and Rygiel, 2006:193). Zones thus differ from frontiers because they are internally dispersed abject spaces that are marked by 'some form of conditional freedom and surveillance' (ibid.). Isin and Rygiel's definition of frontiers and zones runs parallel to the analysis in this book, because it similarly draws attention to pre-emptive or preventative techniques of interdiction that are extended at an 'external' or extraterritorial level, as well as to punitive techniques of isolation and containment that are diffused at an 'internal' level. While Isin and Rygiel primarily conceive 'internal' processes of containment and isolation in relation to detention, the analysis in this book develops a more far-reaching account of the containment and isolation of asylum seekers. Indeed, such a reading is supported by Isin and Rygiel who, after listing accommodation centres, induction centres and removal centres as key examples of abject zones (ibid.:193–4), also point to a more diffuse processes of containment and isolation that extend deeply into the social fabric of the city and the state. In particular, they point to rejected asylum seekers as abjects who are rendered invisible and inaudible through their inhabitation of zones. The analysis of dispersal in Chapter 6 supports this reading of the zone as a dispersed abject space that is 'nestled within cities and states' (ibid.:193, 195), while extending the list of subjects that inhabit such spaces to include dispersed asylum seekers whose claims are in process. Thus we saw how techniques of containment and isolation that constitute the punitive technology of dispersal render it increasingly difficult for asylum seekers to engage within the daily life of the regions within which they are located. Even when they are not subject to the technology of detention, asylum seekers are thus subject to physical restriction and surveillance in terms that substantially limit their engagement within the city or state. It is in this respect that many of the social engagements of the asylum seekers that were interviewed – be it through religious organisations such as the church, through the education system or through informal working – can be interpreted as political acts of solidarity. Specifically, they can be conceived of as political acts that contest both the inscription of asylum seekers as 'culpable' subjects who do not have the right to complain and who are fortunate not to be physically detained, as well as the inscription of asylum seekers as 'inexistent' subjects who are denied speech and visibility.

What an analysis of the frontier and the zone would seem to suggest is that the exclusionary operations of sovereign-bio-power are not only widely practiced, but are also widely contested. Rather than being an all consuming 'given' that is impossible to transcend, sovereign-bio-power is thus perhaps better conceptualised in terms of exclusionary rationalities and technologies that come together through the interrelation of various discursive operations and in accordance with a logic of selective opposition. In this reading, these operations precariously reconstruct (and increasingly dislocate) state governance and national belonging through selectively opposing those 'turbulences' that precede, and often *exceed*, a territorial frame of reference. The cracks in Agamben's picture of sovereign-bio-power thus appear to be more disruptive than can be contained. Indeed, these cracks increasingly exceed the territorial frame. Ironically, in the reactionary struggle to cover over such cracks, the operations of sovereign-bio-power move in an extraterritorial or aterritorial direction. As Isin and Rygiel suggest, this is evident where sovereign states enter into 'reciprocal relationships' with one another in the struggle to create extraterritorial frontiers and zones (ibid.:185). Such is the nature of sovereign power, which turns both extraterritorial and biopolitical in its exclusionary operations that transform the asylum-seeker-cum-illegal-immigrant from a 'threatening' subject into an inexistent one. Irregular migrants (including asylum seekers) play an important role in contesting these exclusionary processes, because the turbulence that cross-border mobility creates for a territorial order positions them as political subjects that contest the reactionary renderings of sovereign power. This is by no means to romanticise or heroise the figure of the irregular migrant or mobile subject, nor is it to define human existence in essentially mobile terms. Rather, it is to suggest that, where irregular migrants engage critically against the operations of sovereign-bio-power, their prior resistance to an (extra)territorial order is effectively transformed into a political contestation. Indeed, it is only in maintaining contending political engagements that irregular migrants, alongside various others, exceed the (extra)territorial parameters of sovereign-bio-power.

Critically inhabiting abject spaces: Proliferating contestations of the exclusionary politics of asylum

While the first part of this chapter focused on the proliferation of abject spaces that struggle to render 'threatening' subjects inexistent, this part of the chapter focuses on the proliferation of contending political engagements that challenge such exclusionary processes. Specifically, it considers how the critical inhabitation of abject spaces by politically engaged subjects constitutes political community, governance and belonging in terms that exceed an exclusionary (extra)territorial frame. There are two parts to this argument. The first part examines Jenny Edkins and Veronique Pin-Fat's Agambenian analysis of the resistance of asylum seekers to the biopolitical workings of sovereign power. It argues that, while Edkins and Pin-Fat are right to draw attention to lip sewing as a powerful contestation of the exclusionary politics of asylum, an emphasis on sovereign power over resistance leaves their analysis caught within an exclusionary frame. Suggesting that a conception of contestation in terms of acts of solidarity, rather than in terms of individualised bodily resistance, is critical to the surpassing of exclusionary politics, the second part of the analysis focuses on contestations that enact political community, governance and belonging in post-territorial terms. In so doing, the analysis reads Jacques Ranciere's notion of 'the part with no part' through Engin Isin and Greg Nielsen's conceptualisation of 'acts of citizenship', in order to draw attention to the critical importance of contestations in which both rights and obligations are claimed in terms that are misplaced according to a territorial frame.

Contesting the exclusionary politics of asylum

The work of Jenny Edkins and Veronique Pin-Fat (2004, 2005) is particularly relevant to the analysis in this chapter, because it engages with questions of sovereign power and resistance in relation to the exclusionary politics of asylum specifically. Edkins and Pin-Fat position their work as sitting between Foucault and Agamben (2004:4–11). Thus, while they acknowledge that resistance is always inevitable where relations of power exist, they also draw attention to the limitations of resistance where sovereign power draws lines in terms that regulate bare life. That is, they claim that sovereign power in its biopolitical form constitutes bare life as a powerless life, thus limiting the scope for resistance (ibid.:7–9). In so doing, Edkins and Pin-Fat make a clear move into the Agambenian camp, by taking as their starting point sovereign power rather than resistance. Struggling to reinstate resistance to its 'proper' position, Edkins and Pin-Fat claim that there is a need to develop political relations so as to counter a violence in which the possibilities of resistance have become practically negligible. They do this specifically by drawing attention to those resistances that are marked both by a refusal of sovereign distinctions as well as by an acceptance of bare life (2004:3–17).

Following Agamben, Edkins and Pin-Fat conceptualise the refugee as a 'limit figure' from which a 'new politics' might be developed. Thus, they focus on the case of Abbas Amini, an Iranian seeking refuge in the UK who, by going on hunger strike in 2003 and by sewing his own eyes, ears and mouth closed with a thread, protested against the UK government's repressive treatment of asylum seekers. Edkins and

Pin-Fat suggest that this resistance was an effective one in breaking a seemingly all-consuming system of violence. Specifically, they see it as such because Amini successfully drew attention to the violent workings of sovereign power in accepting his own reduction to bare life, while at the same time as which he subverted sovereign power's grip through regaining his political voice (2004:16–17; 2005:16–23). In Edkins and Pin-Fat's reading, Amini's protest is thus a powerful one because it embodies both an acceptance and a refusal: an acceptance of his body as a tool of resistance, and a refusal of the sovereign's inscription of him as bare life. This, they suggest, signals a return of political relations and a refusal of the erasure of power and resistance by a sovereign power turned biopolitical. Indeed, Edkins and Pin-Fat importantly highlight the way in which Abbas Amini's affirmative defiance of restrictive controls facilitate his self-constitution as a subject with rights, who contends the UK government's attempt to render him, like all those in his position, as an inexistent subject. In this respect, Edkins and Pin-Fat are right to draw attention to lip sewing as a powerful contestation of the exclusionary politics of asylum, even if it relies on a somewhat disturbing (but nonetheless critical) mimicry of sovereign violence.

While the analysis that Edkins and Pin-Fat develops is provocative and insightful, their Agambenian reading nevertheless remains problematic on various counts. By emphasising sovereign power over resistance, Edkins and Pin-Fat fail to recognise the multitude of cracks of resistance and contestation that were highlighted in the first part of this chapter. Indeed, their analysis seems to remain trapped within an exclusionary frame, because it takes as its starting point sovereign power rather than resistance or 'turbulence'. Edkins and Pin-Fat recoil from the task of exploring alternative conceptions of political community, governance and belonging that might exceed the reactive (extra)territorial frame of sovereign-bio-power, arguably because of their refusal to be lured into 'drawing any lines of the sort that sovereign power demands' (Edkins and Pin-Fat, 2004:13; see Prozorov, 2005:104). This refusal is understandable in terms of their struggle to think of a non-totalising alternative to the totalising workings of sovereign power. However, such an approach is cut through with difficulties, and it remains both unclear as to what such a strategy entails as well as questionable whether it can have any critical effect. Perhaps one could say that Edkins and Pin-Fat become lured by the promise of transcending sovereign power to the point that their privileging of the negative moment of refusal becomes excessively limiting. Thus, they fail to engage any alternative account either of asylum or of political community, while their analysis of resistance remains focused on the bodily resistance of the individual asylum seeker rather than on the wider mobilisations that are so crucial to the politicisation of such resistances (Huysmans, 2008:179). It is in this sense that Edkins and Pin-Fat do not go far enough in examining the proliferating contestations of the exclusionary politics of asylum that are evident at the contemporary juncture.

Contending conceptions of political community, governance and belonging

In refusing the limited conception of contestation that emerges where sovereign power is reified and where resistance is underestimated, this part of the chapter moves beyond one in which individual bodies are taken as the primary site of resistance. Specifically, it explores those contestations that both challenge the exclusionary politics of asylum while simultaneously reconstructing political community, governance and belonging in contending terms. These contestations are conceptualised here as mobilisations that entail *acts of solidarity*. In particular, acts of solidarity are conceived as those in which political relations are reconstructed in terms that contest the exclusionary renderings of a (de)territorialised order, which is precariously constituted through the reactive ideological operations of sovereign-bio-power. Such a notion engages the political philosophy of Jacque Rancière (1999) through drawing on Engin Isin and Greg Nielsen's (2008) work on 'acts of citizenship'. In so doing, it invokes a conception of politics that 'turns on equality as its principle' and that has as its critical focus those with 'no-part' of the political community. Specifically, it considers how those without the right to speak make themselves heard through articulating a grievance as being equal to those who do have a part (Rancière, 1999:27–30). Rather than remaining focused on those with 'no-part' in isolation, however, this analysis develops a political account of the two-way relationships between those with and those without a part of the territorial political community. In so doing, it explores the solidaristic political relations that emerge both in and around the abject spaces of frontiers and zones.

Engin Isin and Greg Nielson's theory of the citizenship 'act' is heavily influenced by Rancière, because it similarly focuses on those 'disruptive moments' in which settled conceptions and practices of political community, governance and belonging become unsettled. Acts of citizenship are defined by Engin Isin and Greg Nielson as deeds that constitute subjects as 'those to whom the right to have rights is due' (2008:2). Specifically, they argue that such acts are marked by a creative moment in which *habitus* (i.e. engrained habitual practice) is disrupted, and in which institutionally embedded citizenship practices become open to question. Following Rancière, those with 'no part' who claim rights as equal members of the community emerge as exemplary political agents in the theory of citizenship acts. In particular, non-status migrants can be interpreted as one such discounted or excluded group of abjects, who create a breach in the territorial order through a 'misplaced' claiming of rights (see Nyers, 2003, 2008). This part of the chapter shows how the 'misplaced' claiming of rights by those without formal citizenship status may be more effective in moving from a transitory disruption to a more enduring *interruption* when met by a 'misplaced' claiming of obligations by those with formal citizenship status. This can be conceptualised in Rancièrian terms as a process in which worlds 'in between' are created; worlds that are invisible and inaudible according to the territorial frame of sovereign power.

This Rancièrian reading of citizenship acts thus brings the notion of *solidarity* to the fore. By focusing on political engagements that are created through misplaced rights *and* misplaced obligation claims, this analysis is interested in drawing attention to contending conceptions of political community, governance and belonging that emerge as alternatives to a (extra)territorial frame, which is reactively inscribed through an opposition to asylum-cum-illegal-immigration by the exclusionary ideological operations of sovereign-bio-power. There are various mobilisations that we could look at in the UK to examine these alternative renderings, such as the *Cities of Sanctuary* movement. However, in this part of the chapter we focus specifically on the enactment of solidarity by the *No Borders* (NB) and the *No One Is Illegal* (NOII) movements, which are both UK-based groups as well as being linked up to wider movements of activists at the European and global levels. There are close associations between NB and NOII and both have engaged within the *European Social Forum* (ESF), which is a broader umbrella network comprising a series of activists groups and networks. Membership of both movements is difficult to gauge due to the informal membership structure of localised groups and the dispersed and floating nature of the activist networks. However, what is clear is that the groups are composed of people of various statuses (citizens, refugees and migrants) who come together to support those who are denied status or who are denied the right of free movement. Both NB and NOII refuse to distinguish between members in terms of their legal and migration status, although some of the campaign material suggests that core members are citizens or migrants with status. NOII in particular differs from NB in the UK, because it is made up of several founding members with status who produce documents and offer guidance to local activist groups. This renders the political theory of NOII more coherent and explicit than that of NB, with the latter produced by a diverse network of activists rather than by a unified group of activists.

Both NB and NOII come together in their mutual call for the removal of all immigration controls. The movements develop a 'no borders' and an 'open borders' approach respectively, with NB campaigning for 'the freedom of movement and for the equal rights for all' and with NOII campaigning for 'free movement for all and unity between all'. As such, both NB and NOII challenge the restrictive controls that this book has shown to be central to the exclusionary politics of asylum. This challenge is explicitly developed by NOII as a critique of the territorial articulation of governance and belonging. Thus, it is claimed on the website that 'No one owns, no one has a franchise, over England or anywhere else'.[1] NB also challenges a territorial conception of governance and belonging, and goes on to develop a more explicitly anti-capitalist stance by emphasising the importance of challenging relations of exploitation that emerge where state controls are dispersed both internally and at the external border. Thus, NB argues that 'we have the reality of the constant mobilization of migrants, of their challenge to the borders of Europe and to other borders in the world, of their refusal to submit their mobility to the supposed 'laws' of the labour market' (NB, 2004). The NB movement in particular thus struggles to render visible and audible the acts of irregular migrants that challenge both a neoliberal economic order, and a territorial political order.

Both NB and NOII conceive migration as normal, rather than exceptional, and in this respect could be said to challenge a territorial framing of politics. Nevertheless, the movements differ as to how they conceptualise this 'normality'. NB, in particular, often tends to approach mobility as the 'foundational norm' of a neoliberal economic order. The movement thus indirectly challenges a nationalistic discourse in which asylum seekers and migrants are constituted as 'culpable' or 'inexistent' subjects by suggesting that migrants are differentially subject to inclusion/exclusion according to the market mechanisms. The position developed by NOII is more ambiguous. On the one hand, the movement challenges a nationalistic discourse by portraying migration as a 'normal' dimension of British life. Thus, the NOII manifesto (NOII, 2003) argues that 'Britain has been constructed out of waves of migration – the very idea of there being an 'indigenous' population is both politically racist and historically nonsensical.' On the other hand, NOII suggests that 'the reality is that the vast majority of people prefer to stay where they are if this is at all possible'. In this respect, NOII challenges the 'nomadism' that sometimes emerges within NB texts. Thus, it is argued in the manifesto that 'Many if not all of the arguments used to justify immigration controls are simply ludicrous and are more the result of racist-inspired moral panic than of any connection with reality. Such is the notion that the entire world population would come to this country if there were no controls: even if such an absurd notion were true, it should prompt concern for their reasons for coming, rather than fear'. There are clearly differences in the politics of NOII and NB when it comes to their conceptualising of mobility and migration. However, what is important for our purposes is that they come together in their definition of mobility as a normal feature of human existence. Both movements thus challenge the territorial framing of politics, in which social interaction is primarily conceived of in terms of sedentary individuals and groups and in which governance and belonging are inscribed according to the state and nation. In so doing, they challenge the exclusionary politics of asylum; a politics that is characterised by processes of securitisation, criminalisation and abjection, which effectively transform 'undesirable' mobile subjects into 'threatening' and 'culpable' subjects before moving them in the direction of 'inexistence'.

Both NB and NOII challenge the identification of migrants or refugees as 'threatening', 'culpable' and 'inexistent' subjects by foregrounding their political agency. For example, the NOII manifesto brings attention to migratory 'push' factors while acknowledging the refugee or migrant's active role in making decisions and taking actions that produce their mobility. Thus, it defines refugees and migrants as agents that either 'attempt to flee wars and repression, or to improve their situation through migration'. Going further, NB focuses attention on the 'turbulent' agency of refugees and migrants. Thus, it claims that, in moving 'for a better life and against the hierarchies of exploitation, [m]igrations undermine the border regimes and create networks and communities beyond all nation states, from countries of origin through transit- to the target-countries' (NB, 2007a). For NB, refugees and migrants are conceived of as active political subjects who constitute political communities that exceed the territorial frame of the nation state.

Indeed, in calling for citizens to struggle in unison with refugees and migrants against restrictive migration controls, both movements strive to create solidaristic political engagements between those with status and those without status. In discourse theoretical terms, these engagements might be conceived of as working more according to a logic of difference, in which political space is pluralised, than according to a logic of equivalence, which has been suggested to characterise exclusionary politics (see Chapter 2).[2] Thus, the NOII manifesto calls for 'solidarity not pity', and claims a 'misplaced' obligation through extending unconditional support for 'the right of all people to stay here if they wish to, and irrespective of their personal circumstances'. Similarly, NB claims the fight against detention and deportation is related to a wider struggle to 'break' borders, and calls for 'a radical movement against the system of control, dividing us into citizens and non-citizens' (NB, 2007b). In so doing, NB demands 'the end of the border regime for everyone ... [in order] to enable us to live another way, without fear, racism and nationalism' (ibid.). Both NB and NOII could thus be described as struggling to create 'worlds in-between' in which those with status and those without status come together. Specifically, they do so through the solidaristic claiming of rights and obligations in terms that are misplaced according to a territorial frame.

What is notable about the mobilisations through which these acts of solidarity emerge is that they are primarily located within and around the abject spaces that we discussed in the first part of this chapter. One important example of this critical inhabitation of abject spaces is the NB camp. The NB movement has been composed of a series of camps that, to use Isin and Rygiel's (2006) terms, are variously located in the vicinity of European frontiers and zones. A recent example of this type of mobilisation is the Gatwick (UK) No Borders Camp, which was enacted in solidarity with irregular migrants in September 2007. From observation, the Gatwick camp was primarily attended by citizens of EU member states – perhaps unsurprising given the risks and difficulties involved for those without status to attend. The camp was enacted at a rural site near to the 'border point' of Gatwick airport as a protest against the development of a new detention centre near the existing Tinsley House detention centre at Gatwick. The camp ran over five days, with various practical activist workshops running throughout and with ideas and information being exchanged at an international forum on detention and deportation. In addition, activists demonstrated against detention and deportation on a march from Crawley town centre to the Tinsley House detention centre (NB, 2007b). In this respect, the acts of solidarity carried out as part of the Gatwick No Border Camp can be interpreted as critical inhabitations of zones, primarily by those who were 'misplaced' in so doing according to a territorial frame of reference.

The Gatwick No Border Camp can be interpreted as an event that renders visible the everyday struggles of activists – both of those with and of those without status. Indeed, struggles to act in solidarity against the exclusionary politics of asylum are not particular to the camp event, but also take place in the everyday enactments of various NB activists who contest the detention and deportation of irregular migrants by the British state. Thus, NB suggests that the 'transnational expression of migrants' struggles against the "monster" of migration controls must be [seen as] something more than a one day event once a year ... [it is a] unified space of migrants' struggles, happening everyday and right now' (2008). The NB camp crystallises this multitude of everyday protests in a spectacular event that creates a dramatic breach in the territorial frame. Indeed, that the camp occurred on land which is normally used as farming pasture symbolically disrupts the territorial imaginary of a nation state. That the 'owners' of this land (both 'the English' and 'the farmer') 'gave it over' to the cause of irregular migrants merely adds insult to injury. However, what is perhaps most critical is that this disruptive event symbolises a range of more concrete and everyday acts of solidarity that create political relations between those with status and those without. It is against the backdrop of these everyday struggles that the camp becomes critically effective in *interrupting* the territorial framing of political community that is reactively inscribed through the exclusionary politics of asylum. By drawing attention to the proliferation of worlds in-between that are created by those with and without status who come together in a multitude of abject spaces to contest exclusionary politics, the camp shows how the claiming of obligation by those with status and the claiming of rights by those without status are radically 'misplaced' according to a territorial frame. That is, it shows how post-territorial conceptions of political community are enacted on a daily basis in terms that transform the turbulence that precedes sovereign power into a politics that exceeds it. It is that the operations of sovereign power emerge in *reaction* to such processes that renders the exclusionary battle a more precarious affair than it would often appear to be.

Conclusion

While the analysis in Parts II and III of this book explored the increasing dominance and decontestation of an exclusionary politics that differentially includes and selectively excludes 'undesirables' such as asylum seekers, the analysis in this chapter has taken the first steps towards

considering how these exclusionary politics might be critically interceded. Specifically, it has shown how a reading of irregular migration
as resistance or 'turbulence' *preceding* the exclusionary operations of a
reactive sovereign-bio-power enables us to conceive irregular migrants
as engaging in terms that potentially *exceed* the territorial frame of
state governance and national belonging. Specifically, it has argued
that these critical interruptions entail solidaristic political relations that
interrupt the exclusionary equivalences that are drawn where a territorial
order is reconstructed in opposition to asylum-cum-illegal-immigration.
Although the focus in this chapter has been on acts of solidarity by
the *No Borders* and the *No One is Illegal* movements, a range of such
solidaristic acts can be identified in, and beyond, the UK today. As
we saw in Chapter 4, a range of contestations-in-solidarity with those
who are subject to the exclusionary politics of asylum have developed
over recent years that potentially reframe political community in post-
territorial terms. Indeed, solidaristic engagements also emerge within
the micropractices of exclusionary technologies such as dispersal. This
is evident, for example, in the self-identification of an asylum support
worker as a 'befriender' of 'people', rather than as a policeman of asylum seekers (Individual interview 1, Appendix 2, see Chapter 6).

By developing an analysis of acts of solidarity that bring those with and
those without status into a relation of mutual contention, this chapter
has critically engaged Giorgio Agamben's theory of sovereign power. It
has suggested that Agamben's work is important, because it helps us
to critically diagnose an exclusionary politics that seemingly entails
an extension of the operations of sovereign-bio-power in all directions
(biometric and extraterritorial). This allows us to further understand
how a deterrent rationality moves to reduce 'threatening' and 'culpable'
subjects to a condition of abject inexistence (see Chapter 6). However,
the chapter has also argued that Agamben's work is highly problematic,
because it takes as its analytical starting point sovereign power, rather
than resistance. This, it has been suggested, leaves Agamben caught
within the totalising grip of a sovereign power, which is played out on
the physical bodies of those who are denied political voice or visibility.
Indeed, the chapter has shown how an Agambenian analysis of resistance can become reduced to a critical mimicry of sovereign power's
physical violence, rather than an analysis that draws to the fore the
multitude of solidaristic acts that render such resistances so powerful.
As an alternative to the Agambenian reading of the camp as a space of
abjection, the analysis has thus drawn on Engin Isin and Kim Rygiel's
theorisation of the zone and the frontier as abject spaces. By examining

these abject spaces from the analytical starting point resistance, rather than sovereign power, the chapter has developed a political reading of the acts of refugees and migrants *qua* irregular migrants, as well as of citizens-in-solidarity with those denied status and the right to free movement. While asylum-seekers-cum-illegal-immigrants can be seen as subjects who are targeted by exclusionary processes of securitisation, criminalisation, dehumanisation and depoliticisation, the analysis suggests that they can by no means seen as dehumanised and depoliticised abjects to a point of no return.

By approaching irregular migrants as political agents whose engagements potentially have a transformative effect, the analysis in this chapter has suggested that the moment when 'undesirables' act as though they have rights is a disruptive moment in which asylum-seekers-cum-illegal-immigrants become irregular migrants through radically opening the territorial frame to question. Similarly, the analysis has suggested that the moment when those with rights claim an obligation to those without rights is equally disruptive. Indeed, in a context where the operations of sovereign power have turned both biopolitical and extraterritorial, it is critical that the disruptive acts of those without status (those with 'no-part' of the political community) are joined with the disruptive acts of those with status (or those with a part of the political community). After all, it is only through such political engagements that a post-territorial order can be developed in terms that effectively *intercede* the exclusionary politics of asylum. While temporary disruptions may be a good starting point in challenging the exclusionary politics of asylum, they need to be critically engaged as more lasting discursive and institutional interruptions if the exclusionary operations of a territorial order are to be critically interceded. It is through the 'misplaced' political engagements of those with and without status that such a task may be achieved. While there is no magical route to a new political realm of authenticity where abjectifying processes of dehumanisation and depoliticisation and exclusionary processes of securitisation and criminalisation are unimaginable, there is always scope for the ongoing struggle against an exclusionary politics to become more critically effective. The analysis in this book suggests that it is through those political engagements in which 'worlds in-between' are created that the exclusionary politics of asylum can be most effectively interceded. While this will always be a struggle, the analysis suggests that the struggle is in itself a critical one in which political subjects, among others, constitute themselves as such through acts of solidarity.

8

Rethinking Asylum, Rethinking Citizenship: Moving Beyond Exclusionary Politics

The exclusionary politics of asylum would seem to be symptomatic of an ambiguous state of affairs. Marked by the logic of selective opposition which, in an alternative form, functions as a logic of differential inclusion, exclusionary politics play a central role in reconstructing a territorial order in the face of its dissolution. Indeed, it is often in the very process of this reconstruction that deterritorialising processes of governance and belonging emerge as internal disruptions of the territorial order. The territorial political community is thus *precariously* reconstructed through the exclusionary politics of asylum, the latter of which emerges in reactive ideological terms against those 'turbulent' migratory processes that precede and exceed governmental control. Whether such 'turbulences' are conceived of in economic terms (as labour) or in social terms (as mobility), this book suggests that exclusionary politics can be interpreted as a reactionary form of politics that produces scapegoats for 'problems' that are, in a sense, the sovereign state's 'own'.

The asylum seeker has emerged as a key figure in this exclusionary process. In being addressed as a 'threatening' or 'culpable' subject who is placed on the fast track towards inexistence, s/he is first prohibited and subsequently punished for the state's failure to maintain total control over the 'turbulence' of migration. More than this, s/he is punished for the state's inability to deal with a wider range of social problems, while being held up as a cover for its territorial transgressions. It is in this regard that the exclusionary politics of asylum are marked by reactive ideological operations that constitute the asylum seeker as a scapegoat. The figure of the 'bogus' asylum seeker plays a central role in this process, even where the term is not openly used. The exclusionary politics of asylum, in other words, are now so firmly sedimented or embedded that the exclusionary speech act need not even occur for its effects to ensue.

In telling two stories, this book has moved from the depoliticising tale of the reactive sovereign state to the contending tale of the irregular migrant's political engagements. That the asylum seeker is produced as 'threatening', 'culpable' and 'inexistent' through the operational adaptations of the territorial state does not reduce the asylum-seeker-cum-illegal-immigrant to such a depoliticised status. Rather, s/he can mobilise around his/her ambiguous position in terms that radically open to question the exclusionary depoliticisations that are central to the reactive ideological operations of the state (and its subsidiaries). This, it would seem, is the critical potential that the mobile figure of the irregular migrant holds today, as a distinctly political subject that moves within, between and across states and nations. Yet the story cannot stop here, for its ending still remains unclear. If the exclusionary politics of asylum are to be critically interceded, we need to go even further in order to consider how an 'inclusionary' alternative might be effectively developed. This, the chapter suggests, requires a rethinking and a re-enactment of both asylum and citizenship alike.

Having set ourselves this somewhat challenging task, let us first outline the journey. The first part of this chapter retraces the critical analysis of the exclusionary politics of asylum developed in this book, and shows how a dual-pronged critique of the territorial reconstruction of political community creates the distance required for a critical rethinking of asylum and citizenship. Suggesting that a simple movement beyond the territorial frame of governance and belonging is inadequate to this task, it draws attention to the ambiguous nature of an exclusionary territorial politics that is simultaneously a deterritorialising politics of differential inclusion. In so doing, the analysis highlights three moves that are critical to any effective challenge of the exclusionary politics charted throughout the course of this book, each of which are expressly political. First, it is suggested an effective critique needs to challenge the reactive and ideological (or totalising) impetus of an exclusionary politics that is organised according to the logic of selective opposition. Second, an effective critique needs to challenge the depoliticising managerial operations of an exclusionary politics that is organised according to a rationality of deterrence. Finally, it is suggested that an effective critique needs to challenge the territorial operations of an exclusionary politics that is organised around the state and the nation. In short, it is argued an 'inclusionary' post-territorial alternative needs to effectively challenge an exclusionary territorial politics that is simultaneously reactionary, depoliticising and divisive.

This clears the ground for the second part of the chapter, which considers how asylum and citizenship can be constructively rethought and re-enacted in terms that critically intercede an exclusionary politics. Drawing attention to the limitations of human rights and open borders approaches in developing a post-territorial alternative that effectively challenges exclusionary politics, it suggests that a more thoroughly *political* approach is required if the totalising, depoliticising and divisive politics that have been charted in this book are to be critically interceded. This requires a rethinking of citizenship through contestation and solidarity. Such an approach opens the possibility for a movement beyond an exclusionary politics of differential inclusion while acknowledging the more difficult political engagements that are inherent to such a process. Closing with some preliminary reflections on the way in which such an alternative might be practically engaged, the analysis points to the European Union as a fertile ground for a political enactment of post-territorial citizenship, which entails acts of solidarity between variously-mobile subjects who engage in mutual contention with one another. Enacting citizenship through mobility, it concludes, potentially opens the space for a politically engaged dialogue surrounding asylum that does not become caught in a reactionary cycle.

Challenging the exclusionary politics of asylum

This book has undertaken a dual-pronged critique of the exclusionary politics of asylum, which can be described as a reactive and ideological form of politics that reconstructs the territorial order in opposition to the asylum-seeker-cum-illegal-immigrant. In so doing, it has charted the increasing dominance of an exclusionary discourse of the asylum 'problem' in the UK, and it has critically examined both the operations and the effects of this process of discursive sedimentation and institutionalised embedding. A critical analysis of the *operations* of the asylum discourse has shown that exclusionary politics are marked by the narrative construction and technical constitution of asylum seekers as 'threatening' and 'culpable' subjects, against which a morally benevolent and socially stable territorial political community is precariously and ambiguously defined. This process, it has been argued, is a highly depoliticising one that entails the exclusionary interaction of technical and narrative operations. Specifically, these exclusionary interactions are indicative of a self-fulfilling cycle of securitisation and criminalisation, which further sediments and embeds an exclusionary politics as part of a precarious territorial order.

The second level of this critique can be seen in terms of a critical analysis of the *effects* of exclusionary politics. This has entailed two movements. Initially, the critique remained internal to a territorial politics and focused on drawing attention to its internal contradictions. Specifically, it showed how the exclusionary politics of asylum entail a shrinking commitment to asylum (despite the UK and the EU's ongoing 'benevolent' commitment to the 1951 Geneva Convention), and it showed how this shrinking commitment is reflected in the hostile reception of 'in-country' and 'at-port' asylum seekers (despite the purportedly 'generous' nature of the 'socially stable' 'host' community). Indeed, the analysis draws attention to the development of a decidedly inconsiderate and unwelcoming response to asylum both at the UK and the EU levels, as well as across the political, popular, public and technical levels. Nevertheless, it is in moving to a position of critical distance from this ambiguous rendering of asylum that this critique has critically examined the *effects* of the contradictory territorial reconstruction of political community. Specifically, it has argued that these contradictory articulations effectively reconstruct a territorial order of state governance and national belonging in the face of its dissolution, by projecting political community's failures and transgressions onto the asylum seeker. Indeed, this belies a less straightforwardly exclusionary politics than may initially appear to be the case, and requires that any challenge to the exclusionary politics of a territorial order is coupled with a challenge of the differential inclusions of a (de)territorialising order.

Challenging the exclusionary politics of a territorial order

Let us first further consider the way in which the book has challenged the exclusionary politics of a territorial order, before we go on to consider how it has challenged the differentially inclusive politics of a (de)territorialising order. The analysis suggests that the asylum seeker has emerged as a key figure against whom political community is constructed in territorial terms; particularly in the late 1990s and the early to mid-2000s during which time the exclusionary politics of asylum were at their height in the UK. In suggesting that this exclusionary politics can be interpreted as a reactive ideological discourse, the book shows how the territorial political community is precariously constructed through its articulation in opposition to the asylum-seeker-cum-illegal-immigrant. Thus, it shows how the figure of the asylum seeker is securitised and criminalised through a range of exclusionary narratives within European and domestic political debates (Chapter 3), as well as within popular and public debates more widely (Chapter 4). Specifically, it shows how these narratives construct the asylum seeker as a 'threatening' or 'culpable' subject in terms that legitimise an extension of restrictive controls while simultaneously defining political community as morally benevolent and socially stable. Indeed, the analysis has suggested that these exclusionary narratives are particularly effective in covering over tensions that emerge where the national political community is redefined along European lines. In so doing, this analysis of asylum discourse tells a reactive ideological story of the precarious territorial reconstruction of political community in conditions of heightened dislocation.

It is through a critical analysis of the operations of exclusionary asylum discourse that the book has developed a dual-pronged critique of the territorial framing of political community. Firstly, the book develops a critique of the territorial construction of political community in 'its own terms', by challenging its dominant articulation as socially stable and morally benevolent. The analysis would often seem to tell the story of a society that is marked by social and cultural hostility more than integration or cohesion, as well as of a government that tends to be concerned with economic productivity over the benevolent protection of refugees. Thus, it suggests that the exclusionary politics of asylum effectively aggravates social and inter-racial tensions (Chapter 6), while at the same time it practically erodes the institution of asylum (Chapter 5). On this reading, the articulation of political community as socially stable and morally benevolent is misleading. Yet the analysis here does not simply 'show the lie' of political rhetoric. Rather, it draws attention to the way in which political community is constructed as stable and benevolent (and, indeed, productive) precisely through an exclusionary politics that criminalises and securitises those that are not deemed worthy of integration or protection. In this regard, it can be seen as developing a critique of a distinctly liberal rendering of territorial political community, through which 'inclusion' is articulated in highly exclusionary terms.[1]

This leads into the book's second line of critique, which challenges the exclusionary politics of a territorial order from a position of critical distance. It is difficult, if not impossible, to think political community 'beyond' territoriality, because the very concept of political community invites us to think in terms of a closed polity or society that is defined according to the geographical boundaries of a state. Indeed, until recent years these geographical boundaries were largely presumed to map both onto a shared national culture as well as onto an economic unit, thus rendering the polity, the state, the economy and the nation in a relation of territorial mutuality. Although many of these founding assumptions have been challenged over recent years (Sassen, 1998), it seems that the will-to-closure of political community remains difficult to effectively interrupt. The analysis in this book challenges this imperative by highlighting the indistinct boundaries between the inside and outside of political community (cf. Walker, 1993; Campbell, 1992, 1998; Lapid, 2001). In so doing, it shows how a political community that is often defined as relatively 'inclusive' in a liberal and multicultural sense remains exclusionary in its territorial delimitation. In this book, this play of inclusion/exclusion is conceived as indicative of a deep-rooted tension that is inherent to the territorial formation of liberal governance and belonging; namely that exclusionary politics play a constitutive role in defining political community's limits.

A consideration of the way in which this exclusionary constitution of limits emerges through complex processes of inclusion/exclusion in relation to asylum discourse is telling. It is important to note that an individual asylum seeker can move swiftly from his or her inscription as a 'threatening' or 'culpable' subject to a position of acceptance or inexistence (see Chapters 6 and 7). If their asylum claim is accepted, individuals are included as 'genuine' refugees, or as 'vulnerable' people with temporary protection status. Prior to this, however, their assumed 'culpability' entails a range of criminalising, securitising and abjectifying processes through which the asylum seeker is inscribed as a 'threatening' subject of a 'bogus' type. The transition from exclusion to inclusion, in this regard, is perhaps less swift and clear-cut than may initially appear to be the case. Indeed, the play of inclusion and exclusion is significantly more complex than a cursory glance would suggest. Although it is correct to say that asylum seekers are excluded where they are constructed as 'culpable' or 'threatening' subjects, this is not to say that asylum seekers are *simply* excluded as such. Rather, asylum seekers are temporarily incorporated within a territorial order through their construction as a 'threatening supplement', whereby they are included through their exclusion. Subsequently, their position is redefined in an inclusive or an exclusive direction. On the one hand, asylum seekers who 'successfully' demonstrate that they are not 'threatening' are excluded through their inclusion as 'genuine' refugees. On the other hand, asylum seekers who are unable to prove that they are not 'threatening' become included *or* excluded through their further exclusion.

So how can we understand the difference between those moments where 'failed asylum seekers' are included through their exclusion, and those moments where asylum seekers are excluded through their exclusion? From the first angle, one could perhaps say that inclusion through exclusion emerges where 'failed asylum seekers' effectively become a part of political community despite their formal exclusion. In practical terms, an example in this regard emerges where the unsupported asylum seeker decides to take up work rather than to suffer destitution. In this regard, s/he is repositioned as a member of the working public (albeit one that is not officially recognised), thus ambiguously moving in the direction of 'inclusion through exclusion'. Exclusionary processes of criminalisation and securitisation clearly remain in play here, but one could say that abjection is resisted by the asylum seeker who enacts citizenship through his or her 'mis-placed' engagement as a worker (see Chapter 6). From the second angle, one could say that exclusion through exclusion occurs where the 'failed asylum seeker' is subject to destitution, detention or removal, which narrows his or her ability to constitute himself or herself as a political subject (see Chapter 7). This is not to say that depoliticisation and dehumanisation serve as the end result of this process, as the analysis in Chapter 7 clearly argued. However, it is to say that an even more troubling form of exclusionary politics emerges where the excluded are excluded (Balibar, 2002); one that would seem to move even further in a totalising direction by moving through reactive processes of securitisation and criminalisation towards abjectifying processes of dehumanisation and depoliticisation. It is in challenging these various exclusionary operations that this critique seeks to move beyond the reactive and abjectifying ideological operations that are central to a territorial order of governance and belonging.

Challenging the differential inclusions of a (de)territorialising order

This critical reading of the exclusionary politics of asylum would seem to suggest that exclusionary politics are not quite what they seem, for they entail a range of complex processes of inclusion/exclusion. The analysis in this book suggests that asylum seekers may now be subject to processes of depoliticisation and dehumanisation as much as they are subject to processes of securitisation and criminalisation, and this perhaps goes some way in explaining why asylum is no longer such a visible issue in contemporary political debate in the UK. However, the analysis also suggests that not all refugees and migrants are conceived of in such oppositional terms. It is for this reason that this critique cannot stop at showing how the exclusionary politics of asylum are constitutive of a territorial political community that it is defined in liberal terms. Rather, a critique also needs to be developed in order to challenge the converse of an exclusionary politics of selective opposition; namely the exclusionary politics of differential inclusion.

It is here that the *selectivity* of the oppositional logic of securitisation and criminalisation comes to the fore, and that the uneven manifestation of a deterrent rationality becomes visible. If the territorial construction of political community relies on a logic of selective opposition that defines asylum seekers as the moving targets of processes of securitisation and criminalisation (if not of processes of dehumanisation and depoliticisation), it thus also relies on a logic of differential inclusion that defines mobile subjects in more variegated, hierarchical terms.

If exclusionary politics are selective, rather than all-encompassing, they can be approached in terms of a wider politics of differential inclusion that distinguishes between mobile subjects through various divisive practices (Mezzadra and Nielson, 2008). The analysis here highlights the political effectiveness of this wider politics, in which the constitution of asylum seekers as 'culpable' or 'threatening' subjects entails both an enactment of territoriality and a covering over of deterritorialising transgressions that differentially include and selectively exclude various mobile subjects. Going further, this analysis also highlights the economic effectiveness of such a process, in terms of its production of exploitable abject subjects (see Part III). As such, this book does not only contribute to a theoretical field of research that considers the political role that the figure of the refugee plays in constituting a territorial order (Owen, 2005). It also contributes to a theoretical and empirical field of research that explores both the political and the economic effectiveness of the body of the undocumented migrant in precariously constituting such an order (De Genova, 2002, 2004; McNevin, 2007; Mezzadra and Nielson, 2008; Nyers, 2008). Specifically, the claim that 'culpable' subjects are often reconstructed as abject subjects and put on the fast track to 'inexistence' is suggestive of an intertwinement of these political and economic effects (Chapters 6 and 7). On this reading, the exclusionary politics of asylum are inseparable from a wider divisive and hierarchical politics of differential inclusion; a politics that has both a political and an economic effectiveness in the separation of mobile subjects into their 'threatening', 'non-threatening' and 'inexistent' variants.

An important dimension that this wider politics of differential inclusion brings into view is the 'internal disruptions' or territorial transgressions of political community that the state itself entails, which might be conceptualised in terms of a movement beyond sovereignty (Dillon, 2007). These internal disruptions can be understood in two forms, both of which are related to managerialism (see Chapter 2). First, internal territorial disruptions can be conceived of in terms of the state's transgression of territorial governance. This relates to the discussion of extended and diffuse managerial renderings of migration control in Part III, which brings in a range of subsidiary agents to make up for the sovereign state's inability to gain total control over the 'external turbulence' of cross-border mobilities. From private security firms, through voluntary and charitable sector agencies, to third countries, the story that this book has told is one of the territorial extension of the institutional and technical operations of the state. These extensions signal the incorporation of both private and non-private agencies as part of the state's managerial response to migration, and move in both a subnational or regional direction and also in an international or global direction to disperse and extend controls.

There is also a second way in which these internal territorial transgressions can be conceived, which relates more to the complex processes of inclusion/exclusion that are inherent to a managerial approach to migration (see Chapter 2). Specifically, the analysis turns here to the internal disruptions of a territorial order through which national belonging is transgressed. Political community *qua* belonging often exceeds its national and territorial frame where an exclusionary politics of differential inclusion is engaged, because various mobile subjects are differentially incorporated within the socio-economic fabric. For example, undocumented migrants are incorporated (albeit surreptitiously) by employers as a part of the working public, while refugees are incorporated (albeit in select positions) by local communities as part of the resident public. While the management of migration entails a highly exclusionary dimension, it thus simultaneously creates the conditions for a reconstruction of political community along post-national or post-territorial lines. It is here, however, that any 'inclusionary' post-territorial alternative comes face to face with exclusionary politics. In this book, exclusionary politics are not inevitable, not even in conditions of dislocation (see Chapter 2). While dislocation tends to exacerbate the social and political desire for a 'scapegoat' figure such as the asylum seeker (Doty, 2003), this book works from the assumption that there are alternative ways in which political community can be constituted in order to avoid the excesses of a dislocated territorial order that creates scapegoats for its internal failures and transgressions (see Isin, 2002). This not only requires a rethinking of asylum, for an exclusionary politics can always turn to the mobile Muslim (in the context of the 'war on terror') or the Polish migrant (in the context of European integration) as alternative scapegoat figures. Rather, it requires a critical rethinking and mobile re-enactment of citizenship at large.

Effectively challenging the exclusionary politics of differential inclusion

Before we go on to consider some of the possible directions in which a critical rethinking of citizenship and asylum might move, it is important to draw attention to three critical moves that any 'inclusionary' post-territorial alternative needs to make if it is to effectively challenge an exclusionary politics. The exclusionary politics of differential inclusion that have been the focus of this book are ambiguous and troubling and, in this analysis require careful engagement from a position of critical distance (see Chapter 2). Indeed, this book can be read as a process of creating critical distance between us and the object of our study: the exclusionary politics of asylum, which is simultaneously a managerial politics of differential inclusion, as well as a liberal politics of territorial governance and belonging. Throughout this process, several key dimensions have come to the fore, which are specific to the exclusionary politics of asylum but are also of wider relevance to a reactive, liberal and managerial rendering of territorial governance and belonging. The analysis suggests that any effective challenge of the exclusionary politics of asylum needs to maintain careful distance from these dimensions, while at the same time critically interceding in their operations in distinctly political terms.

The first dimension of an exclusionary politics that needs to be critically interceded is the *logic of selective opposition*, which can be conceived of as a reactionary political logic or strategy (see Chapter 2). The logic of selective opposition is characterised by a drawing of equivalences between 'threats', which are opposed to territorial 'referents' such as the nation and the state. This logic, it would seem, is central to the exclusionary reconstruction of a territorial order, the discursive operations of which coalesce around the 'empty signifier' of political community (see Chapter 2). Indeed, selective opposition might be seen as a defining feature of exclusionary politics at large, conceptualised in terms of a totalising logic characterised by the imperative of closure (Bauman, 1991). More specifically, the book has defined this logic as a reactionary one composed of both an ideological and a reactive dimension. Thus, it has been argued that such a logic emerges to cover over or to mask the dislocations of a territorial order by reactively inscribing limits through the production of 'threatening' or 'culpable' subjects. In so doing, internal disruptions of the territorial order are projected onto disruptive or 'turbulent' figures such as the asylum-seeker-cum-illegal-immigrant. Political community *qua* governance and belonging is thus both constructed and constituted according to the exclusionary logic of selective opposition through intertwined processes of securitisation and criminalisation. The analysis has shown that this logic is sedimented and embedded both in legislative and technical practices, as well as in political and popular debate. On this reading, any critical engagement with the exclusionary politics of asylum needs to effectively challenge the *reactionary* nature of an exclusionary politics that is organised according to the logic of selective opposition.

The second dimension of an exclusionary politics that this book has drawn critical attention to is the *rationality of deterrence*, which is conceived to be fundamentally depoliticising in its technical and technological operations. Deterrence is central to the legislative and technical operations of a managerial approach to migration, and works in accordance with the logic of selective opposition. This analysis has suggested that deterrence is a complex rationality that entails both eliminative and preventative dimensions, and that moves through interdictive technologies to incorporate punitive technologies within its exclusionary remit. In this regard the rationality of deterrence belies complex processes of bordering (Walters, 2006). Indeed, its operations are both extensive and intensive, in the sense that the selective inclusions/ exclusions that it entails move ever outward and inward in the attempt to gain total control over the 'turbulence' of migration that becomes internal to (rather than simply external to) its workings. An effective challenge to the exclusionary politics of asylum does not only have to critically intercede the selectively oppositional logic of a reactionary politics, from this perspective, but it also has to critically intercede the *depoliticising* tendencies of a managerial politics that operate according to a rationality of deterrence.

The third dimension of an exclusionary politics that this book has drawn critical attention to is the *territorial* organisation of governance and belonging, which is conceived here as divisive and hierarchical in its liberal articulation. Our analysis suggests that the territorial organisation of governance and belonging is not *simply* territorial, but rather governance and belonging are increasingly constructed in complex and contradictory ways. How we challenge the exclusionary territorial organisation of governance and belonging thus remains a complex question that this book can only begin to consider here. What is clear, however, is that a liberal articulation of territorial governance and belonging in accordance with the nation and the state is highly problematic. The denial (or limited incorporation) of cross-border mobilities is problematic from this perspective because it serves to reify the nation and the state while differentiating between mobile subjects on an uneven or hierarchical basis. Any effective interruption of the exclusionary politics of asylum also thus requires a challenge to the *divisive* liberal politics through which an exclusionary territorial articulation of state governance and national belonging ensues.

Mutually engaging post-territorial citizenship

The discussion in the first part of this chapter suggested that a simple movement beyond the territorial framing of political community is inadequate to the task of rethinking asylum in more 'inclusionary' terms, because it fails to properly grasp the nature of an exclusionary politics that is simultaneously a politics of differential inclusion. Specifically, a critical analysis of the exclusionary politics of asylum has suggested that any attempt to move beyond such an approach must simultaneously intercede in a reactive ideological or *reactionary* politics, in a *depoliticising* managerial politics and in a *divisive* liberal politics. In this concluding part of the book we make the first steps beyond the exclusionary politics of asylum towards a mobile post-territorial citizenship, in an attempt to critically intercede each of these dimensions. This entails two critical moves. First, it entails a critical engagement with 'human rights' and 'open borders' as alternative frameworks that potentially rethink both asylum and political community along post-territorial lines. The analysis shows that, despite taking mobility seriously, these approaches remain limited in their critical engagement of post-territorial citizenship because they generally fail to effectively challenge the depoliticising and reactionary tendencies of an exclusionary politics. By suggesting that a rethinking of political community through citizenship is required to facilitate such a political engagement, the analysis moves to consider how the depoliticising effects of an exclusionary managerial politics might be interrupted. This requires both a re-engagement with the 'limits' of political community through solidaristic mobile engagements as well as the opening up of managerial operations in the area of asylum to engage political dialogue. Pointing to European citizenship as an important starting point for such engagements, the analysis goes on to show how a mobile post-territorial citizenship engages us all as political actors in mutual contention of the depoliticisations of exclusionary politics.

Critically interceding open borders and human rights

Two approaches that potentially serve as alternative frameworks for a critical rethinking of asylum and citizenship are the 'open borders' and 'human rights' perspectives. These approaches are relevant here, because they potentially move beyond the liberal rendering of territorial governance and belonging that have been examined in this book by taking cross-border mobility and/or global citizenship seriously. However, there remain critical limitations with each of these approaches in terms of the effective challenge that they pose to the exclusionary politics of asylum. Specifically, this book suggests that neither human rights nor open borders approaches properly address the reactionary and depoliticising processes that emerge as part of an exclusionary politics of differential inclusion. Rather, they strive to either limit the excesses (human rights) or challenge the oppositional encounters (open borders) of exclusionary politics through removing the external limits of political community, and in so doing expand the territorial reach of the polity in an attempt to do away with the 'constitutive outside'. The problem with this, from the perspective developed here, is that it assumes that the 'outside' is something that can eventually be incorporated within the territorial order, rather than a feature that plays a constitutive role in its very formation. By approaching the 'outside' as constitutive this analysis takes an alternative route, which is more concerned with rethinking the *relations* between the inside and outside (between those with a part of the territorial political community and those without a part of the territorial political community). This entails a distinctly political rearticulation of citizenship.

We will first examine the potential and limitations of an open borders approach, before doing the same with the human rights perspective. By calling for the removal of border controls, an open borders approach potentially serves as a critical alternative to the exclusionary approach to migration that has been charted here. Advocates of open borders dispute an exclusionary territorial articulation of political community by arguing that exclusion is not justifiable (Carens, 1987). In so doing, they offer a strong challenge to communitarians who conservatively reaffirm the national boundaries of a territorial political community (Miller, 2005). Indeed, in taking mobility seriously, open borders advocates potentially open up the way for a post-territorial rearticulation of political community. Despite the critical purchase of an open borders approach, however, it remains limited in several ways. While we do not have the space to engage in detail with various open border approaches here, it is nevertheless important to consider some of the general limitations of such an approach in relation to this analysis of exclusionary politics.

Any critical interruption of the technical and narrative operations of the exclusionary politics of asylum needs to do more than open borders if it is to take mobility seriously. It also needs to challenge the divisive and depoliticising practices that emerge where the state and the nation are reified by reactionary managerial means. This is the challenge that we face where a rationality of deterrence and a logic of selective opposition become discursively sedimented and institutionally embedded within the technical workings of political community. That an open borders approach can effectively intervene in these politics is not clear. While open borders advocates often conceive such an approach as potentially challenging the divisions and inequalities associated with the exclusionary politics of differential inclusion, they do not offer any adequate theorisation of how or why such 'inclusionary' re-renderings might be developed. By giving mobility a 'free run', advocates of open borders thus tend to assume that the removal of state immigration controls will naturally iron out division and inequality (Harris, 2003), and that the oppositional encounters occurring at the limits of political community will be transcended by removing borders (Hayter, 2000). In this respect, they do not adequately challenge the depoliticising and reactionary tendencies of the exclusionary politics that have been charted here. Rather they strive to challenge the oppositional encounters of exclusionary politics through removing the external limits of political community. This, however, fails to acknowledge that limits of some sort play a constitutive role in the formation of political community.

While a human rights approach differs from open borders in terms of its specific relevance to asylum, it similarly remains limited in its ability to critically challenge the exclusionary politics of asylum. It is, of course, important to note that legal recourse to human rights is practically useful in challenging the abjectification of asylum seekers. However, human rights cases tend to ameliorate the excesses of exclusionary politics, more than moving in a direction of effectively challenging their operations. Moreover, human rights are particularly problematic when they are framed as a challenge to abjectification *qua* dehumanisation, rather than as a challenge to abjectification *qua* depoliticisation. It is where human rights are developed in 'anti-territorial' humanitarian terms that they are particularly limiting, because it is here that asylum seekers are reconstituted as 'vulnerable' or 'threatened' subjects without political voice. As Jacques Rancière (2004) suggests, this humanitarian rendering of human rights profoundly disempowers and depoliticises abject subjects, who are conceived of as the apolitical 'victims' of a territorial order.

From a Rancièrian perspective, it is only when human rights are claimed by a politicised abject that the disruptive conditions for a movement beyond an exclusionary politics of differential inclusion are created (see Isin and Nielsen, 2008). However, this requires more than an individualised politicisation based on a 'misplaced' demand for legal rights. It also requires a political act of solidarity in which those with and without a part of the territorial political community engage with one another in relations of mutual contention. This requires a wider social mobilisation than human rights claims alone entail. As the analysis in Chapter 7 shows, the actions of the *No Borders* and the *No One Is Illegal* movements can be interpreted as examples of such mobilisations. Human rights claims may feature within such political engagements, but only if they form part of a wider mobilisation in which contending relations of mutuality are created that critically intercede the exclusionary politics of differential inclusion. It is in this direction that this analysis moves in rethinking asylum in terms of a mobile political engagement through which citizenship can potentially be reframed in interruptive post-territorial terms.[2]

Creating mobile solidaristic relations

Like human rights and open borders advocates, this book attempts to challenge the exclusionary politics of asylum by moving beyond a territorial political frame of reference. However, in contrast to many human rights and open borders advocates, it does not simply conceive such a move in terms of a removal of border controls or in terms of the assertion of basic rights for all humans. Rather, it suggests that any move in an 'inclusionary' direction requires the development of contending political engagements that take mobility seriously; engagements that critically intercede in the exclusionary politics of differential inclusion whereby some mobile subjects are inscribed as 'desirable' only for others to be inscribed as 'undesirable', 'culpable' and 'threatening'. Specifically, it conceives these engagements in terms of mobilisations that create 'misplaced' political relations through a range of mobile social and economic engagements that transgress the limits of a territorial frame (Aradau, Huysmans and Squire, forthcoming). While human rights and open borders advocates draw attention to the way in which the territorial frame might be exceeded through a global reframing of political community, they do not adequately consider how taking mobility seriously can critically interrupt the reactionary relations and depoliticising operations that this book has shown to be central to the exclusionary politics of asylum. Any 'inclusionary' alternative to an exclusionary politics of differential inclusion requires a critical interruption of a reactionary, depoliticising and divisive politics in order that the 'constitutive outside' is neither objectified nor reactively reinscribed along new lines. This entails a distinctly political and a continuously mobile re-enactment of citizenship and asylum.

While this analysis suggests that the tendency to reconstruct political community in exclusionary terms will always exist (particularly under conditions of dislocation), it is important to note that exclusionary politics are *not* inevitable under *any* conditions. Rather, the mediation of disruption and turbulence at the limits of any political community can take various forms. This book suggests that limits are denied and avoided where an exclusionary politics are dominant, and that political engagements are replaced by oppositional encounters. By approaching limits as constitutive, however, this analysis has pointed to an alternative mediation of limits that emerges where acts of solidarity bring those 'with a part' of the political community in a relation of mutual contention with those who have 'no-part' (Rancière, 1999; see Chapter 7). From a discourse theoretical perspective, this focus on mutual contention is indicative of a movement beyond a 'radical democractic' alternative that a return to the 'logic of difference' would entail (Mouffe, 1996; see Chapter 2). A radical democratic alternative importantly focuses attention of the pluralisation of political space (Laclau and Mouffe, 2001), but risks being pulled back into political community's imperative of closure if it is simply conceived of in terms of plural identities. By focusing on solidaristic relations of mutual engagement, this analysis thus moves to consider how mobility can be mobilised in the very mediation of limits.

Such a reading of the solidaristic mediation of limits entails two interrelated moves, both of which are decidedly political. The first move is one that takes us out of the realm of political community and into the realm of citizenship acts. This entails a distinction between citizenship as a governmental technology (Hindess, 1998) and citizenship as a mode of disruptive claims-making (Isin and Nielson, 2008). Both of these dimensions emerge in a relation of constitutive tension with one another in the construction of governance and belonging. However, the former can be conceived in ideological terms in relation to the imperative of closure, while the latter can be conceived in creative terms as associated with the constitution of political and politicised subjects (Isin, 2008). It is in thinking citizenship according to the latter framework that this book conceives the possibility for the creation of solidaristic relations. Indeed, by starting with an analysis of citizenship acts we are able to explore how 'mis-placed' acts of claims- and obligations-making effectively break with the exclusionary relations of differential inclusion that have become increasingly sedimented and embedded over time. Re-sedimentations will, of course, always occur, but these do not have to be of the oppositional form that this analysis has shown to be the case in relation to asylum. Nor do they have to be of the assimilative form that emerges in relation to 'desirable' migration (Squire, 2005). Rather, it would seem that the building of *mobility* into the discursive and institutional operations of political community might effectively preclude a totalising closure. Specifically, it can do so by embedding engagements of mutual contention at the limit as alternatives to the reactive and divisive encounters that are characterised by opposition and denial. This requires both a rethinking and re-enactment of governance and belonging in creative and dynamic terms.

This is related to a second move, which takes us out of the realm of managerialism and into the realm of politics. Managerial operations are depoliticising on various counts. They are depoliticising in terms of their technical operational, and they are depoliticising in terms of their dispersion (extensive and intensive) throughout the discursive and institutional social fabric. Indeed, they are depoliticising in their naturalisation and normalisation of an exclusionary politics of differential inclusion, through which a separation of the 'desirable' from the 'undesirable' is put beyond debate. The analysis in this book suggests that it is these processes of depoliticisation that are the most troubling dimension of an exclusionary politics of asylum. What the analysis has also shown, however, is that exclusionary politics are not pre-given or handed down 'from above'. Technical operations are highly regulated, but they are also carried out by *people* who have the potential to become political beings through 'misplaced' claims and obligations. In this regard, the engagement of solidaristic relations of mutual contention at the level of technical operation can potentially have a disruptive effect. To engage such relations is highly challenging, as is the process of creating the conditions for such relations to occur. However, what this analysis of the exclusionary interactions of technical and narrative operations suggests is that the cycle might be critically interrupted or turned around by various means, whether at the level of political or popular debate *or* at the level of technical regulation. Indeed, it can be broken in numerous daily actions. Political dialogue, it would seem, can be opened up through solidaristic engagements *anywhere* and at *anytime*.

So where does this leave us in terms of the rethinking of citizenship? At a philosophical level, we are left with a specifically mobile 'post-territorial' conception of citizenship based on acts of solidarity. At a practical level, we are left with various disruptive possibilities that require discursive and institutional embedding. One potential site that is fertile ground for such contending movements is Europe. Various critical analysts have pointed to the potential of the European Union as a space of post-national citizenship (Habermas, 1992, 1998; Soysal, 1994). This interest in Europe often rests on its discursive institutionalisation of citizenship in terms of mobility. Citizenship within the EU is founded on a constitutive tension between free movement or mobility and nationality or territoriality, and this opens up a range of possibilities for the mobilisation around mobility (Aradau, Huysmans and Squire, forthcoming). The (partial) institutionalisation of European citizenship in terms of free movement renders the disruptive claims of mobile subjects uniquely positioned in terms of their potential to produce a more sustained and far-reaching interruption of an exclusionary territorial order. While the analysis in Chapter 3 draws attention to the way in which attempts to constitute the EU as a political community have relied on an exclusionary politics, a critical rereading of Europe as a dynamic, moving and highly contested space of mobility draws attention to its potential for the political re-enactment of citizenship in terms that move beyond an exclusionary politics. After all, if mobility is at the heart of European citizenship, then disruptive mobilisations of exclusionary territorial politics potentially find a discursive and institutional foothold in the shifting space of the European Union.

How, then, does this mobile reworking of citizenship facilitate a rethinking of asylum? This book suggests that a distinctly *mobile* discursive and institutional re-enactment of citizenship based on solidaristic relations facilitates the engagement of asylum seekers as political subjects. Specifically, it entails a rethinking of asylum in relation to political engagements of *mutual contention*, which create solidaristic relations between asylum seekers and various others in distinctly mobile terms. Let us consider this further. Mutual contention can refer to a complex range of political engagements, but at base comes down to a constitutive tension between contestation and solidarity, or between disagreement and equality (Rancière, 1999). This tension can be conceived of as mitigating against exclusionary politics, which entail oppositional relations that preclude the political engagement required to come together in solidaristic relations of contestation. An example in this regard is evident in the analysis in Chapter 7, which pointed to solidaristic relations of mutual contestation that are constituted between irregular migrants and citizens against exclusionary politics. It is in framing these solidaristic relations in terms of mobility, rather than territoriality, that this book conceives the potential for the institution of a more dynamic relation between solidarity and contestation at the limits of political community. This potentially mitigates against an exclusionary politics of asylum by ensuring that reactionary and divisive politics are always open to question.

Where, then, is this more 'inclusionary' reading of asylum left? It is located, it would seem, in a distinctly political position. What the analysis in this book does *not* signal is the end of reactionary politics. Reactionary politics will always emerge in various guises, along with all its depoliticising and divisive tendencies. However, this analysis does signal the possibility of a political re-enactment of asylum that effectively interrupts a discursively sedimented and institutionally embedded exclusionary politics; a politics that is put *beyond question*. In short, an inclusionary alternative opens the ground for political dialogue and engagement so that alternative renderings of asylum come into contact with one another through relations of mutual contention. Solidaristic relations are not necessarily marked by agreement, in this regard, but they are marked by mutual acceptance. Moving beyond exclusionary politics is, in other words, fraught with difficulties and entails engagements that many of us might prefer not to have. What the analysis in this book suggests, however, is that such engagements are a necessary dimension of a dynamic social life that, if avoided through denial and opposition, take us to a realm that many would describe as inhuman. This book interprets such a realm as apolitical, and focuses attention to the potential that we all have in critically interceding exclusionary politics on a daily basis. The asylum seeker, in this analysis, is not reduced to the position of an apolitical abject *qua* asylum-seeker-cum-illegal-immigrant. Rather, s/he is a political subject *qua* irregular migrant who, in his/her engagements, reminds us that we are *all* mobile subjects of one kind or another.

Conclusion

In drawing a long journey to a close, this chapter has opened the door to a mobile citizenship. A post-territorial rethinking of governance and belonging, it has suggested, can be conceived of as engaging citizenship in mobile terms through solidaristic acts in mutual contention of an exclusionary politics that denies us all political agency. This does not signal the end of the state or the nation, nor does it signal the end of reactionary politics. What it does signal, however, is the interruption of an exclusionary politics that has become both discursively sedimented and institutionally embedded at the political, popular, public and technical levels. So why is it so pressing that we critically intercede in such a politics? There are various reasons. If we are committed to refugee protection, as it is so often said that we are, this book tells us that something needs to change. If we are committed to political dialogue over reactionary politics and managerial operations, this book also tells us that something needs to change. Even if we resist both refugee protection and political dialogue, this book tells us that something has to change. Indeed, it already has. The story that this book has told is not simply one of an exclusionary politics, but is also one of various mobile operations that take us beyond the territorial order. Whether a mobile (dis)order worries or excites us, it is an order of our own making. To blame the asylum seeker for its limitations is thus wrong.

Rather than detailing normative prescriptions or policy suggestions as an alternative to the exclusionary politics of asylum, this book has developed a specifically political answer to the question of what we can do in order to move asylum discourse in a more 'inclusionary' direction. By taking mobility seriously, it has attempted to contribute to the process of creating a more open space in which politically engaged asylum seekers are able play an active role in the construction of a post-territorial order. It is in rethinking citizenship in terms of mobility that the potential for this engagement emerges, allowing for dialogues and enactments that do not become caught in the reactionary cycle of the exclusionary politics that have been charted throughout the course of this book. This repoliticisation not only mitigates against the securitisation and criminalisation of those who are positioned at the limits of political community, but so also does it entail a repoliticisation of those that are pushed beyond its limits as abjects. In this regard, it potentially intercedes in the repoliticisation of asylum seeking from a radically new direction. Whether we take on this challenge with courage or shy away in fear is a personal decision that has (a)social and (a)political effects. How we take on this challenge is dependent on our position and locale, and thus remains mobile. What the analysis in this book suggests is that we are all mobile social actors whose words, actions and organisations have far-reaching effects. It is thus by politically engaging others in mutual contention that we can speak, out and mobilise in terms that effectively challenge an exclusionary politics; a politics that is simultaneously reactionary, depoliticising and divisive, both in its operation and in its effect.

Appendices

Appendix 1

Interviews[1]

Interview 1: Individual interview with the Project Manager of the original Project IMMpact in BiH and of IMMpact 2 in Serbia and Montenegro, carried out at the Immigration and Nationality Directorate Intelligence Service, London, November 2003.

Interview 2: Group interview with two UK immigration officers seconded from the Home Office to the European Union Police Mission (EUPM), both of whom were directly or indirectly involved with the project, and one of whom was a member of the original IMMpact team, carried out in Sarajevo, August 2003.

Appendix 2

Interview data[2]

Service providers

Individual interview 1: A senior local authority housing manager involved with the provision of support to dispersed asylum seekers. Carried out in April 2005.

Individual interview 2: A local authority asylum support worker. Carried out in February 2005.

Individual interview 3: A regional manager responsible for supporting dispersed asylum seekers in Birmingham through a private provider. Carried out in June 2005.

Asylum seekers/refugees

Individual interview 4: 'SUSANNE': A female asylum seeker from Cameroon who was dispersed from Kent to Birmingham 2003, who is housed in privately managed accommodation, and is receiving NASS support. Carried out in April 2005.

Individual interview 5: 'GUY': A male refugee from the Democratic Republic of Congo who was housed in an emergency accommodation in Birmingham for two months, who has lived in Birmingham on receiving refugee status since that time and who *works as a crisis support worker at a voluntary organisation supporting asylum seekers.* Carried out in May 2005.

Individual interview 6: 'P': A male asylum seeker with dual citizenship (Congolese and Ivory Coast) who was housed in an emergency accommodation in Birmingham during 2001 before being supported intermittently by NASS in publicly managed dispersal accommodation, and who *volunteers with a local organisation in Birmingham that supports asylum seekers and refugees.* Carried out in April 2005.

Group interview 1:

'ROCKY': A male asylum seeker from Congo Brazzaville who was supported in an emergency accommodation by NASS in Birmingham during 2004 and is supported by social services in Birmingham. Carried out in April 2005.

'DAVID': A male refugee from Angola who was dispersed from an emergency accommodation in Birmingham to dispersal accommodation in Manchester during 2004 and who lives in Birmingham. Carried out in April 2005.

'JOHN': A male refugee from Congo Brazzaville who was dispersed from emergency accommodation in London to privately managed dispersal accommodation in Newcastle during 2003 and who lives in Birmingham. Carried out in April 2005.

Group interview 2:

'ABBAS': A male asylum seeker from Iraq who has reached end of process without status, who was dispersed from London to Doncaster during 2000, who has lived in Birmingham for four years, and who has worked as a translator for asylum seekers since arriving in the region. Carried out in April 2005.

'ARI': A male Kurdish refugee from Iraq who came to the UK in 1998, who has lived in Birmingham for five years, and who has *worked for various organisations supporting asylum seekers on NASS support in and around the Birmingham area.* Carried out in April 2005.

Local community members

Group interview 3:

'REPRESENTATIVE 1': A female local community representative who was granted refugee status 15 years ago, and who lives and works in a key area of dispersal within Birmingham. Carried out in April 2005.

'REPRESENTATIVE 2': The male Vice Chairman of a local community association, a refugee community group which has been established for approximately 20 years in a key area of dispersal in Birmingham. Carried out in April 2005.

Notes

1. A Dislocated Territorial Order? Introducing the Asylum 'Problem'

1. Indeed, it would seem to have taken on a new target in this context, namely one in which the Muslim (particularly, though by no means solely, the Muslim migrant) is articulated as the primary 'threat'.
2. The analysis in this book does not focus on anti-terrorism legislation specifically, but rather examines the way in which the narrative and technical articulation of asylum within a broad security frame entails processes of both securitisation *and* criminalisation that are indicative of an exclusionary politics.
3. The UK did not sign up to the original Convention, but does opt to law-enforcement and judicial aspects of Schengen. It also participates in moves to integrate immigration and asylum policies, as we will see in Chapters 3 and 5.
4. The UK's focus on asylum can also be explained by historical factors, such as the UK's long-standing colonial ties with a range of countries from which asylum seekers originate. Such ties are likely to render the UK a more 'attractive' destination for those seeking refuge than destinations that do not have any ties with their home state, because it potentially provides existing community support structures and/or is more accessible in terms of language.

2. Challenging Managerial Operations: Developing a Discursive Theory of Securitisation

1. When Laclau and Mouffe state that negativity 'has gained a form of presence' they mean that the limit or antagonism is dealt with through a logic of equivalence, whereby a chain of differential terms become identical in their construction as the negative reverse to this 'external something' (2001:29). This is defined as a paratactical approach that constitutes popular subject positions through the simplistic division of political space into two antagonistic camps (2001:132-3).
2. This is defined as a differential approach that constitutes democratic subject positions and relegates division to the margins of society. Laclau and Mouffe suggest that 'there is a lessening of the charge of negativity attaching to the antagonism' where the logic of difference predominates (2001:132).

3. Moving to Europe: Charting the Emergence of Exclusionary Asylum Discourse

1. Castles and Miller suggest that the flow of migrants invited from Europe was 'not major' in the late 1940s and early 1950s and that colonial workers were

seen as more convenient in terms of labour recruitment practices after 1951 (1998:68). Nevertheless, if we take into consideration Hayter's separation of Irish immigration from colonial immigration, it is perhaps possible to reconcile what would initially appear to be conflicting readings.

2. The 1962 Commonwealth Immigration Act re-devised categories of British passport holders and introduced work vouchers.

3. The 1968 Commonwealth Immigration Act increased control over UK passport holders who were not (or whose grandparent or parent were not) born, adopted or naturalised in the UK, while the 1969 Immigration Appeals Act enforced stricter restrictions and introduced the legal requirement for entry certificates.

4. Randall Hansen suggests that the UK's response over the Ugandan Asian 'crisis' under the then Prime Minister Edward Heath is evidence of the ongoing relevance of a liberal politics.

5. This Act revised the colonial system of categorisation, which was replaced by the categories of 'patrials' (who were free from restrictions) and 'non-patrials' (who, whether from the Commonwealth or not, were subject to immigration controls). Patrials were defined as British or Commonwealth citizens who were born or naturalised in the UK or who had a parent – or a grandparent in the case of British citizens – who were born or naturalised in the UK. The category also included British or Commonwealth citizens who had settled in the UK for five years and had registered or applied to register as British citizens. What this meant in effect was that citizenship criteria became biased and in line with migration controls (Spencer, 1997:143).

6. While this book conceives the 1971 legislation as a continuation of the exclusionary politics, Hansen and King (2000:399) argue that this legislation signals a racist turn in the UK's tradition of citizenship, with the 1971 Act effectively excluding British subjects from 'New' Commonwealth countries in Asia and Africa over those from 'Old' Commonwealth countries with largely white populations, such as Canada and Australia.

7. This articulation of illegal immigration as a target for controls intensified rapidly, particularly from 1989–92 through the Trevi group. Trevi drew up four key documents during this period. First, the Palma Document, agreed in 1989, described as 'essential action' a system of surveillance and control at external frontiers; the improved cooperation and exchange of information; and the 'combating illegal immigration networks'. Second, the 1989 Declaration of Trevi group Ministers set out principles of free movement while mapping four areas of cooperation for 'public order and internal security' (including the introduction of external frontier controls). Third, the 1990 Programme of Action noted 'clandestine immigration networks' and the 'identification of [unwanted] aliens' as an area needing cooperation. Finally, the 1992 Palma Report set out a progress report including a focus on action at 'external borders' and at 'internal frontiers' (Bunyan, 1993:195–6).

8. The External Borders Convention never reached the signature stage due to contention between Spain and the UK over Gibralta. The Dublin Convention was signed in 1990 and came into force for signatories (including the UK) in 1997. It was designed to ensure that asylum seekers only claim asylum in one member state, and has since been revised as the Dublin II Regulation in order to ensure that asylum seekers claim asylum in the first place of entrance.

9. The UK did, however, participate in an international Ad Hoc Group on Immigration on which the European Community sat as a member. Set up in 1986 in order to 'end abuses of the asylum process', the group proposed a raft of measures between 1987 and 1992 that included sanctions on airlines carrying illegal immigrants, the finger printing of asylum seekers, and the development of criteria for 'manifestly unfounded' claims (Webber, 1993:144). In participating in an international forum it would seem that asylum and illegal immigration were opposed by the UK in strictly state-centric terms, with the development of European controls resisted at this time. The European Commission (EC) had no recognised competence to deal with immigration and asylum issues during this period and the group operated under international rather than EC law. The Ad Hoc Group was replaced as the 1992 Maastricht Treaty of the European Union (EU) took force from November 1993, as competency was granted to the EU.

10. The UK announced its decision to 'opt-in' to parts of the Schengen acquis and parts of the Free movement Chapter at the meeting of the Justice and Home Affairs Council in Brussels on 12 March 1999. The then UK Home Secretary Jack Straw said the UK would maintain its frontier controls, specifically covered in a Protocol in the Amsterdam Treaty.

11. At the time of writing, the Draft (partial) Immigration and Citizenship Bill, 2008 was under consideration.

12. In this respect, Amsterdam was of importance in at least two ways. Firstly, it initiated a shift in institutional power from the Heads of the member states within the European Council towards the EC, with the latter given the sole right to propose asylum and immigration legislation. It also provided the EU with several legislative instruments not requiring procedures of national ratification. Secondly, Amsterdam was important in terms of articulating the need for *common* asylum and immigration policies, with the Treaty stipulating that these were necessary in developing the Union as an area of 'freedom, security and justice' for 'Europe's citizens and legal long-term residents'. The future of the pillar system remains, at the time of writing, uncertain in light of the wider uncertainty surrounding institutional reform.

13. These include legislation regarding 'rules governing which Member state is responsible for considering the application for asylum by each asylum-seeker in the EU; minimum rules on reception conditions for asylum-seekers; minimum rules on procedures for considering applications for asylum; minimum rules on the definition of "refugee"; minimum rules on "temporary protection"; minimum rules on "subsidiary protection"; and illegal immigration'.

14. This is based on Article 33 of the Geneva Convention with regard to the prohibition of expulsion or return. This article states that '1. No Contracting State shall expel or return ("refouler") a refugee in any manner whatsoever to the frontiers of territories where his life or freedom would be threatened on account of his race, religion, nationality, membership of a particular social group or political opinion. 2. The benefit of the present provision may not, however, be claimed by a refugee whom there are reasonable grounds for regarding as a danger to the security of the country in which he is, or who, having been convicted by a final judgement of a particularly serious crime, constitutes a danger to the community of that country'.

The term 'reasonable grounds for regarding' in the second statement here is, of course, crucial in terms of the deportation of suspected terrorists in the post-11-September context (UNHCR [1951]).

15. Franco Frattini stepped down as Commissioner in 2008 and was replaced by Jacques Barrot.

4. Restricting Contestations: Exclusionary Narratives and the Dominance of Restriction

1. The analysis is based on newspaper articles that were generated over a week-long period during the run up to the 2005 election, specifically those produced by two broadsheets and two tabloids from opposite ends of the political spectrum: *The Independent* and *The Mirror* towards the Left, and *The Telegraph* and *The Mail* towards the Right. The period chosen (from 6th–12th February 2005 inclusive) coincides with the presentation of the five-year plan on 7th February 2005. The search was carried out using the Lexis Nexis (Executive) database of news stories. Stories containing 'asylum' or 'immigration' from the specified papers were included in the sample, which was initially narrowed down through discarding articles that only referenced asylum or immigration in passing. Foreign news stories were also discarded from the analysis. This left a total of 78 articles. In the interest of space we only include, in the Bibliography, those texts that are directly referenced.

2. It is important to note that the analysis in this chapter remains suggestive rather than conclusive. Nevertheless, although it is not possible to make more general claims regarding the extent to which there is a convergence of party political responses to asylum or a dominance of anti-asylum narratives within political and popular debate based on this analysis alone, an indication as to the direction in which party political discourse is heading can be drawn from statements during election campaigns. This is particularly the case given the heightened political nature of the issue during such periods, although care does need to be taken to contextualise such an analysis.

3. A coalition of organisations including Save the Children UK, Bail for Immigration Detainees, the Refugee Council, the Scottish Refugee Council and the Welsh Refugee Council set up the 'no place for a child' campaign in 2006 following the publishing of various reports by the Chief Inspector of Prisons in 2005 and the Children's Commissioner report on Yarlswood in December 2005.

4. Tony Blair took personal responsibility for the issue of asylum, and in February 2003 pledged to cut asylum applications by 30–40 per cent 'in the next few months' and to halve them by September 2003.

5. This decision was later defended by the High Court. Two High Court rulings have been made in this case, the first claiming that the deportation of the Afghans would threaten their safety and the more recent claiming that they should be able to remain in the UK. A subsequent ruling by the Court of Appeal rejected the government's attempt to impose temporary admission status on the individuals, which would effectively deny them freedoms such as the right to work and to receive travel documents.

6. This measure was announced in March 2006, resulting in outrage in the welfare sector.

7. For example, the then General Secretary of the Transport and General Workers Union Bill Morris expressed concerns regarding accommodation centres on 1 October 2002, while the Lords added a clause within the bill stating that accommodation centres must be situated in a 'suitable' area.

8. This move would also seem to reflect the fact that there has recently been decreasing numbers of asylum applications, with spaces available in dispersal accommodation across the country.

9. For example, Section 55 prompted the tabling of an early day motion by the Labour backbencher Lynne Jones on its implementation in January 2003, as well as a joint statement of opposition from housing and welfare charities. This included the following organisations: The Refugee Council, Shelter, Amnesty International UK, Asylum Rights Campaign, Crisis, Jewish Council for Racial Equality (JCORE), the Joint Council for the Welfare of Immigrants (JCWI), Maternity Alliance, Medical Foundation for the Care of Victims of Torture, Migrant Helpline, Oxfam, Refugee Action and Refugee Arrivals Project (Refugee Council, 2003).

10. Local authorities and social workers were concerned regarding their role in implementing the policy, while groups such as the Refugee Children's Consortium lobbied against the measure during the passage of the Act. Members of this consortium are as follows: The Asphaelia Project, Bail for Immigration Detainees, Barnardos, British Association for Adoption and Fostering (BAAF), Children's Rights Alliance for England, The Children's Society, The Immigration Law Practitioners' Association (ILPA), The Medical Foundation for the Care of Victims of Torture, NCB, NCH, Refugee Council, Refugee Arrivals Project, and Save the Children UK. The British Red Cross, UNICEF UK and UNHCR have observer status.

11. This follows the UK's reaffirmation of its commitment to the Convention alongside over 80 other states in December 2001.

12. Indeed, the extreme right-wing party, the British National Party, was alone in calling for 'an immediate halt to all further immigration' in 2005 (BNP, 2005).

13. In 2005 the party changes its emphasis from the progressive movement to a more open response by stressing that migration is a right only 'as far as is practical' (Green Party, 2005b).

14. The analysis in this section focuses on party political and press texts produced during the 2005 campaign in particular.

15. While some of these representations emerge in letters pages (e.g. the 'strain on the infrastructure) or a part of a critique of right-wing discourse (e.g. the 'deluge'), it is nevertheless clear that a popular discourse of the asylum 'threat' or 'problem' is relatively widespread.

5. Interception as Criminalisation: The Extension of Interdictive 'external' Controls

1. As a co-operative EU initiative led by the UK, Project IMMpact was largely funded by domestic immigration agencies. At any one time, six or seven full-time UK immigration officers from the Home Office's Immigration Service worked on the project, these being joined on a temporary basis by delegates

'from seven EU member states' (INDIS, 2003). In this respect, the initiative serves as a good example of an interceptive initiative that extends both EU and domestic control through interception.

2. The project continued in Serbia and Montenegro until December 2003. This extension of the project's remit is said to reflect the difficulties that BiH had, as a new state, in controlling its international border of 1600 km and its 432 crossings (SFOR, 2002a).

3. A range of development-migration programmes have been set up by the EU over recent years. For example, the Balkans Community Assistance for Reconstruction, Development and Stabilisation (CARDS) regional programme involves Albania, Bosnia and Herzegovina, Croatia, Federal Republic of Yugoslavia (FRY), and Former Yugoslav Republic of Macedonia (FYROM). Requiring the participation of countries involved with the Stabilisation and Association Process (SAP), the aim is to foster regional cooperation within the realm of Justice and Home Affairs (see Samers, 2004).

4. Frontex has budgetry and operational autonomy and, although its budget is not huge (€42 million in 2007) it has increased each year thus far. While the UK only participates in Frontex-organised joint operations on a case-by-case basis, its commitment to the development of EU border controls is evident in its position as host of a related *ad hoc* centre for control and surveillance technologies (Wolf, 2008). The way in which EU border controls develop under Frontex remains to be seen, but what is evident at this stage is that intergovernmental co-operation remains the preferred norm of many of the member states. As Sarah Wolf (2008) suggests, in the light of an 'unwillingness to create a European Corps of Border Guards like the European Commission initially proposed' some 'member states sought to lower their transaction costs and through Frontex to opt for the less integrationist solution'. Although it may signal a move towards a more supranational approach to border control (Neal, 2009), Frontex thus largely continues a co-operative model of EU border controls that was initiated on a more *ad hoc* basis by projects such as IMMpact.

5. It may be more appropriate to conceive deterrence as composed of distinct intertwined rationalities (preventative and eliminative), rather than a single rationality that brings these two dimensions together. This requires further consideration than can be developed here, however. Rather, this book focuses on how these dimensions come together as part of a wider exclusionary politics.

6. Indeed, a more detailed analysis of technical processes of securitisation and criminalisation would need to go further than this book can in examining this two-way process.

7. Notably, SIS II is one element of the Schengen *acquis* to which the UK has 'opted-in'.

8. Examples in this regard are the statistical office, Eurostat; the Centre for Information, Discussion and Exchange on the Crossing of Frontiers and Immigration (Cirefi); and the Centre for Information, Discussion and Exchange on Asylum (Cirea), which has more recently been replaced by a network of experts known as Eurasil.

9. The UK has enthusiastically contributed to this network. In 2003, for example, the then British Immigration Minister Beverley Hughes (2003) claimed that in the Balkans region 'the UK has posted nine Immigration Liaison Officers

to disrupt trafficking and organised immigration crime'. This delegation, she said, is overseen by the domestic multiagency Project Reflex that was set up in 2000 and which (1) coordinates enforcement through intelligence and strategic planning; (2) is led by the National Crime Squad; and (3) has close organisation links with Europol (which houses a 'dedicated UK liaison officer').

10. The European Union Police Mission (EUPM) took over from the post-war IPTF from 1st January 2003, and was the first EU operation carried out under the European Security and Defence Policy (ESDP), launched by the British Prime Minister and President Chirac in December 1998. Project IMMpact can be directly linked to this body in terms of its personnel, with at least one British immigration officer from the project having been seconded from the Home Office to the EUPM since it was set up. This crossover of personnel is also evident in terms of the EUPM, Project IMMpact and a joint British–Romanian project known as Reflex Romania, with the same leader heading the latter two projects and with at least one British immigration officer involved with Reflex Romania having been seconded from the Home Office to the EUPM. A crossover of personnel between policing and immigration agencies is particularly telling in terms of the institutional and technical analysis of securitisation and criminalisation in the first part of this chapter.

11. In 2001 there were 6805 Iraqi, 3740 Turkish, 2810 Pakistani and 2415 Chinese asylum applicants in the UK. From 'Asylum statistics 2001', accessed at the Refugee Council at http://www.refugeecouncil.org.uk/downloads/stats/summary_2001.pdf on 16.6.2006.

12. The author is indebted to Sandro Mezzadra for drawing attention to the innovative term 'pre-emptive refoulement'. Refoulement refers here to the return of refugees or irregular migrants to persecution. It thus draws on the term *non-refoulement*, which was introduced in the 1951 Refugee Convention in order to ensure that those seeking refuge are not returned to persecution.

6. Dispersal as Abjectification: The Diffusion of Punitive 'internal' Controls

1. These include Greater London, South West, South East and Central, East of England, East Midlands, West Midlands, North West, Yorkshire and Humberside, North East, Wales, Scotland and Northern Ireland.

2. It is important to acknowledge that dispersal has often been developed in pragmatic terms according to the availability of accommodation, as much according to the principle of dilution. Dispersal was initially introduced according to a 'clustering' model in order to facilitate the provision of services to groups of asylum seekers and in order to locate asylum seekers in regions that were already successful in integrating ethnic minorities (see Pearl and Zetter, 2002:235). However, the clustering approach faced significant difficulties (Home Office, 2001:12), and was limited both by the development of dispersal according to the availability of cheap accommodation as well as by the abandonment of plans to house asylum seekers in rural accommodation

centres in the face of significant opposition by local communities (sees Hubbard, 2004; Malloch and Stanley, 2005).
3. Out of those interviewed, three of the asylum seekers who arrived in the South East were dispersed after approximately one month, while those three who arrived in Birmingham spent longer periods of four, five and eight months in emergency accommodation. This would seem to be a fairly common experience, with one public sector asylum support worker claiming that 'it is not uncommon for people to be in there for months, or even at one point years' (Individual interview 1, Appendix 2).
4. A failure to recognise P on the system was a problem highlighted here, with support being stopped without notification and with forms not registered as being received despite P having faxed them several times.

7. Sovereign Power, Abject Spaces and Resistance: Contending Accounts of Asylum

1. See www.noii.org.uk
2. In this book, Laclau and Mouffe's 'radical democractic' approach is important to, but insufficient in, challenging the exclusionary politics of asylum. Specifically, the pluralisation of political space is necessary to an 'inclusionary' mobile alternative, but it does not go far enough in challenging the reactive and depoliticising processes to which this analysis draws attention. (see Chapter 8).

8. Rethinking Asylum, Rethinking Citizenship: Moving Beyond Exclusionary Politics

1. The critique of the exclusionary territorial renderings of the sovereign state is inseparable from the critique of the exclusionary territorial renderings of the liberal state. From the perspective developed in this book, the two can be analysed at the same time. Nevertheless, a more careful distinction between the territorial and the liberal state may be important in critically thinking beyond exclusionary politics towards post-territorial citizenship. This book only has the scope to offer a preliminary introduction here.
2. The author is heavily indebted to her colleagues at the Open University for the argument developed in this section, much of which draws on provocative discussions the group has had surrounding issues of citizenship and mobility. In particular, thanks are extended to Rutvica Andrijasevic, Claudia Aradau, Jef Huysmans, Engin Isin and Mike Saward, for their numerous invigorating conversations on these themes.

Appendices

1. All interviews were undertaken without the use of recording material on the request of the interviewees. Notes were made during the interviews and these were supplemented with additional notes directly following the interviews.

As such all referencing of interview material may be replicated in slightly different wording as was originally the case. All interviewees were asked as to how they would like to be referred to in order to ensure their anonymity if required, and instructions have been followed as agreed.

2. All interviewees were asked as to how they would like to be referred to in order to ensure their anonymity if required, and instructions have been followed as agreed. All of the asylum seekers interviewed were asked to provide a false name, and are identified by this throughout the analysis.

Bibliography

Agamben, G. (1994), 'We refugees' (Trans. Michael Rocke), http://www.egs.edu/faculty/agamben/agamben-we-refugees.html, accessed on 15 August 2006.

Agamben, G. (1997), 'The camp as nomos of the modern', in H. de Vries and S. Weber (Eds), *Violence, Identity and Self-determination* (Stanford: Stanford University Press).

Agamben, G. (1998), *Homo Sacer: Sovereign Power and Bare Life*. (Trans. Daniel heller-Roazen) (Stanford: Stanford University Press).

Agamben, G. (2005), *State of Exception* (Chicago: University of Chicago Press).

Ahmed, S. (2004), *The Cultural Politics of Emotion* (London: Routledge).

Andrijasevic, R. (2009), *Sex Moves: Migration, Agency and Citizenship in Sex-Trafficking* (forthcoming).

Appadurai, A. (1996), *Modernity at Large: Cultural Dimensions of Globalisation* (Minneapolis: University of Minnesota Press).

Aradau, C. (2004a), 'Security and the democratic scene: Desecuritisation and emancipation', *Journal of International Relations and Development* 7, 388–413.

Aradau, C. (2004b), 'The perverse politics of four letter words: Risk and pity in the securitisation of human trafficking', *Millennium: Journal of International Studies* 33(2), 251–77.

Aradau, C. (2008), *Rethinking Trafficking in Women: Politics out of Security* (Basingstoke: Palgrave Macmillan).

Aradau, C. and van Munster, R. (2007), 'Governing terrorism through risk: Taking precautions (un)knowing the future', *European Journal of International Relations* 13(1), 89–115.

Aradau, C. and van Munster, R. (2008), 'Security, technologies of risk, and the political', *Security Dialogue* 39(2–3), 147–54.

Aradau, C. Huysmans, J. and Squire, V. (forthcoming), 'Acts of European citizenship: From a politics of integration to a politics of mobility', *International Studies Association*, February 2009.

Ashley, R. (1988), 'Untying the sovereign state: A double reading of the anarchy problematique', *Millennium: Journal of International Studies* 17(2), 227–62.

Audit Commission (2000), 'Another country: Implementing dispersal under the Immigration and Asylum Act 1999' (England and Wales: Audit Commission).

Austin, J. (1975), *How to do Things with Words* (Oxford: Oxford University Press).

Bail for Immigration Detainees (BID) (2008), *Briefing Paper on the Detained Fast-Track*, http://www.detention-in-europe.org/images/stories/bid%20briefing%20on%20uk%20fast%20track%20for%20asy%20skrs.pdf, accessed on 3 June 2008.

Balibar, E. and Wallerstein, I. (1991), *Race, Nation, Class: Ambiguous Identities* (London: Verso).

Balibar, E. (2002), *We, the People of Europe? Reflections on Transnational Citizenship* (Princeton, NJ: Princeton University Press).

Balzacq, T. (2008), 'The policy tools of securitization: Information, exchange, EU foreign and internal policies', *Journal of Common Market Studies* 46(1), 75–100.

Barnardos (2005), *The End of the Road*, www.barnardos.com (home page), accessed on 1 June 2006.

Bartleson, J. (1995), *A Genealogy of Sovereignty* (Cambridge: Cambridge University Press).

Bauman, Z. (1991), *Modernity and Ambivalence* (Cambridge: Polity Press).

BBC (2003), 'Ministers back down on asylum pledge', 10 February 2003, www.bbc.co.uk (home page), accessed on 15 August 2006.

BBC (2005), *Detention Undercover – The Real Story*, 2 March 2005, BBC1.

Bhabha, J. (1999), 'Belonging in Europe: Citizenship and post-national rights', *International Social Science Journal* 51(159), 11–23.

Bigo, D. (2000a), 'When two become one: Internal and external securitisations in Europe', in M. Kelstrup and M. C. Williams (Eds), *International Theory and the Politics of European Integration: Power, Security and Community*, London: Routledge, 171–204.

Bigo, D. (2000b), 'Liaison officers in Europe, new actors in the European security field', in Sheptycki et al. (Eds), *Issues in Transnational Policing*, London: Routledge, 66–99.

Bigo, D. (2002), 'Security and immigration: Toward a critique of the governmentality of unease', *Alternatives* 27, 63–92.

Bigo, D. (2004), 'Criminalisation of "migrants": The side effect of the will to control the frontiers and the Sovereign Illusion', in Barbara Bogusz, Ryszard Cholewinski, Adam Cygan and Erika Szyszczak (Eds), *Irregular Migration and Human Rights: Theoretical, European and International Perspectives* (Leiden, Martinus Nijhof Publishers), 61–92.

Bigo, D. (2005), 'Globalised-in-security: The field and the ban-opticon', in John Solomon and Naoki Sakai, *Translation, Philosophy and Colonial Difference*, Traces: A Multilingual Series of Cultural Theory (4) (Hong Kong: Hong Kong University Press), 109–57.

Bigo, D. and Tsoukala, A. (2006) (Eds), *The Illiberal Practices of Liberal States*, (Paris: L'Harmattan).

Blair, T. (2001), 'Prime minister's speech on Europe', presented to the European Research Institute (Birmingham University) on 23 November 2001, http://www.pm.gov.uk (home page), accessed on 2 August 2002.

Blair, T. (2002a), 'A clear course for Europe', presented on 28 November 2002 http://www.number-10.gov.uk (home page), accessed on 6 May 2003.

Blair, T. (2002b), House of Commons parliamentary debate 24 June 2002, Column 615, http://www.publications.parliament.uk/pa/cm/cmhansrd.htm on 21.5.2003, accessed on 2 August 2002.

Blair, T. (2005), 'Foreword to the five year strategy for immigration and asylum', *Controlling Our Borders: Making Migration Work for Britain*, February 2005. HMSO: Norwich, 5–6.

Bloch, A. (2000), 'A new era or more of the same? Asylum policy in the UK', *Journal of Refugee Studies* 13(1), 29–42.

Bloch, A. and Schuster, L. (2005), 'Asylum Policy under New Labour', *Benefits* 43(13:2), 115–18.

Blunkett, D. (2002), cited in Immigration and Nationality Directorate's latest information, 'UK proposals for EU common asylum and migration policy published', 12 June 2002. http://194.203.40.90/news.asp?NewsId=157&SectionId=1, accessed on 2 August 2002.

BMA (2002), British Medical Association Board of Science and Education, *Asylum Seekers: Meeting their Healthcare Needs*, www.bma.org.uk (home page), accessed on 15 August 2006.

Bohmer, C. and Shuman, A. (2007), 'Producing epistemologies of ignorance in the political asylum application process', *Identities* 14(5), 603–29.

Boswell, C. (2001), *Spreading the Costs of Asylum Seekers: A Critical Assessment of Dispersal Policies in Germany and the UK* (London: Anglo-German Foundation).

Boswell, C. (2003a), *European Migration Policies in Flux: Changing Patterns of Inclusion and Exclusion* (Oxford: Blackwell).

Boswell, C. (2003b), 'The external dimension of EU immigration and asylum policy', *International Affairs* 79(3), 619–38.

Boswell, C. (2003c), 'Burden-sharing in the European Union: Lessons from the German and UK experience', *Journal of Refugee Studies* 16(3), 316–35.

Boswell, C. (2007), 'Migration control in Europe after 9/11: Explaining the absence of securitisation', *Journal of Common Market Studies* 45(3), 589–610.

Boswell, C. (2008), 'Migration, security and legitimacy: Some reflections', in T. Givens, G. Freeman and D. Leal (Eds), *Immigration Policy and Security: U.S., European and Commonwealth Perspectives* (London: Routledge).

British National Party, the (BNP) (2005), 'What we stand for: Immigration – Time to say ENOUGH', www.bnp.org.uk (home page), accessed on 9 March 2005.

Brubaker, W. R. (1989), *Immigration and the Politics of Citizenship in Europe and North America* (New York: Rowman & Littlefield).

Bunyan, T. (1993), *Statewatching the New Europe: A Handbook on the European State* (London: Statewatch).

Butler, J. (2006), *Precarious Lives: The Powers of Mourning and Violence* (London: Verso).

Buzan, B., Wæver, O. and de Wilde, J. (1998), *Security: A New Framework of Analysis* (Boulder: Lynne Reiner).

Campbell, D. (1992), *Writing Security* (Manchester: Manchester University Press).

Campbell, D. (1998), *National Deconstruction: Violence, Identity and Justice in Bosnia* (Minnesota: Minnesota University Press).

Carens, J. (1987), 'Aliens and citizens: The case for open borders', *The Review of Politics* 49(2), 251–73.

c.a.s.e. collective (2006), 'Critical approaches to security in Europe: A networked manifesto', in *Security Dialogue* 37(4), 443–87.

Castles, S. and Davidson, A. (2000), *Citizenship and Migration: Globalisation and the Politics of Belonging* (Basingstoke: Palgrave Macmillan).

Castles, S. and Miller, M. (1998), *The Age of Migration* (2nd edn) (Basingstoke: Palgrave Macmillan).

Cesarani, D. (1996), *Citizenship, Nationality and Migration in Europe* (Routledge: London).

Church of England (2006), 'Rich-poor divide a disgrace, says church report', www.ekklesia.co.uk (home page), accessed on 1 June 2006.

Clarke, C. (2005), 'Foreword to the five year strategy for immigration and asylum' *Controlling Our Borders: Making Migration Work for Britain*, February 2005. HMSO: Norwich, 7–8.

Clarke, J. and Neuman, J. (1997), *The Managerial State: Power, Politics and Ideology in the Re-making of Social Welfare* (London: Sage).

Cohen, R. (1994), *Frontiers of Identity: The British and the Others* (London: Longman).

Collyer, M. (2005), 'Secret agents: Anarchists, Islamists, and politically active refugees in London', *Journal of Ethnic and Migration Studies* 28, 278–303.

Conservative Party (2001), *The Conservative General Election Party Manifesto* (The Conservative Party).

Conservative Party (2005), *The Conservative Party General Election Manifesto* (The Conservative Party).

Crawley, H. (2005), 'Europe: Fortress or refuge?', *Forced Migration Review* 23, 14–16.

Crisp, J. (2003), 'A new asylum paradigm? Globalisation, migration and the uncertain future of the international refugee regime', *New Issues in Refugee Research*, Working Paper No. 100, UNHCR.

Cuneen, C. (2000), *Conflict, Politics and Crime* (Crows Nest: Allen and Unwin).

Daily Mail, The (2005a), 'I work hard and I can't understand why more Scots don't', article by Graham Grant, p.21, 9 February 2005.

Daily Mail, The (2005b), '"Trickle" that became a torrent', article by Matthew Hickley, p.21, 10 February 2005.

Daily Mail, The (2005c), 'The toll on homeowners', article, p. 7, 8 February 2005.

Daily Telegraph, The (2005a), '"Rattled" Blair to set tough tests for migrants', news, p.1, 7 February 2005.

Daily Telegraph, The (2005b), 'Labour's plan will not control the influx', leading article, p.19, 7 February 2005.

Davis, D. (2005), 'Controlled Immigration and a firm but fair asylum system', http://www.conservatives.com (home page), accessed on 9 March 2005.

De Genova, N. (2002), 'Migrant "illegality" and deportability in everyday life', *Annual Review of Anthropology* 31, 419–47.

De Genova, N. (2004), 'The legal production of Mexican/migrant "illegality"', *Latino Studies* 2, 160–85.

De Genova, N. (2007), 'The production of culprits: From deportability to detainability in the aftermath of homeland security?', *Citizenship Studies* 11(5), 421–48.

Derrida, J. (1997), *Of Grammatology.* (trans. Gayatri Chakravorty Spivak), (London: The John Hopkins University Press).

Diez, T. and Squire, V. (2008), 'Traditions of citizenship and the securitisation of migration in Germany and Britain, *Citizenship Studies* 12(6), 565–81.

Dillon, M. (2007), 'Governing terror: The state of emergency of biopolitical emergence', *International Political Sociology*, 1(1), 7–28.

Dobrowolsky, A. with Lister, R. (2006), 'Social exclusion and changes to citizenship: Women and children, minorities and migrants in Britain', in E. Tastsoglou and A. Dobrowolsky (Eds), *Women, Migration and Citizenship* (Aldershot: Ashgate), 149–82.

Doty, R. L. (1996a), 'Immigration and national identity', *Review of International Studies* (22), 235–55.

Doty, R. L. (1996b), 'Sovereignty and the Nation: Constructing the Boundaries of National Identity', in T. J. Biersteker and C. Weber (Eds), *State Sovereignty as Social Construct* (Cambridge: Cambridge University Press), 121–47.

Doty, R. L. (2003), *Anti-Immigrantism in Western Democracies: Statecraft, Desire and the Politics of Exclusion* (London: Routledge).

Duvell, F. (2003), 'The globalization of migration control', *Open Democracy*, www.openDemocracy.net, date accessed 3rd February 2004.

Edkins, J. (2002), 'After the subject of international security', in A. Finlayson and J. Valentine (Eds), *Politics and Poststructuralism: An Introduction* (Edinburgh: Edinburgh University Press), 66–80.

Edkins, J. and Pin Fat, V. (2004), 'Introduction: Life, Power, Resistance', in J. Edkins and V. Pin-Fat (Eds), *Sovereign Lives: Power in Global Politics* (London: Routledge), 1–22.

Edkins, J. and Pin Fat, V. (2005), 'Through the wire: Relations of power and relations of violence', *Millennium: Journal of International Studies* 34(1), 1–24.

Epstein, C. (2007), 'Guilty bodies, productive bodies, destructive bodies: Crossing the biometric borders', *International Political Sociology* 1(2), 149–64.

Europa (2004), 'The Hague programme: Ten priorities for the next five years', www.europa.eu (home page), accessed on 18 June 2006.

Europa (2008), http://ec.europa.eu/justice_home/fsj/immigration/illegal/fsj_immigration_illegal_en.htm, accessed on 15 May 2008.

European Council (1999), *Presidency Conclusions of the Tampere European Council*, 15 and 16 October 1999, www.europa.eu.int (home page), accessed on 18 September 2003.

European Council (2001), *Presidency Conclusions of the Laeken European Council*, 14 and 15 December 2001, www.europa.eu.int (home page), accessed on 18 September 2003.

European Council (2002), *Presidency Conclusions of the Seville European Council*, 21 and 22 June 2002, www.europa.eu.int (home page), accessed on 18 September 2003.

European Council (2003), *Presidency Conclusions of the Thessaloniki European Council*, 19 and 20 June 2003, www.europa.eu.int (home page), accessed on 18 September 2003.

European Union (2005), 'Introduction to the UK Presidency of the EU', www.eu2005.gov.uk (home page), accessed on 18 June 2006.

European Council on Refugees and Exiles (2008), Statistics fact file, www.ecre.org (home page), accessed on 15 January 2008.

European Security and Defence Assembly (2005), 'Surveillance of the maritime and coastal areas of European states', http://www.assembly-weu.org/en/documents/sessions_ordinaires/rpt/2005/1920.html, accessed on 15 June 2006.

Flynn, D. (2005), 'New borders, new management: The dilemmas of modern immigration policies', *Ethnic and Racial Studies* 28(3), 463–90.

Foot, P. (1965), *Immigration and Race in British Politics* (Harmondsworth: Penguin).

Frattini, F. (2005), Speech at University of Harvard on 'Legal migration and the follow-up to the Green paper and on the fight against illegal immigration', 7 November 2005, http://europa.eu.int (home page), accessed on 21 June 2006.

Frattini, F. (2006), Press release on 'Commission moves to strengthen practical cooperation between member states on asylum management', 17 February 2006, http://europa.eu.int (home page), accessed on 21 June 2006.

Frontex (2008a), http://www.frontex.europa.eu/origin_and_tasks/origin/, accessed on 15 May 2008.

Frontex (2008b), http://www.frontex.europa.eu/newsroom/news_releases/art35.html, accessed on 15 May 2008.

Frontex (2008c), http://www.frontex.europa.eu/border_tech/, accessed on 15 May 2008.

Frost, D. (2007), 'The enemy within? Asylum, racial violence and "race hate" in Britain today', *21st Century* 2(3), 227–48.

Garland, D. (2001), *The Culture of Control: Crime and Social Order in Contemporary Society* (Chicago: University of Chicago Press).

Geddes, A. (2000), *Immigration and European Integration: Towards Fortress Europe?* (Manchester University Press: Manchester).

Geddes, A. (2003), *The Politics of Migration and Immigration in Europe* (London: Sage).

Gibney, M. (2004), *The Ethics and Politics of Asylum* (Cambridge: Cambridge University Press).

Gibney, M. (2008), 'Asylum and the expansion of deportation in the United Kingdom', *Government and Opposition*, 43(2), 146–67.

Gilroy, P. (1987), *There Ain't No Black in the Union Jack: The Cultural Politics of Race and Nation* (London: Hutchinson).

Glynos, J. (2001), 'The grip of ideology: A Lacanian approach to the theory of ideology', *Journal of Political Ideologies* 6(2), 191–214.

Glynos, J. and Howarth, D. (2007), *Logics of Critical Explanation in Social and Political Theory* (London: Routledge).

Goodwin-Gill, G. (2001), 'After the Cold War: Asylum and the refugee concept move on', *Forced Migration Review* 10, 14–16.

Goodwin-Gill, G. (1996), *The Refugee in International Law* (Oxford: Clarendon Press).

Gordon (2006), 'Home Secretary loses hijacker appeal', *The Independent*, 4 August 2006. www.independent.co.uk (home page), accessed on 15 August 2008.

Green Party (2001), *The Green Party General Election Manifesto* (The Green Party).

Green Party (2005a), *The Green Party General Election Manifesto* (The Green Party).

Green Party (2005b), 'EU & UK policy, Green positions and Jean Lambert's work', www.greenparty.org.uk (home page), accessed on 9 March 2005.

Griffiths, D., Sigona, N. and Zetter, R. (2005), *Refugee Community Organisations and Dispersal: Networks, Resources and Social Capital* (Bristol: Policy Press).

Guild, E. and Niessen, (1996), *The Developing Immigration and Asylum Policies of the European Union* (London: Martinus Nijhoff Publishers).

Guild, E. (2003), 'International terrorism and EU immigration, asylum and borders policy: The unexpected victims of September 11', *European Foreign Affairs Review* 8, 331–46.

Guiraudon, V. (2003), 'Before the EU border: Remote control of the "huddled masses"', in K. Groenendijk, E. Guild and P. Minderhoud (Eds), *In Search of Europe's Borders* (Kluwer: The Hague), 191–214.

Habermas, J. (1992), 'Citizenship and national identity: Some reflections on the future of Europe', *Praxis International* 12(1), 1–19.

Habermas, J. (1998), 'Why Europe needs a constitution', in R. Rogowski and C. Turner (Eds), *The Shape of the New Europe* (Cambridge: Cambridge University Press), 25–55.

Hall, S., Critcher, C., Jefferson, T., Clarke, J. and Robert, B. (1979), *Policing the Crisis: Mugging, the State, and Law and Order* (Basingstoke: Palgrave Macmillan).

Hall, S. (1983), 'The great moving right show', in S. Hall and M. Jacques (Eds), *The Politics of Thatcherism* (London: Lawrence and Wishart), 19–39.

Hampshire, J. and Saggar, S. (2006), 'Migration, integration and security in the UK since July 7', *Migration Information Source* www.migrationinformation.org (home page), accessed on 13 December 2007.

Hampshire, J. (2005), *Citizenship and Belonging* (Basingstoke: Palgrave Macmillan).

Hampshire, J. (2008), 'Disembedding liberalism? Immigration politics and security in Britain post-9/11', in T. Givens, G. Freeman and D. Leal (Eds), *Immigration Policy and Security: U.S., European and Commonwealth Perspectives* (London: Routledge).

Hansen, L. (2006), *Security as Practice: Discourse Analysis and the Bosnian War* (London: Routledge).

Hansen, R. (2000), *Citizenship and Immigration in Post-war Britain: The Institutional Origins of a Multicultural Nation.* (Oxford: Oxford University Press).

Hansen, R. and King, D. (2000), 'Illiberalism and the new politics of asylum: Liberalism's dark side', *The Political Quarterly* 71(4), 396–403.

Harris, N. (2003), *Thinking the Unthinkable* (London: IB Taurus).

Hayter, T. (2000), *Open Borders: The Case Against Immigration Controls* (London: Pluto Press).

Heath and Jeffries (2005), 'Asylum statistics: United Kingdom 2004', *National Statistics Report 13/05*, 23 August 2005 (London: Home Office).

Hindess, B. (1998), 'Divide and rule: The international character of modern citizenship', *European Journal of Social Theory* 1(1), 57–70.

HOL (2006), *House of Lords Parliamentary Debate*, 15 March 2006, columns 60–2, www.publications.parliament.uk (home page), accessed on 15 December 2006.

Home Office (2001), 'Report of the operational reviews of the voucher and dispersal schemes of the national asylum support service' (London: Home Office).

Home Office (2003), 'UK Leads International Drive to Tackle Spread of Organised Crime in the Balkans', at the Home Office website http://www.drugs.gov.uk/News/PressReleases/1038218995, accessed on 28 July 2003.

Home Office (2005), *Controlling Our Borders: Making Migration Work for Britain* (Norwich: HMSO).

Home Office (2006), 'The New Asylum Model: Swifter decisions – faster removals', www.homeoffice.gov.uk (home page), accessed on 2 June 2008.

Home Office (2007), 'Asylum statistics: First quarter 2007 United Kingdom', www.homeoffice.gov.uk (home page), accessed on 2 June 2008.

Honig, B. (2001), *Democracy and the Foreigner* (Princeton NJ: Princeton University Press).

Howard, M. (2005a), 'I believe we must limit immigration', *The Telegraph* 23, January 2005, www.telegraph.co.uk (home), accessed on 9 March 2005.

Howard, M. (2005b), 'The cost of Tony Blair's chaotic asylum system', 28 January 2005, www.conservatives.com (home page), accessed on 9 March 2005.

Howarth, D. (2000), *Discourse*, (Buckingham: Open University Press).

Hubbard, P. (2004), 'Inappropriate and incongruous: Opposition to asylum centers in the English countryside', *Journal of Rural Studies*, 21(1), 3–17.

Hughes, B. (2002), Hansard Written Answers, 8.7.2002, Beverley Hughes columns 739–42W. http://www.publications.parliament.uk/pa/cm/cmhansrd. htm, accessed on 21 May 2003.

Huysmans, J. (1995a), 'Migrants as a security problem: Dangers of "securitising" societal issues', in R. Miles and D. Thränhardt (Eds), *Migration and European Integration: The Dynamics of Inclusion and Exclusion* (London: Pinter), 53–72.

Huysmans, J. (2006), *The Politics of Insecurity: Fear, Migration and Asylum in the EU* (London: Routledge).

Huysmans, J. (2008), 'The jargon of exception: On Schmitt, Agamben and the absence of political society', *International Political Sociology* 2, 165–83.

Huysmans, J. and Buonfino, A. (2008), 'Politics of exception and unease: Immigration, asylum and terrorism in parliamentary debates in the UK', *Political Studies* 56(4), 766–88.

Hyndman, J. and Mountz, H. (2008), 'Another brick in the wall? Non-*refoulement* and the externalization of asylum by Australia and Europe', *Government and Opposition* 43(20), 249–76.

Immigration and Nationality Directorate Intelligence Service (INDIS) (2003), 'PROJECT IMMpact information and appraisal sheet', obtained from the project leader on 21 November 2003.

Immigration and Nationality Directorate (IND) (2005a), 'NASS in the regions', www.ind.homeoffice.gov.uk (home page), accessed on 21 May 2005.

Immigration and Nationality Directorate (IND) (2005b), 'NASS regional offices', www.ind.homeoffice.gov.uk (home page), accessed on 21 May 2005.

Immigration and Nationality Directorate (IND) (2005c), 'NASS: History', www.ind.homeoffice.gov.uk (home page), accessed on 21 May 2005.

Immigration and Nationality Directorate (IND) (2005d), 'What do IND really do?', www.ind.homeoffice.gov.uk (home page), accessed on 21 May 2005.

Immigration and Nationality Directorate (IND) (2005e), 'NASS policy bulletin 55', www.asylumsupport.info (home page), accessed on 13 May 2005.

Independent, The (2005a), 'Village that gives the lie to the scare stories about immigration', news report by Jonathan Brown, p.3, 12 February 2005.

Independent, The (2005b), 'The desperate plight of a disposed people: The seizure of three boatloads of African migrants off the canary', title page article by P. Popham, pp.1–4, 7 February 2005.

Independent Asylum Commission (2008), *Deserving Dignity* www.independentasylumcommission.org.uk (home page), accessed on 13 July 2008.

Isin, E. (2002), *Being Political: Genealogies of Citizenship* (Minneapolis: University of Minnesota Press).

Isin, E. (2008), 'Theorising acts of citizenship', in E. Isin and G. Nielsen, *Acts of Citizenship* (London: Zed Books), 15–43.

Isin, E. and Nielsen, G. (2008), *Acts of Citizenship* (London: Zed Books).

Isin, E. and Rygiel, K. (2006), 'Abject spaces: Frontiers, zones and camps', in E. Dauphinee and C. Masters, *Logics of Biopower and the War on Terror* (Basingstoke: Palgrave Macmillan), 181–203.

JCHR (2004), *Joint Committee on Human Rights: Fifth Report*, www.publications.parliament.uk (home page), accessed on 15 March 2006.

Jennings, W. (2005), 'Responsive risk regulation? Immigration and asylum', in *Risk and Regulation* No. 9, www.lse.ac.uk (home), accessed on 15 January 2008.

Joint Committee on Human Rights (2006), *Thirty-Second Report* (London: HM Government).

Joly, D. (1996), *Haven or Hell: Asylum Policies and Refugees in Europe* (Basingstoke: Palgrave Macmillan).

Joly, D., Kelly, L. and Nettleton, C. (1997), *Refugees in Europe: A Hostile New Agenda* (London: Minority Rights Group).

Joppke, C. (1998), 'Immigration challenges to the nation-state', in C. Joppke (Ed.) *Challenge to the Nation-state: Immigration in Western Europe and the United States* (Oxford: Oxford University Press), 5–46.

Joppke, C. (1999), *Immigration and the Nation-State* (Oxford: Oxford University Press).

Kaye, D. (1998), 'Redefining the refugee: UK media portrayal of asylum seekers', in K. Koser and H. Lutz (Eds), *The New Migration: Social Constructions and Social Policy* (Basingstoke: Palgrave Macmillan).

Kaye, D. (1999), 'The politics of exclusion: The withdrawal of social welfare benefits from asylum seekers in the UK', *Contemporary Politics* 5(1), 25–43.

Kernerman. G. (2008), 'Refugee Interdiction before Heaven's Gate', *Government and Opposition* 43(2), 230–48.

Klein, J. P. (2001), Special Representative of the Secretary-General and Coordinator of the UN Operations in BiH, 'Speech on the first anniversary of the BiH SBS', SBS Headquarters, Lukavica, 6 June 2001, http://www.unlos-bih.org/news/srsgspe/2001/06jun01.asp, accessed on 28 July 2003.

Koopmans, R., Statham, P., Giugni M. and Passy, F. (2005), *Contested Citizenship: Immigration and Cultural Diversity in Europe* (Minneapolis: University of Minnesota Press).

Koser, K. (2001), 'New approaches to asylum?', *International Migration* 39(6), 85–101.

Kostakopoulou, D. (1998), 'Is there an alternative to Schengenland?', *Political Studies* 46(5), 886–902.

Kostakopoulou, D. and Thomas, R. (2004), 'Unweaving the threats: Territoriality, national ownership of land and asylum policy', *European Journal of Migration and Law* 6(1), 5–26.

Labour Party (2001), *The Labour Party General Election Manifesto* (The Labour Party).

Labour Party (2005a), *The Labour Party General Election Manifesto* (The Labour Party).

Labour Party (2005b), 'The Labour Party: Britain is working. Don't let the Tories wreck it again. Asylum and immigration', www.labour.org.uk (home page), accessed on 9 March 2006.

Laclau, E. and Mouffe, C. (1987), 'Post-Marxism without apologies', *New Left Review* 166, 79–106.

Laclau, E. and Mouffe, C. (2001), *Hegemony and Socialist Strategy* (London: Verso).

Laclau, E. (1990), *New Reflections on the Revolution of Our Time* (London: Verso).

Laclau, E. (1993), 'Discourse', in R. Gooding and P. Petit (Eds), *The Blackwell Companion to Contemporary Political Philosophy* (Oxford: Blackwell), 431–7.

Laclau, E. (1996), *Emancipations* (London: Verso).

Lapid, Y. (2001), 'Identities, borders, orders: Nudging International Relations theory in a new direction', in M. Albert, D. Jacobsen and Y. Lapid (Eds), *Identities, Borders, Orders* (Minnesota: University of Minnesota Press), 1–20.

Lavenex, S. (1999), *Safe Third Countries: Extending the EU Asylum Policies to Central and Eastern Europe* (Budapest: Central European University Press).

Lavenex, S. (2004), 'EU external governance in "wider Europe"', *Journal of European Public Policy* 11(4), 680–700.

Lavenex, S. (2006), 'Shifting up and out: The foreign policy of European immigration control', *Western European Politics* 29(2), 329–50.

Lavenex, S. and Uçarer, E. (2004), 'The external dimension of Europeanisation', *Cooperation and Conflict* 39(4), 417–43.

Layton-Henry, Z. (1992), *The Politics of Immigration* (Oxford: Blackwell).

Lewis, G. and Neal, S. (2005), 'Contemporary political contexts, changing terrains and revisited discourses', *Ethnic and Racial Studies* 28(3), 423–44.

Liberal Democrats (2001), *The Liberal Democrats General Election Manifesto* (The Liberal Democrats).

Liberal Democrats (2005a), *The Liberal Democrats General Election Manifesto* (The Liberal Democrats).

Liberal Democrats (2005b), 'Liberal Democrats Policy Briefing 12: Safe havens', January 2005, www.libdems.org.uk (home page), accessed at on 9 March 2005.

Linklater, A. (1998), *The Transformation of Political Community* (Cambridge: Polity Press).

Linklater, A. (2007), *Critical Theory and World Politics: Citizenship, Sovereignty and Humanity* (London: Routledge).

Lister, R. (2001), 'New Labour: A study of ambiguity from a position of ambivalence', *Critical Social Policy* 21(4), 425–47.

Malloch, M. and Stanley, E. (2005), 'The detention of asylum seekers in the UK', *Punishment and Society* 7(1), 53–71.

Mezzadra, S. and Nielson, B. (2003), 'Né qui, né altrove – migration, detention, desertion: A dialogue', *Borderlands* 2(1) www.borderlandsejournal.adelaide.edu.au (home page), accessed on 15 May 2008.

Mezzadra, S. and Nielsen, B. (2008), 'Border as method, or the multiplication of labor' accessed at http://eipcp.net/transversal/0608/mezzadraneilson/en on 13.1.2009.

McMaster, M. (2001), *Asylum Seekers: Australia's Response to Refugees* (Melbourne: Melbourne University Press).

McNevin, A. (2006), 'Political belonging in a neo-liberal era: The struggle of the *sans papiers*', *Citizenship Studies* 10(2), 135–51.

McNevin, A. (2007), 'The liberal paradox and the politics of asylum in Australia', *Australian Journal of Political Science* 42(4), 611–30.

McShane, D. (2003), Parliamentary Under-Secretary of State for Foreign and Commonwealth Affairs, House of Commons, column 656, 10 July 2001, http://www.parliament.the-stationary-office.co.uk (home page), accessed on 28 July 2003.

Migration Watch UK (2003), 'Reduction of asylum applications masks a failure to remove', www.migrationwatchuk.co.uk (home page), accessed on 15 August 2006.

Mirror, The (2005a), 'Voice of the Daily Mirror: It will work for Britain', Leader, p.6, 8 February 2005.

Miller, D. (2005), 'Immigration: The case for limits', in A. I. Coher and C. H. Wellman (Eds), *Contemporary Debates in Applied Ethics* (Oxford: Blackwell), 193–206.

MORI (2003), 'The MORI poll Refugee Week 2003: A survey of 15–24 year olds', www.mori.com (home page), accessed on 15 January 2008.

Morris, L. (2002), *Managing Migration: Civic Stratification and Migrants Rights* (Oxon: Routledge).

Mouffe, C. (1996), *Dimensions of Radical Democracy: Pluralism, Citizenship, Community* (London: Verso).

Muller, B. (2005), 'Borders, bodies and biometrics: Towards identity management', in Elia Zureik and Mark B. Salter (Eds), *Global Surveillance and Policing: Borders, Security, Identity* (Devon: Willan Publishing), 83–96.

van Munster, R. (2005), 'Logics of security: The Copenhagen School, risk management, and the war on terror', *Political Science Publication*, 10/2005, University of Southern Denmark.

van Munster, R. (2009), *Immigration, Security and the Politics of Risk in the EU* (Basingstoke: Palgrave Macmillan).

NASS secretariat (2005), 'Correspondence from the NASS Secretariat, Immigration and Nationality Directorate Ref. T0/Gen/Corr/VS', received by email as a response to an interview request, 23 May 2005.

Neal, A. (2009), 'Securitization and risk at the EU border: The origins of FRONTEX', *Journal of Common Market Studies* 47(2), 333–56.

Newman, D. (2003), 'Boundaries, borders and barriers: Changing geographic perspectives on territorial lines', in M. Albert, D. Jacobson and Y. Lapid (Eds), *Identities, Borders, Orders: Re-thinking International Relations Theory* (Minneapolis: University of Minnesota Press), 137–51.

Nickels, H. (2007), 'Framing asylum policy discourse in Luxembourg', *Journal of Refugee Studies* 20(1), 37–59.

No Borders (NB) (2004), 'Seminar @ ESF'04: Migration as social movement'. Accessed on 19.3.2008 at the No Borders website http://www.noborder.org/item.php?id=317

No Borders (NB) (2007a), 'Crossing Borders: Movements and struggles of migration', (January 2007) Accessed on 19.3.2008 at the No Borders website http://www.noborder.org/crossing_borders/newsletter02en.pdf

No Borders (NB) (2007b), 'Overview of the no borders camp 2007'. Accessed on 19.3.2008 at the No Borders website, http://noborders.org.uk/Static/CampProgramOverview

No Borders (NB) (2008), 'Fighting the borderregime! Transnationalization now!', Accessed on 19.3.2008 at the No Borders website http://www.noborder.org/item.php?id=407

No One Is Illegal (NOII) (2003), 'No one is illegal manifesto'. Accessed on 19.3.2008 at the No One Is Illegal website http://www.noii.org.uk/no-one-is-illegal-manifesto/

Norval, A. (1997), 'Frontiers in question', *Acta Philosophica* 18(2), 51–75.

Norval, A. (2000), 'Trajectories of future research in discourse theory', in D. Howarth, A. Norval and Y. Stavrakakis (Eds), *Discourse Theory and Political Analysis* (Manchester: Manchester University Press), 219–36.

Nyers, P. (2003), 'Abject cosmopolitanism: The politics of protection in the anti-deportation movement', *Third World Quarterly*, 24(6), 1069–93.

Nyers, P. (2006), *Rethinking Refugees* (London: Routledge).

Nyers, P. (2008), 'No one is illegal between city and nation', in E. Isin and G. Nielsen (Eds), *Acts of Citizenship* (London: Zed Books), 160–81.

Nyers, P. and Moulins, C. (2007), '"We live in the country of UNHCR": Refugee protests and global political society', *International Political Sociology* 1(4), 356–72.

Owen, D. (2005), 'Resistance in movement: Illegal immigrants and global government', Keynote presentation at the Sixth Graduate Conference in Political Theory, *Difference, Borders, Others*, 13th May 2005.

Oxfam (2005), *Foreign Territory: The internationalization of EU asylum policy* (Eynsham: Oxfam).

Oxfam (2006), 'Scrap it!: Summary of the vouchers campaign', www.oxfam.org. uk (home page), accessed on 1 June 2006.

Papastergiadis, N. (2000), *The Turbulence of Migration: Globalization, Deterritorialization and Hybridity*. (Polity: Cambridge).

Pearl, M. and Zetter, R. (2002), 'From refuge to Exclusion: Housing as an instrument of social exclusion for refugees and asylum seekers', in P. Somerville, A. Steel (Eds), *'Race', Housing and Social Exclusion* (London: Jessica Kingsley publishers), 226–45.

Peers, S. (2003), 'Statewatch analysis: EU immigration and asylum discussions', www.statewatch.org (home page), accessed on 6 June 2003.

Perera, S. (2002), 'What is a camp?', *Borderlands* 1(1), www.borderlandsejournal. adelaide.edu.au (home page), accessed on 12 July 2007.

Pickering, S. and Weber, L. (2006), *Borders, Mobility and Technologies of Control* (Springer: Dordrecht).

Pirouet, L. (2001), *Whatever Happened to Asylum in Britain? A Tale of Two Walls* (Oxford: Berghahn Books).

Pratt, A. (2005), *Securing Borders: Detention and Deportation in Canada* (Vancouver: University of British Columbia Press).

Přibáň, J. (2005), 'European Union constitution-making, political identity and central European reflections', *European Law Journal* 11(2), 135–53.

Prodi, R. (2002a), 'Priorities for Seville: Better Regulation and Immigration' to the European Parliament Strasbourg, 12 June 2002, http://europa.eu.int (home page), accessed on 18 September 2003.

Prodi, R. (2002b), 'Speech on the Seville Summit: Enlargement, Immigration and Reform', 2 July 2002, http://europa.eu.int (home page), accessed on 18 September 2003.

Prodi, R. (2002c), 'Intervention on Asylum and Immigration: Morning Session of the European Council', 21 June 2002, http://europa.eu.int (home page), accessed on 18 September 2003.

Prozorov, S. (2005), 'X/Xs: Towards a general theory of the exception', *Alternatives* 30, 81–112.

Puumala, E. (2008), 'Skin feelings of the international: Narratives of failed asylum and the politics of becoming', paper presented at International Studies Association conference, San Francisco, March 2008.

Rancière, J. (1999), *Dis-agreement* (Minnesota: University of Minnesota Press).

Rancière, J. (2004), 'Who is the subject of the rights of man?', *The South Atlantic Quarterly* 103, 297–310.

Refugee Council (2001) *Asylum Statistics 2001* http://www.refugeecouncil.org. uk/downloads/stats/summary_2001.pdf, accessed on 16 June 2006.

Refugee Council (2003), 'A joint statement on the withdrawal of asylum support for in-country applicants', www.refugeecouncil.org.uk (home page), accessed on 1 June 2006.

Refugee Council (2005), 'The National Asylum Support Service', www. refugeecouncil.org.uk (home page), accessed on 18 April 2005.

Refugee Council (2006), 'Section 55: An overview', www.refugeecouncil.org.uk (home page), accessed on 1 June 2006.

Refugee Council and Refugee Action (2006), 'Inhumane and ineffective: Section 9 in practice', www.refugeecouncil.org.uk (home page), accessed on 1 June 2006.

RESPECT Coalition, the (2005a), *The RESPECT Coalition General Election Manifesto* (The RESPECT Coalition).

RESPECT Coalition, the (2005b), 'Establishment parties slammed over cruel and inhuman immigration policy', 15 February 2005, http:///www.respectcoalition.com (home page), accessed on 9 March 2005.

Robinson, V., Andersson, R. and Musterd, S. (2003), *Spreading the Burden: A Review of Policies to Disperse Asylum Seekers and Refugees* (Bristol: Policy Press).

Sales, R. (2002), 'The deserving and the undeserving: Refugees, asylum seekers and welfare in Britain', *Critical Social Policy* 22(1), 456–78.

Sales, R. (2005), 'Secure borders, safe haven: A contradiction in terms?', *Ethnic and Racial Studies* 28(3), 445–62.

Sales, R. (2007), *Understanding Immigration and Refugee Policy: Contradictions and Continuities* (Bristol: Policy Press).

Samers, M. (2004), 'An Emerging Geopolitics of Illegal Immigration in the European Union', *European Journal of Migration and Law* 6(1), 27–45.

Sassen, S. (1998), *Globalisation and its Discontents: Essays on the New Mobility of People and Money* (New York: New Press).

Savage, S. J. (2005), 'The efficacy and justifiability of policies to disperse asylum seekers: A case study of dispersal under the UK's Immigration and Asylum Act of 1999', in A. Bolesta (Ed.), *Refugee Crises and International Responses: Towards Permanent Solutions?* (Leon Kozminski Academy of Entrepreneurship and Management: Warsaw), 217–46.

Schmitt, C. (1996), *The Concept of the Political* (Chicago: University of Chicago Press).

Schmitt, C. (2005), *Political Theology: Four Chapters on the Concept of Sovereignty* (Chicago: University of Chicago Press).

Schuster, L. (2003a), *The Use and Abuse of Political Asylum* (London: Frank Cass).

Schuster, L. (2003b), 'Common sense or racism? The treatment of asylum-seekers in Europe', *Patterns of Prejudice* 37(3), 233–55.

Schuster, L. (2005a), 'The realities of a new asylum paradigm', *Centre on Migration, Policy and Society*, Working paper no. 20, University of Oxford.

Schuster, L. (2005b), 'A sledgehammer to crack a nut: Deportation, detention and dispersal in Europe', *Social Policy and Administration*, 39(6), 606–21.

Schuster, L. and Solomos, J. (2004), 'Race, immigration and asylum', *Ethnicities* 4, 267–86.

Schuster, L. and Welch M. (2005), 'Detention of asylum seekers in the UK and US: Deciphering noisy and quiet constructions', in Chas Critcher (Ed.), *Moral Panics* (London: Open University Press).

SFOR Informer (2002a), Online news service 'SFOR INFORMER 142', 4 July 2002, http://www.nato.int/sfor/indexinf/142/p14a/t02p14a.htm on 28.7.2003 accessed on 28 July 2003.

SFOR Informer (2002b), Online news service 'SFOR INFORMER 141', 20 June 2002, http://www.nato.int/sfor/indexinf/141/p14a/t02p14a.htm, accessed on 28 July 2003.

Smith, A. M. (1994), *New Right Discourse on Race and Sexuality* (Cambridge: Cambridge University Press).

Smith, K. (2005), 'The outsiders: The European neighbourhood policy', *International Affairs* 81(4), 757–73.

Sondhi, R. (1983), 'Immigration and citizenship in post-war Britain', in C. Fried (Ed.), *Minorities, Community and Identity* (New York: Springer Verlag), 255–68.

South East Europe Security Cooperation Steering Group (2002), Speech jointly presented by the Head of organised crime analysis and the Inspector of Immigration and leader of Project IMMpact, 'Civil-Military management of non-military risks: The perspective of the United Kingdom', speech for a Euro-Atlantic Partnership Model/South East Europe Security Cooperation Steering Group (part of the North Atlantic Treaty Organisation) security management workshop: Civil-Military Interaction in Security Management: The Case of South East Europe, 27–8.6.2002, http://www.isn.ethz.ch/pfpdc/documents/2002/06_02_sofia/leese_mcarthur.htm on 28 July 2003.

Soysal, Y. (1994), *Limits of Citizenship: Migrants and Postnational Membership in Europe* (Chicago University of Chicago Press).

Spencer, I. (1997), *British Immigration Policy since 1939: The Making of Multi-racial Britain* (Routledge: London).

Spencer, S. (1994), *Strangers and Citizens: A Positive Approach to Migrants and Refugees* (London: Rivers Oram Press).

Spencer, S. (2003), 'Introduction', *Political Quarterly* 74(1) 1–24.

Squire, V. (2005), '"Integration with diversity in modern Britain": New Labour on nationality, immigration and asylum', *Journal of Political Ideologies* 10(1), 51–74.

Squire, V. (2008), 'Accounting for the dominance of control: Inter-party dynamics and restrictive asylum policy in contemporary Britain', *British Politics* 3(2), 241–61.

Straw, J. (2001), 'An effective protection regime for the twenty-first century', Speech to the Institute for Public Policy Research, 6 February 2001, accessed at www.asylumrights.net (home page), on 21 March 2005.

Tastsoglou, E. and Dobrowolsky, A. (2006) (Eds), *Women, Migration and Citizenship* (Aldershot: Ashgate).

Thompson, G. (2000), *A Globalising World? Culture, Economics, Politics* (London: Routledge).

Torfing, J. (1999), *New Theories of Discourse: Laclau, Mouffe and Zizek* (Oxford: Blackwell).

United Kingdom Independence Party, the (UKIP) (2001), *General Election Manifesto* (the UKIP).

United Kingdom Independence Party, the (UKIP) (2005), 'UKIP immigration policy', www.independenceuk.org.uk (home page), accessed on 9 March 2005.

United Nations High Commissioner for Refugees (UNHCR) (1996 [1951]), *Convention and Protocol Related to the Status of Refugees*, www.unhcr.org (home page) accessed on 16 March 2003.

UNMIBH (2001), Online news service, 'Borderline 9', September–October 2001, www.unmibh.org (home page), accessed on 28 July 2003.

UNMIBH (2002), Online news service, 'Borderline 11', January–February 2002, www.unmibh.org (home page), accessed on 28.7.2003.

Veenkamp, T. Buonfino, A. and Bentley, T. (2003), 'People flow: Migration and Europe', *Open Democracy*, www.openDemocracy.net, date accessed 3rd February 2004.

Veritas (2005), 'Statement by Robert Kilroy-Silk', www.veritasparty.co.uk (home page), accessed on 9 March 2005.

Vitorino, A. (2003), 'Asylum is a right, economic migration is an opportunity', European Parliament Strasbourg, 11 February 2003, http://europa.eu.int (home page), accessed on 18 September 2003.

Wæver, O. (1995), 'Securitisation and desecuritisation', in R. Lipschutz (Ed.), *On Security* (New York: Columbia University Press), 46–86.

Wæver, O. (1997), *Concepts of Security* (Copenhagen: University of Copenhagen Press).

Wæver, O., Buzan, B., Kelstrup, M. and Lemaitre, P. (1993), *Identity, Migration, and the New Security Agenda in Europe* (London: Pinter).

Walker, R. (1993), *Inside/Outside: International Relations as Political Theory* (Cambridge: Cambridge University Press).

Walters, W. (2006), 'Rethinking borders beyond the state', *Comparative European Politics* 4, 141–59.

Webber, F. (1993), 'European conventions on immigration', in T. Bunyan (Ed.), *Statewatching the New Europe: A Handbook on the European State* (London: Statewatch), 142–53.

Weiner, A. (1998), *'European' Citizenship Practice: Building Institutions of a Non-State* (Boulder: Westview Press).

Welch, M. and Schuster, L. (2005), 'Detention of asylum seekers in the UK, France, Germany and Italy: A critical view of the globalizing culture of control', *Criminal Justice* 5(4), 331–55.

Wolf, S. (2008), 'Border management in the Mediterranean: Internal, external and ethical challenges', *Cambridge Review of International Affairs* 21(2), 253–71.

Zetter, R., Griffiths, D. and Signona, N. (2005), 'Social capital or social exclusion? The impact of asylum-seeker dispersal on refugee community organisations', *Community Development Journal* 40(2), 169–81.

Zetter, R. (2007), 'More labels, fewer refugees: Remaking the refugee label in an era of globalisation', *Journal of Refugee Studies* 20(2), 172–92.

Zizek, S. (1990), 'Beyond discourse analysis', in E. Laclau (Ed.), *New Reflections on the Revolution of Our Time* (London: Verso), 249–60.

Zureik, E. and Salter, M. (2005), *Global Surveillance and Policing: Borders, Security, Identity* (Uffculme: Willan).

Index

CPSIA information can be obtained at www.ICGtesting.com
Printed in the USA
LVOW080123080512

280762LV00005B/6/P